Foxtrots of the Indian Navy

P.R. Franklin

Copyright © 2015 P.R. Franklin
ISBN 13: 978-81-930055-7-6 ISBN 10: 81-930055-7-0
All rights reserved.

Published by

Frontier India Technology
No 22, 4th Floor, MK Joshi Building, Devi Chowk, Shastri Nagar,
Dombivli West, Maharashtra, India. 421202
http://frontierindia.org
https://www.facebook.com/frontierindiapublishing
The views expressed in this book are those of the author and not at all of the publisher. The publisher is not responsible for the views of the author and authenticity of the data, in any way whatsoever. Cataloging / listing of this book for re-sale purpose can be done, only by the authorised companies. Cataloging /listing or sale by unauthorized distributors / bookshops /booksellers etc., is strictly prohibited and will be legally prosecuted. All disputes are subject to Thane, Maharashtra jurisdiction only.

VANSHALI

Extracts From

"Diesel Boats Forever"

Author: E. A. Ransom (1972)

It seems it's now that time of year
When once again we shed a tear
To see some Diesels - proud before
That now will put to sea no more.

> As for the men who made them run,
> They're submariners unsurpassed
> Who've spent their years before the mast.
> Making sure the job's done right
> And keeping reputations bright.

The wives behind these valiant men,
Are now, as they have always been,
An inspiration to us all,
They've aided us to stand tall.

> New boats come and old boats go,
> And men and wives move on, and do,
> As for a time, our friendships sever,
> Remember "DIESEL BOATS
> FOREVER."

CONTENTS

Acknowledgement	
Preface	001
Introduction	003
The Grey Lady of Tallinn	008
Pre-Commissioning Revelries	011
The Commissioning	017
Acceptance and Work Up	024
Homeward Bound	036
Warmer Climes	049
Lagos and Christmas	058
South Atlantic and the Horn of Africa	065
The Coming of Age	073
The Indian Ocean – At Last!	078
Complexities of Undersea Warfare	083
A New Way Of Life	088
A Trip To The Andaman Islands	094
Girija!	103
Fleet Exercises	106
Catching Smugglers	119
Collision!	123
War Patrol	133
Bottom Cleaning In Company	144
Support Organisations	147
Off For A Mid-Life Update	150
Vladivostok	157
The Inspection	160
Stripe Wetting	166
The Piggery	169
The Rogue Torpedo	173
Operational Missions	177
A Foreign Cruise	185
VIP's Onboard	189
Relegation To Second Line	193
The Final Countdown	196
Epilogue	198

ACKNOWLEDGMENTS

This book is devoted to my superiors, my subordinates, my teachers both senior and junior, and to all those who ran, supported, refitted, and repaired, the 'Foxtrot' Class submarines of the Indian Navy from the birth of the Submarine Arm, to the sequential decommissioning process of the magnificent 'Eight'.

It is also a tribute to the families who stood by these adventurous men who earned and wore the 'dolphins', and without whose support the high standards of professionalism woven round the 'esprit de corps' of a very close-knit family could not have been set.

My thanks is also due to my wife, Joya, who had to postpone many programs to allow me to bang away at the keyboard, to my talented young niece, Varsha, who has provided the sketches, and to the editor and the publishers for making this book possible.

PREFACE

When the British left India, the Admiralty had envisaged a role for the newly emerging navy of an independent nation, and recommended the size and shape of a maritime force that would fulfill the envisaged tasks. It was to be a gradual build up. It included acquisition of submarines. However, with the departure of the British Admirals, acquisition of ships took priority, and the creation of a 'submarine arm' lapsed into the background for want of funding. It was the late Admiral A.K Chatterjee, the first Indian Chief of the Naval Staff with the rank of a full Admiral, who took up the cause for acquiring submarines, and gave it the impetus it deserved. All or most of the Indian surface acquisitions at that time were WW II veteran ships that the Royal Navy wanted to discard, as they were downsizing their assets.

We asked for the 'Oberon' class submarines for our navy. They were of post-war design. The British were initially inclined to give them, and some of our personnel went to the United Kingdom for submarine training. They trained on submarines of different classes of WW II vintage. When the time came to sign the contract for the first Oberon Class submarine, India asked for a deferred payment scheme to pay the five million pounds for it. The British government did a volte-face and offered a surviving WW II submarine returned by Australia, which was due for scrapping. Fortuitously at that time, the Soviets stepped in and offered their 'Foxtrot' class submarines which were of late 50s / early 60s design. What's more, the payment terms were so relaxed that it was jocularly remarked that they were being paid for with 'bananas and shoes'! The costs worked out much cheaper than the costs for the 'Oberons' that were asked for in hard-currency. The 'Foxtrots' were offered at three Crore rupees (a crore being the Indian equivalent of ten million) apiece. India turned away from the British and decided to go in for the Soviet submarines. This marked the turn away from Western to Soviet acquisitions for the Indian Armed Forces for many years to come.

Years later, when I was posted as the Naval Advisor to the High Commissioner of India in London, during one of the many one-to-one meetings with the First Sea Lord, I asked him whether he was aware that the British were responsible for India turning away from the West and seeking Arms from the Soviets by the refusal to part with one Oberon class submarine on deferred payment. He looked at me quizzically and promised to look into this more deeply. I requested him to share the reason for denying us the 'Oberon's' at that time, as many years had passed and the information must have been de-classified. The Indian version was known and has been documented in unclassified form. The British version has not been openly published. I met him again and again innumerable times and occasionally reminded him of his promise to give me an answer. Admiral Jock Slater retired from Service without giving me the answer.

The 'Foxtrot' class submarine as it was known in the West, or the I-641 class submarine as it was referred to by the Soviets, was designed to travel great distances and operate far away from its homeport. It was designed to move away from Soviet ports, cross the Atlantic or the Pacific oceans, and operate off the American coast. It therefore had tremendous endurance, staying power, and survivability factors woven into its design. It could go 36,000 nautical miles or halfway round the world without re-fuelling! The West acknowledged it as one of the most successful designs ever produced in its category. It was a very forgiving submarine with a high level of redundancy, and an ideal platform to learn the art of operating submarines. The scope for surviving mistakes and averting danger was high. The Indian Navy's first submarines were these very 'Foxtrots'. During our learning phase, we committed our share of mistakes, some of which would have proved fatal in other designs. In hindsight, the choice was the best, and the safety record of the submarine arm of the Indian Navy operating these boats tells it all. We brought eight of them back from Soviet waters. At that time, the Suez Canal was shut because of the Arab- Israel wars, and so we had to bring them back all the way around Africa. That was an experience by itself, and mentioned in part in this book.

This is a story compiled from some of the exploits of these submarines during the formative years of the Submarine Arm of the Indian Navy, told in such a fashion that the reader can enjoy the life and anecdotes without any specialist background.

As they do not relate to any specific boat, the name is fictitious - but not without a connection to the eight boats we acquired. One alphabet from each of their names has been taken and anagrammed to arrive at the name – VANSHALI.

INTRODUCTION

The watertight portion of a submarine is what is inside the Pressure hull. Men live and work inside this pressure hull. Around the pressure hull is the outer hull that consists of external tanks and free flooding spaces that are not accessible when the submarine is under water. The 'Foxtrots' had seven compartments and a Conning Tower on top of the third compartment, all of them inside the pressure hull. The First, or the forward most, compartment was named the **Fore-Ends**. It had six torpedo tubes and racks behind them to carry twelve more torpedoes as re-loads. A total of eighteen torpedoes could be carried in this compartment. Torpedoes are fired at both ships and other submarines, with destruction of the target more or less assured with a direct hit. Alternatively, thirty-six mines could be carried. These are laid on the seabed in the intended path of enemy ships and submarines before they transit through the area. When not carrying a full outfit of torpedo re-loads or mines on the racks, the space was available for a variety of uses like carrying extra stores, rigging clothes lines to put clothes up on hangars, or putting out extra sleeping mattresses for those not too happy with the 'hot bunking' system. It was a very cool compartment with the air-conditioning working at its very best. But it was also where you felt the roll and pitch or the 'corkscrew' effects of the submarine the most, particularly when it was transiting on the surface, in rough weather. Seasick prone sailors avoided sleeping in the Fore Ends if they could help it, or slept with buckets close at hand to puke into. On one occasion, the space served to accommodate the crew of a dhow caught with contraband items onboard while transiting from the Persian Gulf to Indian shores. How that came about has been explained elsewhere and is not being elaborated here. On many other occasions that space was used to accommodate extra personnel from other than naval sources who were required to be transported in a submarine, clandestinely. The Fore Ends also had a hatch on the upper portion of the pressure hull that was angled at sixty degrees, through which torpedoes, mines, and other stores could be received from outside and taken onboard.

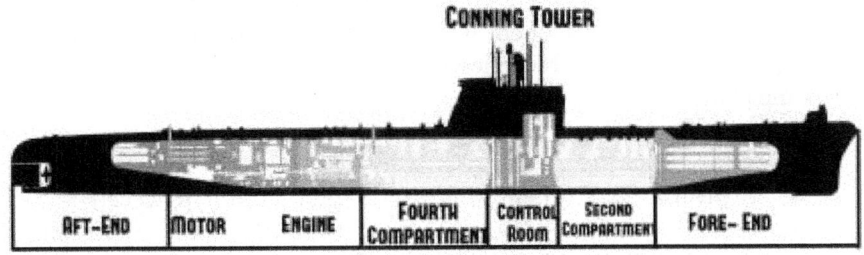

The **Second Compartment** was the forward Battery Compartment. The total number of batteries onboard for underwater propulsion was divided into two groups. The first, or 'forward group', was located in this compartment in the lowermost portion of the pressure hull, in two tiers. The deck above the batteries, accommodated the Commanding Officer's cabin, a four-bed officer's cabin on the Port side, another four-bed officer's cabin on the Starboard side, the officer's Wardroom, and a two-bed cabin for the Executive Officer and the Engineer Officer who, in this class of submarines, were destined to be closeted together, immaterial of their affinity or otherwise for each other! The Ward Room also served as an Operation Theatre for the Medical Officer's use in an emergency. During silent hours, the seating in the Ward Room could be converted into two, two-tiered beds for the extra officers who were carried onboard as supernumeraries, for training. The compartment also had the Sound Room and a very cramped Wash Room. The Sound Room was, literally, the eyes and ears of the submarine underwater. It got all inputs from the sonar sensors and passed on filtered information to the Control Room. Needless to say it was manned round the clock at sea.

The Third Compartment was the nerve center of the submarine and aptly referred to as the **Control Room**. One could say that almost all operations could be directly or remotely triggered from here. It had the main access to the submarine from outside, through the Bridge and the Conning Tower above it. The compartment was divided into two with an upper and lower portion by a deck. The Navigating Officer's Chart-house, the Radar and Electronic Warfare Operator's cabin, the Fire Control Computer, the Flooding and Blowing Panels, and the Rudder and Planes Operators were all located in the upper portion of the compartment. Also, on the upper deck of this compartment was one of only two Heads (WCs) that existed onboard for the entire crew! The lower deck housed the Cold Room (to keep frozen meat, fish and chicken), the Cool Room (to store fruits and vegetables, juices etc), the main Hydraulic Accumulators, and the controls to operate the main Ballast Pumps. The shafts of all hoists (periscopes, radar mast, Electronic Warfare mast, Snort mast, Communication mast etc) passed through the upper portion, through the deck, and down to the lower portion of this compartment.

The **Fourth Compartment** was also a Battery Compartment that housed the Second Group of Batteries in its lower portion, just like the Second Compartment. The upper portion accommodated the Wireless Office, the central Air Conditioning plant of the submarine, the Galley, and the Senior Sailor's Mess.

The Fifth Compartment was the **Engine Room** that had a forward portion with the engine remote controls, and the aft portion housing three main diesel engines that were run for propulsion on surface or at Periscope

Depth, the two being separated by a bulkhead. Abaft the engines, and close to the aft bulkhead of the compartment were two diesel compressors that were used to top up air in the High Pressure air bottles when the submarine was either running on surface or at Periscope Depth. When the diesels were running, this compartment, without doubt became the noisiest compartment of the submarine. During Snorting regimes, smoking was permitted under controlled conditions in the forward portion. Otherwise, no smoking was permitted at any time inside the submarine.

The Sixth Compartment was the **Motor Room**. In the lower portion it housed three Main Motors - one on each shaft in tandem with the diesel engines ahead. (Between the diesel engines and the motors were the gearboxes that enabled one to disengage one from the other so that the motor could be run underwater without the diesel clutched on to it. On the other hand, when the diesel engine was run, the motor could be clutched on to it so as to act as a generator, generate current, and charge the batteries). The upper deck had the control panels for these motors, the remote control panel for the Economic Speed motor, the electrical compressor, the second of two Heads (WCs) onboard, the only Wash Room with bathing facilities, and ten bunks for junior sailors.

The seventh and last compartment was termed the **Aft Ends**. It had four torpedo tubes that could carry a torpedo each, or two mines per tube. There were no racks for re-loads of any sort. It had bunks for junior sailors, the main hydraulic pumps, the main plant for foam manufacture for firefighting anywhere in the submarine, and the Economic Speed Motor on the center shaft. It also had an access hatch to the Aft Casing and the outside world.

Finally, inside the pressure hull, and above the Control Room, the submarine had a **Conning Tower** from where the two Periscopes were manned. The Attack Periscope was the forward one meant exclusively for the use of the Captain. The aft one was the Search Periscope that was required to be manned constantly by the Officer of the Watch whenever the submarine was at Periscope Depth. The Conning Tower had access to the Control Room down below and the Bridge in the Fin (outside the pressure hull) above. In an emergency, the three hatches i.e. the Torpedo Loading Hatch in the Fore Ends, the Aft Ends Hatch, and the Conning Tower Hatch, could be used for escape from the submarine, in addition to the ten torpedo tubes that could accommodate three humans each at a time in each of them!

An outer casing enveloped the Pressure Hull. The space between the two housed Ballast tanks and other tanks. The casing forward of the Fin was known as the Forward Casing. Consequently, the casing aft of the Fin was referred to as the Aft Casing. At its front end, the submarine had two sonar domes that housed the eyes and ears of the submarine underwater, an underwater sonar communications sensor, and a sensor that assisted in 'screen penetrations' of a formation of warships moving about, screening their main assets. On the Forward Casing was another sensor that measured the bathy profile and enabled the Sound Room to determine the nature of the waters the submarine was transiting through. The Fin housed additional sensors for underwater communications. The space between the Casing and the Pressure Hull, which was open to the sea and got flooded whenever the submarine dived, had pipelines of various systems, the High Pressure Air bottles, the cable holder for the anchor and the Fore Planes in the forward section. Abaft the Fin, outside the casing and well below the waterline, the Aft Hydroplanes, the stabilizers, a single rudder, and three propellers were located.

Specifications

Indian Name:	Kalvari Class
Russian Name:	Project 641-E
NATO Name:	Foxtrot Class
Length:	91.3
Beam:	7.5
Draft:	6 m
Displacement:	1,952 tons surfaced, 2,475 tons submerged
Construction:	3/8 inch outer light hull comprising ballast tanks, 7/8 inch QT28 Nickel Steel pressure hull.
Complement:	11 officers, 69 senior and junior sailors
Max Dive Depth:	985 feet
Speed:	16 knots surfaced, 15 knots submerged, 9 knots snorkeling
Range:	20,000 miles surfaced at 8 knots, 11,000 miles

	snorkeling, 380 miles submerged at 2 knots
Endurance:	3 - 5 days submerged
Propulsion:	3 x 2D42M diesel engines, 2,000 hp each. 3 x electric motors; 2 with 1,350 hp and 1 with 2,700 hp. 1 x auxiliary Eco Speed motor with 180 hp. 3 x propeller shafts, each with 6 bladed propellers.
Torpedoes:	10 tubes (533 mm) 22 Soviet Type 53 torpedoes with active/ passive homing heads
Mines:	44 in lieu of torpedoes
Radar:	Surface search: Snoop Tray; I band
Sonar:	Artika - medium-frequency active/passive, Feniks - passive search/attack.
Electronic Warfare:	Stop Light, Radar Warning, Quad Loop Directional Finder.

With this brief description of a Foxtrot Class submarine, let us now transport ourselves to the world of Vanshali and her experiences while she roamed the seas, both on surface and underwater.

THE GREY LADY OF TALLINN

Autumn was setting in, and the maple trees were beginning to look vibrant in hues of gold and rust. The ground below was covered with a light brown carpet of fallen leaves that had lived their lives, interspersed with tiny patches of green grass stubbornly peeping here and there. The sparse grass patches were a grim reminder of the joys of spring and summer that had gone by, as also of the prospects of a cold winter ahead. A gentle sea breeze was blowing. There was no sunshine. It was beginning to get chilly – certainly chilly for the three officers of the Indian Navy who were used to warmer climes. But here they were in the city of Tallinn in Estonia, undergoing a special three-month course on submarine torpedoes, and as they gazed out to sea from their classroom, they saw a light grey colored 'Foxtrot' Class submarine in the middle of the Bay about a mile away. Grey? That was an unusual color for a submarine! Warships are grey – not submarines. Submarines were normally painted a sinister black, and there are many reasons for the selection of that color, all linked to the need for concealment, camouflage, and surprise. All Soviet submarines were painted black. Could it be the submarine they were going to receive and eventually commission into the Indian Navy?

There was more cause to be curious: Tallinn those days did not have any warships tied up in its Bay. The Bay was a part of the Gulf of Finland that flowed into the Baltic Sea. On a clear day one could see outlines of high-rise buildings of Helsinki silhouetted on the horizon nearly 80 Kilometers across the vast expanse of water from Tallinn's highest point, which was a little over 60 meters above mean sea level, and located in the south-west part of the city. Curiosity now thoroughly aroused, the three officers turned to the Soviet Naval Instructor in the class and asked him why that submarine was painted grey, and what was it doing in the Bay? Equally curious, the tall beady-eyed officer disappeared to get an answer and came back in a short while to announce that it was a submarine currently in use for shooting of a movie, and one of the requirements of the script was that it be 'grey'. Fair enough! Throughout the day it distractingly hung around in the Bay now submerging for awhile and now surfacing amidst wisps of 'white horses' that topped the waves in a grey colored restless sea that reflected the dull color of the sky above. The next day the 'grey lady' was gone, and that was the last the officers saw of her in Tallinn.

This was an unscheduled 'weapons' course that the three officers were attending. In a similar fashion, two Navigating Officers were attending a 'navigation' course in the historical city of Leningrad (St. Petersburg). These courses were not part of 'The Contract' signed between the two nations for training Indian naval personnel and delivering submarines to the Indian

Navy, but was offered at the last minute by the Soviets at no cost to the Indian government, and hence readily accepted. Some confusion ensued in Tallinn. The Indians thought the Soviets would pay the three officers their daily allowances and for their accommodation during their stay in Tallinn. The Soviets rightly assumed that they would have to absorb only the extra training costs, and the Indians would pay for the accommodation and provide the necessary allowances to their officers. The result was that the torpedo officers were not paid by either, and eventually ran out of whatever money they had - even to pay for their SOS phone-calls to the Embassy in Moscow, and for their three daily meals. The only option that loomed large before them was to socialize and get friendly with the locals, and then get invited to dinner! As Indians were well liked in this part of the world, there was every reason for optimism. They were not always successful in this endeavor, but often managed to find a friendly couple who took care of at least one meal – dinner. With the frugal, 'single-sausage', breakfast in the hotel ("Gostineetsa Palaace"), this ensured at least two meals of sorts on lucky days. Lunch was skipped, and during 'lunch hour' the three officers remained in their classroom and translated their rough Russian notes into fair notes in the English language. The Soviet officers in the institution, unaware of their financial predicament, were very impressed and remarked that they had not seen such dedicated officers from any navy in their lives, and they had been training many officers from Socialist and non-socialist countries over the years! The Embassy eventually cleared the hotel bills and paid the officers their allowances as 'arrears', but that was well after they left Tallinn and had mastered the art of 'How to Win Friends & Be Invited To Dinner', and suffered daily hunger pangs.

The Estonians were a friendly people, as long as you were not a Russian. They detested the Russians. Having been ruled at various stages in history also by the Scandinavians and the Germans, it is possible that they hated them too. But, with a healthy mix of bloodlines over centuries from the ruling neighboring countries, they, like the Latvians and Lithuanians, were a very handsome race.

Tallinn, the capital of Estonia was, in those days, a combination of the ancient and the modern. The historic part was a very quaint old city that had preserved much of its medieval features of sloped, tiled, rooftops, and cobbled streets. The names of some of the old streets also reflected the communities that occupied them – Cobbler Street, Carpenter Street, Tailor Street, Baker Street etc, etc. The town's mascot was a funny-faced man with a big moustache, fondly referred to as "Vana Toomas" (Old Thomas). It is a quaint city for the tourist to investigate, and definitely worth a visit.

Having completed the course, the three officers left Tallinn and their 'dinner friends', and headed for Riga, the capital of Latvia, where they rejoined the rest of their colleagues. They were there to take over and commission a brand new submarine for the Indian Navy, and sail it home. The days were getting colder, and spring had already been relieved by the beginnings of autumn even in Riga, just like it had in Tallinn. Riga was to the south of Tallinn. Some species of trees had even raced ahead and shed their leaves, exposing their bare branches in anticipation of lower temperatures, and an early onset of winter snowfall. Central heating kept the Indians indoors and the cold deterred them from venturing out of buildings for too long. No amount of woolies seemed to be enough to keep warm – especially when a strong breeze sprang up. The wind chill factor was severe enough to be felt through layered wear consisting of woolen socks, long johns, woolen trousers, and thick overcoats. They had to accept the submarine and everything that went with it, and sail out from those latitudes before the Gulf of Finland and the Baltic Sea froze, which they did every winter.

The torturous cold was not new to the Indians. They had experienced temperatures down to -30°C coupled with howling Siberian winds spanning two winters, in far eastern Vladivostok during their training there. Still! - This kind of cold took some getting used to. Some of the young, mod, stylish, local girls would come out shivering in fur hats, short coats, attractive miniskirts, and shapely stocking-ed legs. They could be seen jumping up and down and slapping their cheeks to keep their blood circulation active as they waited for trams, trolley buses, and attractive young men. Young men were mostly about in various types of uniforms, doing their conscription service in the Armed Forces or in the auxiliary services. Middle-aged males were rare in the Soviet Union after Hitler's campaign during the Second World War that saw most of them killed. The survivors of the war, now mostly old men and women, were around. They were just as heavily dressed as the Indians. The women out-numbered the male population. The cold was bitter and severe for one and all.

PRE-COMMISSIONING REVELRIES

Actually, the Indian crew was not located in Riga. The capital of Latvia was situated a little inland from the Gulf of Riga at the junction of the Daugava and Ridzene rivers. The Indians were located in a village named Balderai about 15 Kilometers downstream from Riga, at the mouth of the Daugava river, which flowed into the Gulf of Riga. The Gulf of Riga forms the eastern end of the Baltic Sea. The village, at that time, had a very small naval presence – just a few ships of medium size, and some patrol boats. It also had a lone submarine depot ship tied up alongside a rather long jetty, and the Indian crew was accommodated onboard this modest floating hotel. The Soviets had this habit of keeping things out of sight of those who had no business to see them. It would not have been wrong to presume that Balderai normally had more naval ships and that most of them were moved out to keep them away from curious and prying Indian eyes. The married and single accommodation facilities available ashore in the village for naval personnel, and the vast number of berths lying empty in harbor, supported this reasoning.

The depot ship was huge and spacious. It was designed to support four submarines and their crews at a time. It was more than adequate for the Indian submarine crew. Apart from the Russian support staff to look after the Indians, a skeleton Russian maintenance crew of the Depot Ship lived onboard, and generally kept out of the way of the Indians. The ship had a gymnasium, a basketball court, a sauna, and good accommodation. It did not have any propulsion and had to be towed around when the need to move it around arose. It was centrally heated and very cozy. There was no other ship or craft tied up alongside this depot ship which the Indians learned to refer to as 'the PKZ' ('Pay Kay Zay').

No one had seen the new submarine that was to be acquired. It had not arrived; yet the thrill of seeing it soon lent an air of expectancy that could be felt through the corridors, cabins, and mess-decks where the Indian crew lived. There was lots of work to do before its arrival. Stores and tools to be carried onboard had to be mustered box-by-box, and piece-by-piece. Each Department had to muster, mark, and record, sighting of their items. Documents had to be mustered and taken on charge. This was another tedious task, as they had to be page-mustered. The Navigation Department was busy planning the submarine's passage back home, working out 'time and space' and miles to be covered each day, when to enter foreign ports en route, writing to the port authorities there for tugs and a berth, so on and so forth. Indian Consulates had to be contacted in these ports to make all arrangements for the submarine's visit. There were zillions of little things to be done. Such tasks kept the Indian crew busy for most parts of the day.

Mercifully, all this was carried out within the confines of the centrally heated PKZ. The evenings were, however, made available for the crew to relax.

Not used to the vagaries of cold and harsh climates, some useful tips on how to weather them were passed on by the Russians to the Indian crew. Partaking of hard liquor in a centrally heated place and then suddenly stepping out into the bitter cold can result in sudden 'black-outs' and collapse. As a safety precaution, the Indian crew was directed to move about only in groups of two or more. They had to remain in pairs (at least) whenever they stepped out for the evening, and till they returned back to the PKZ by midnight. As part of naval discipline, no one was normally permitted to stay out beyond midnight.

For entertainment, there was nothing the village offered, and the crew would have to go to Riga. It was a young crew with many of them not married. They were full of life and zest. Most of them knew the Russian Language and were comfortable in carrying on a conversation with interested Russian damsels and even taking it a bit further, given the proper encouragement. They couldn't be kept back onboard with a book or only the TV to watch, despite the unwelcome weather. They were eager to go out and bust up whatever little money they had, and seek entertainment after a hard day's work. Taxis and buses were available and affordable. They looked forward to these evenings of quest and adventure. To have a drink, the best place was Hotel Riga, which became a favorite haunt of some of the officers. It had a nice bar and served the local, very attractive drink, named 'Balzaam', apart, of course, from the varieties of Vodkas, Cognacs, Wines, Champagnes, and what-have-you. Balzaam was available in porcelain, rather unattractive looking, opaque, bottles, and was over 70 percent proof! It was drunk neat and in small quantities by the locals, just like vodka by the Russians. The now familiar vodka to seasoned guzzlers was not a patch on the newly discovered Balzaam. The locals also referred to it as 'Samagon', which translated into English to read 'Fire' or 'Flame'! It soon became the popular drink because it gave an extra kick and kept one extra warm in cold environs. The Medical Officer, who was a part of the crew, fell in love with it after his very first sip. He was a sober, modest, endearing fellow, who preferred to treat his patients on the quiet with homeopathic rather than allopathic medicines. He was not a habitual drinker, and was addicted to chewing betel leaf, or 'paan', that he managed to smuggle from India through unbelievable routes on a regular basis. He, nevertheless, took a strong liking for Balzaam. He would drag any willing officer into a cab, and take him to Hotel Riga. He would then order one peg of Balzaam each at the bar. Just one peg, because he couldn't stomach a second one! After that one peg, he would pull his companion out and into a taxi – homeward bound, because he would feel too 'drowsy' to hang around any longer!! A few days later, this drill would be repeated with another hapless 'victim'. Those who accompanied him knew they were condemned to only that one peg for the evening and an assured early dinner back on the PKZ! No one could get him to have a second drink although many tried! Balzaam also had this effect of leaving some in a thoroughly inebriated condition that, in turn, led to many yarns and unbelievable exploits being related, on getting back to the PKZ.

There was this story related by two officers who returned to Balderai in a taxi very late one night after an enjoyable evening in the city, topped up with Balzaam. The taxi had to halt at a railway level crossing and wait for the train to pass. It was a moonlit night and there were no streetlights. The train went past the level crossing slowly – very slowly. Unusually slowly! In the dark, and with the moon on the far side, only the low silhouette of the wagons could be made out. None of the wagons were lit. Obviously it was a freight train. Suddenly, one of the officers in the taxi saw what looked like the silhouette of a 'huge' warship on one of the low-decked wagons. It had its mast folded back. He couldn't believe it, and shook the other officer to bring this strange sight to his attention. The other officer also could not believe what he was seeing through half-closed eyes and rubbed them with disbelief. The taxi driver was noncommittal and only grunted when asked to elucidate. The following morning they related this to the rest of their colleagues. No one believed either of them. It is possible that they had hallucinated. On the other hand, it is possible that they had indeed seen what they had seen. The Soviets had all sorts of contingencies for moving ships from the Baltic Sea to the Black Sea and vice versa. They needed this flexibility as both the seas had 'choke points' at their narrow entrances which an enemy could block, and thereby seal an entire fleet. They moved ships across in man-made canals. It is possible that they also moved the smaller ones by rail.

For an evening of music and dance, there was the "Dom Offitserof" or 'Officer's Club', where the officers could always find someone to dance with. It was frequented by unescorted, bored, ladies out to have an evening of fun. They could be married ladies whose husbands were away on duty to distant places, or they could be young lasses looking for a bit of romance that, with luck, could turn into long-term partnerships. Invariably, there were more women than men in the club on any evening. Every alternate dance was therefore announced as 'lady's choice', so one didn't have to work too hard at getting a partner to dance with! One only had to ensure that one was in the front row of the waiting crowd of men at the edge of the dance floor at the appropriate time!

There were a number of restaurants with dance floors for the sailors to while away their evenings. Their equivalent club for entertainment was known as the "Matroski Klyb" or the 'Sailor's Club'. The scene there was pretty much the same as in the Officer's Club. In a supposedly classless society, there were class distinctions. Sailors could not enter the Officer's Club and vice versa. The Indians had this cliché for them – "In the Communist world, all are equal: some more than others!"

Russian girls got easily attracted to the Indians for a variety of reasons. For one, Russian males were no company. Put a bottle and a girl in front of them and their interest would unwaveringly focus on the bottle. They drank till they got drunk and were not interested in dancing or carrying on a conversation. On a dance floor it was very common to see two Russian girls dancing with each other. As one Russian woman put it, Russian males had this idolized vision of Genghis Khan and his band of marauders who came swooping down to a place, ravaged it, drank till they got drunk, and then took the women of their choice. The average Russian male wanted to emulate this when in an inebriated state. It was a different matter that most of them did not succeed in getting past the drinking stage, and often ended up in the 'clink'. There was no concept of dating or wooing a girl like the romantic French, the serenading Italians, or any other civilized people. Indian males talked to the girls, didn't get drunk, and even danced with them. Yes, they were definitely more interesting. And, of course, they had black hair! - And that was another attraction. The Sikhs were the most attractive of them all, and were often fought over! It did not matter to them whether the Indian was an officer or a sailor. The flip side of the coin was that many Indians found themselves attracted to these girls. They were clear-skinned, pretty, had good figures (before marriage, that is) and were very friendly. There was this officer who would return from an outing and relate the evening's happenings to his mates. His date was 'ravishingly beautiful and pleasant'. Lying in his bed, he would go on mooning over the girl he had just met, with his cronies sitting around listening to a description of this very ravishing damsel. The following week he would go out and meet another girl, come back to his digs and moon over the latest one, the old one forgotten. This would go on and on. A true romantic! Some of the crew eventually fell in love and had visions of marrying their beaus, but didn't know how to go about it. Marrying a foreigner was discouraged in the Indian Navy and required special permission from the highest authorities back home. One officer and another sailor who did marry had to leave the Navy to do so.

Another officer of the Electrical Branch, who was a part of the crew on board the PKZ, did fall hopelessly in love, and applied for permission to marry his Russian girlfriend and continue to serve in the Navy, despite the Captain's advice against it. The request was forwarded to 'higher authorities', through proper channels, at the officer's insistence. Other romantics in the crew waited and watched.

For the culturally inclined, the very impressive Cathedral named

'Domski Sobor' in the heart of the city, held pipe organ and other forms of Western classical music recitals of exceptionally high standards, on a regular weekly basis. Built in the 13th century, this cathedral was reputed to be the largest church in the Baltic States. It had a magnificent pipe organ that was installed in 1844. It had ceased to function as a house of worship during the Communist regime, but was maintained in an immaculate condition by the State.

The Soviets arranged 'cultural outings' for the Indian crews. One definite outing was to what is now known as Kaiserwald, also known as Mezaparks. During the Second World War, the Germans ran a Concentration Camp here, with a capacity to hold around 20,000 prisoners. No pains were spared to emotionally relate horror stories of German atrocities. The visit was most revealing and disturbing, and almost had the desired effect on some.

Another notable outing was to an open-air ethnographic museum set among pine trees by the side of a lake, just outside Riga. Here an entire range of medieval wooden houses from all over the Soviet Union had been assembled, each of the houses typical of an era and a region, all neatly arranged with gardens, picket fences, streams flowing past them, and little bridges across the streams. The ground was thickly carpeted with pine needles that exuded a very pleasant smell. Pensioners were employed to live in these cottages in 'period' costumes, and eat and live as the people of those eras lived. They got a stipend for this, in addition to their pension. A quaint and very old chapel was located at the entrance to this area. It had an organ manually worked by bellows, with a violinist accompanying the organist. The chapel was a relic from the fifteenth century. One could see that a lot of effort had gone into developing the theme and laying out the old houses in that locale.

Then there were excursions to nearby townships of Ventspils, Salispils, and Sigulda that had their own historical importance, complete with old fortresses located in beautiful surroundings. These were enjoyable breaks away from the daily rigors of work, and the Indian crew looked forward to such excursions arranged by the Soviet Navy.

All this apart, the Indian crew was always 'watched' – by 'Ivan's' hidden eyes! Invisible eyes followed them wherever they went, and if they went to places the Soviets did not wish them to enter, they were either apprehended on the spot, and sent back, or a report would come in the following morning to the Officer in Charge of the Indian contingent by way of a complaint and a warning. The Indian crew was used to this, to the point of using it occasionally to their advantage. One amusing incident that took place in Vladivostok while the crew was training there, will elaborate this.

Vladivostok was a restricted city, and not all Russians could visit it those days. It was a strategic city that looked after Soviet maritime interests in the

Pacific Zone. The Indian contingent was allowed to move around within a 19 kilometers' radius from the center of the city. There was no problem with this restriction as one hit the outskirts of the city at the 19th kilometer. Now, at the 19th kilometer, a Sanatorii was located where Russian submariners, amongst others, were sent for a month's rest and recuperation every year. It was a health resort also frequented by Russian girls. Members of the Indian crew went there quite often. On this particular occasion, two Indian sailors were brought back to their barracks escorted by the Russian Militia (police), who claimed that they were apprehended when found crossing the 20th kilometer! Promising to take disciplinary action against them, the Indian Officer-in-Charge took them to task and asked for an explanation.

"Sir, we were in the Sanatorii. We ran out of money and didn't have enough in hand to pay the return-fare. So we decided to walk one kilometer away. That way we got 'picked up' and a free lift back!"

Every sailor knew he was always under watchful eyes. In this case they took advantage of it. Their initiative was secretly admired and they were let off with a mild reprimand.

Balderai and Riga held many pleasant memories for those who went there to commission and bring back submarines to India.

THE COMMISSIONING

Late one evening in autumn, well after sunset and under cover of darkness, the serenity of the PKZ was disturbed by a sudden flurry of activities, coupled with excited orders in Russian over the ship's Main Broadcast, as the Soviet complement ran about helter-skelter on the upper deck. Some craft was approaching the PKZ, to be received and tied up alongside. Far away, it looked small and low in the water. Its navigational lights were bright and hindered a clear view of the vessel's shape. As it came nearer, the outline form of a submarine could be discerned, with Russian sailors on the Forward and Aft Casings handling ropes that were to be passed on to the PKZ for tying her up alongside. The Indian crew scrambled up to the upper deck to get a first view of what was soon going to be theirs! Or was it theirs? It was not painted black but grey! – just like the one painted for shooting a film that the three Torpedo Officers had seen in Tallinn, but this was observed only the following morning. Perhaps it was not their submarine. None of the Russians onboard the PKZ would elucidate, and the submarine crew would not talk! Some confusion prevailed in the minds of the Indians, further compounded by the next order that came – the Indian crew onboard the PKZ was not permitted to step onboard this submarine. Once the boat was tied up alongside the PKZ, everyone scurried below decks to the warmth of their cabins and away from cold. The upper deck looked deserted, as if the frantic activities of the last half an hour or so had never happened.

Below decks, in the Indian section, groups got together to speculate. Some scoffed and stated that it was their boat without a doubt. The three Torpedo officers went to great lengths to explain why it could not be theirs. Others stated that it was not theirs or else they would have been permitted to go onboard to have a look. A few officers went across to the Commanding Officer designate and asked him outright if it was their boat. He looked up surprised from whatever he was reading and stated:

"Of course it is! Where is the doubt? Oafs!" - And he went back to his reading.

Sleep was difficult to come by that night. This was it! – the culmination of going through the volunteering process in India, of being selected as part of the crew, of all that training in classrooms in India and the Soviet Union, and of all the training out at sea in the Sea of Japan (East Sea) in a Soviet submarine! The crew was soon going to have a submarine they could call their own. The homeward bound journey was about to start. A lot of Vodka was downed that night and well into the wee hours of the morning ....

Bleary eyed, and after a good wholesome breakfast, the Indians went to the upper deck the following morning to have a good look at the exterior of the submarine. It had no name! No Pennant number! No identity! It was light grey! Then realization dawned – of course it wouldn't have an identity! All those details was part of the commissioning ceremony that was just a few days away. But first the boat had to be taken over. The procedure for Acceptance Trials had to be gone through for each piece of equipment, and all systems onboard. All those stores and documents mustered and lying around on the PKZ had to be moved into the submarine, each in its proper place. Then sea trials had to be conducted ..... . There were oodles of work ahead, and now the crew would have to work round the clock. The jaunts into Riga became rarer!

The Commissioning Day arrived. It was bitterly cold. The crew was immaculately turned out on the jetty in Indian Naval winter uniform that was quite inadequate for this type of weather. It was meant for Indian winters. Their ears and noses were a purple hue and hurting. Their toes were numb. They were freezing, but bravely making out as if they were comfortable. A Soviet Naval Band was in attendance. VIPs from Moscow and other local dignitaries, all of them invitees, were seated at the appointed time in chairs placed on the jetty opposite the submarine. What, however, took one's breath away was the newly painted, grey majestic sleek-lined submarine that was tied up now behind the PKZ, all by herself and in front of the invitees, in solitary splendor. She had been moved astern of the PKZ and directly alongside the jetty for the ceremony.

The ceremony began. The Soviet National Anthem was played and the Russian Flag and Naval Ensign lowered from the submarine's masts. The Commissioning Warrant, sent from New Delhi, was read out followed by a chant of an invocation in the Sanskrit language. Dignitaries from both countries made speeches. A curtained Name Board was prominent on the submarine's Fin, which was eventually unveiled by the Chief Guest to read "**VANSHALI**", even as the Indian National Flag, the Naval Ensign, and the Commissioning Pennant were hoisted. Hearing the Soviet Naval Band play the Indian National Anthem in that remote part of the world, so far removed from the country the strains of music belonged to, brought a lump to the throats of many of the Indians present. It was a poignant moment that would be remembered by all there, and especially by the crew present.

One exhausted, breathless, elderly, portly, Soviet Admiral, who was short in stature, and who was to be seated in the VVIP enclosure in a prominent seat, could not make it to his chair. Admiral Aistov, the Flag Officer Riga, was visibly upset when he saw a host of uninvited young, pretty Russian girls coming to attend the ceremony. They were informally invited by their Indian boyfriends and had come all the way from Riga to Balderai to witness the show. Such things are not normally done in the Soviet Union. His attempts to shoo them away before the arrival of the

VIPs and his superiors were producing no results. They just refused to go away and insisted that the Indians had invited them. Just off the jetty, and on the far side across the road running parallel to it, were a number of vacant wooden huts that were evenly spaced apart and probably meant to be used by ships on the jetty as temporary storage spaces. He decided to push these girls into these huts and shut them in, as there seemed to be no other solution. They could peep through the windows and watch the ceremony. Along with a few Soviet sailors, he personally participated in this comical pursuit and just about managed to huff and puff and lock up the reluctant girls in, out of sight of the Chief Guest, before the latter drove in. Admiral Aistov stood in one corner and watched the proceedings from afar.

At the start of the ceremony, it was the Soviet crew that was manning the submarine. During the ceremony, there was a switch over, and by the end of the ceremony it was the Indian crew that manned the boat, all of them 'volunteers' from the surface navy who had cleared a very strict medical examination and selection process before they were taken in. They underwent a rigorous training ashore and at sea with the Soviets, in Latitudes that were unfamiliar, and in the process faced hostile weather that generally fluctuated between +14°C and - 20°C. Some of them had volunteered so that they could see and train in a foreign country. Others volunteered in anticipation of new excitement in a yet to be formed branch of the Service. There were others still, who joined for the extra financial benefits this new branch of Service offered. A special 'Submarine Allowance' was offered to all those who qualified for submarine service. They came from all corners of India – some of them from States in mountainous regions, some from the heartland, and a few from the coastal belts of the country – all with different culinary habits, different mother tongues, and ethnic backgrounds. They all, however, spoke Hindi, and most of them understood and spoke the English language well. Now, inside this steel hull, they were required to live and work as one homogenous team, in an environment most of the world was still unfamiliar with – the deep sea with much of its mysteries still to be discovered.

There was still some work ahead as sea trials were far from over. Before its final departure from Latvian shores, the submarine had to complete all trials; the crew had to satisfy themselves that everything was as it should be; and that the Indian Navy was getting a properly constructed fighting platform, with its performance matching expectations. Only the air-conditioning plant's trials would be deferred till she reached Tropical waters, as it was meaningless to test and clear it in the local prevailing weather conditions. During the pre-commissioning outings it was the Soviet crew that had handled the boat while the Indian crew looked on. Now the roles would be reversed and she would sail with the Indians in charge.

After the Commissioning ceremony, and with the departure of all dignitaries, the Indian crew went onboard to have a look at what was going to be their home over the next couple of months. Vanshali looked spick and span and very natty – both inside and outside. There was a combined smell of fresh paint, fresh grease, and Russian cooking! All the tally plates of equipment were in the Russian language and these would have to be changed for Tally plates in English. The Indian crew would have to sit down and work out the translations and give them to the Soviets. Some documents were handed over in the Russian language and the English versions had not arrived onboard. More work!

That evening, while the officers were tied up with commissioning revelries ashore in the form of speeches, toasting, exchange of gifts, and a grand banquet, the men were allowed to go into town and celebrate. Even before the night ended, a tragedy of enormous proportions hit the crew. They lost their cook. He was murdered!

The crew had been paid their salary only the previous day, and was flush with money and eager to go out on a binge. Standard procedures required them to proceed ashore in groups, which they did. The Officer of the Day, who was on duty onboard the submarine, followed the normal procedure and stayed awake till well past midnight to check and confirm that all those who had gone ashore had returned back onboard the PKZ. He got an 'All Correct' report and turned in for the night. A little after 'Hands Call' the following morning, he was told that the morning tea for the crew was not prepared and the cook was missing. A proper search confirmed his worst fears. The cook had gone ashore the previous evening but had not returned. Had he found a girl for the evening and taken the risk of spending a night out with her? On cross-examining the sailor who had accompanied him into town, this was confirmed. He had decided to stay back in town 'for a little fun' and had requested his companion to make a false entry in the 'Liberty Book' to make it appear as if both had returned at the same time. The Captain was informed about the missing cook. So were the Soviets. Around 9AM, the Soviets asked for one of the crew to come and identify 'an unidentifiable body' in the city morgue. It was the hapless cook. His head had been smashed in, making him almost unrecognizable. There were absolutely no documents on him, and all his possessions, including a ring on his finger, had been removed from his person. But it was him – of that there was no doubt.

The hunt for the murderer began. The Soviet organization swung into action. Tracker dogs were brought into the act and some of his clothes from his locker in the PKZ were handed over for identification of scent. Late in the afternoon the same day, the guilty were apprehended – forty kilometers outside Riga, in a snow-bound, isolated shack. There were three of them – a man and two women. The cook's gold ring was recovered from one of them, and so were some crisp, new, rouble currency notes whose serial numbers were verified as those preceding and following the serial numbers of money with personnel above and below the cook's name in the paying out nominal roll in the PKZ. It took their system less than half a day to apprehend the culprits!

The story eventually unfolded. The cook, flush with money in his pockets, had walked into a restaurant. A band was playing and couples were dancing on the floor. The air was thick with smoke and liquor was flowing freely. A young Russian lad, who was seated with two young girls, spotted the cook standing at the entrance. They invited him to join them at their table to make a 'foursome' for the evening. Apparently, the brazen, young local fellow had incurred more expenses than he could pay for, and was concerned about how he was going to clear the bill. In the Soviet system he was assured of very serious consequences, and he was both worried and scared. The Indian cook provided him with the solution. A few dances and some vodkas later, just as the cook was enjoying the evening, the three of them got up to leave and asked the thoroughly inebriated Indian to pay the bill, which in his condition, he did. He, however, made the mistake of trying to follow them in pursuit of further excitement for the evening. The pavements were carpeted with fresh, damp, slippery snow, but he managed to catch up with them. His persistence annoyed the young local lad who, suddenly, spying a loose iron rod on a nearby wrought iron fence, wrenched it out and hit the cook on the head. It was, not meant to be a fatal blow, but tragically, it was, and the cook groaned and collapsed immediately with blood gushing out of his broken skull, rapidly coloring the white snow around him. The immensity of this action suddenly sobered and frightened the wits out of the three of them. They stripped the victim of all his possessions including his identity card, his purse, the buttons on his overcoat, and the ring on his finger. They fled. They were caught later the same day. The Captain of Vanshali was informed that the culprits had been located and arrested. After whatever procedures and investigations the Soviets adopt were carried out, the local lad was declared to be of 'unsound mind and therefore unfit to live in Soviet society'. He was handed over for 'medical research'. Over the months that followed, organs were removed from his body one by one till he was reduced to a vegetable and finally died. His death was also intimated to the submarine through official channels, long after she had reached India. The girls were let off.

The late cook's grieving mother in Madras (Chennai) requested that he be interred in the Soviet Union. As he had belonged to the Catholic faith, the funeral was conducted in a local Latvian Russian Orthodox Church with a proper Service attended by over seventy Latvians and Russians who chanted their prayers in Latin as if they were very familiar with the lines. This was not an act put on for the benefit of the Indians present. It was a revelation of their brave, strong faith that had and was surviving a strict, often intolerant, near Communist environment. This was probably possible in Latvia and other Republic states. Such open worship was not possible in White Russia, or 'Beloroos' as the main central state was referred to in the Russian language. The stocky, bald headed priest must have been over seventy years old, and must have witnessed and lived through the carnages of the 1917 Bolshevik Revolution. His faith in his religion was unshaken and had survived all these years, in a hostile environment. As the body was lowered into the grave in the Cemetery, one aged Russian lady broke down and wept bitterly. It was not a 'put on' act. She walked across to the Indian Naval Attache´ who had come from Moscow, and stated:

"Don't worry son. I will look after the grave of this young man. I will plant flowers around the grave and tend to them regularly. I too lost a son recently at sea, and he was around the same age. His body couldn't be recovered and brought to me for the final rites. I will look after this grave for his mother back in your country."

She kept her promise as long as she was able to visit the cemetery. A subsequent Indian crew, who went to receive another submarine, visited the grave and found it in immaculate condition with flowers blooming in neat, well-maintained beds all around it.

There was gloom for a while in the Indian camp. But a soldier is trained to stoically accept such losses and carry on with his business. The crew began to settle down to spending more and more hours onboard the submarine and less and less onboard the PKZ each day. There was much to do, and time was running out, for the day of final departure to India was now not far away.

Commissioning of a Foxtrot in USSR

P.R. Franklin

ACCEPTANCE AND WORK-UP

Vanshali had gone through a change in crew with a change in nationality too. She had 'drawn blood' on her Commissioning Day itself, with the death of the cook. She had a mean ugly side that was now apparent. Everyone onboard agreed that she was going to be a mean submarine for any 'enemy' to encounter. Mariners all over the world have superstitions and the belief that ships have their own characters and behave in their own individual ways. They believed that certain traits can be discerned in one particular ship that is not visible in a sister ship of identical make. A ship is always referred to as 'she' and never 'it'. Ships have souls and minds of their own. So sailors have believed for centuries. Vanshali's crew thought so too. Vanshali, on her part, did not disagree! She watched this new crew, and formed her own opinions.

"What a motley crew I have, embarked onboard to handle me! They are all inexperienced fellows - at least most of them. I had been watching some of these newcomers during our outings before my Commissioning, when some of them had embarked onboard. Of course I was under the control of my old masters - the same chaps who had put me through the paces after my launch, while these Indians were onboard as 'supernumeraries', in a manner of speaking. I wasn't worried then, as I was in safe hands. Now I am worried and more than nervous! Barring a few who claim to have had some experience in handling the likes of me in the Royal Navy, the others have very little experience, limited to that acquired onboard my distant cousin while training off the Pacific Coast. OK! So I have been christened with a new name and given a new nationality and a new Pennant Number. The name, I was to learn later, was anagrammed from the names of sharks in Sanskrit. I like it – the name, I mean. Will these sods take me safely to my new faraway home in the tropics? The celebrations are over and now serious work lies ahead. There is much to be done before we finally say good-bye to the Baltic shores and my country of birth.

The man in charge, the Commanding Officer - the Captain- is a very short fellow who takes to barking at everybody. It seems to come to him naturally. Psychologically most men of short stature have a chip on their shoulders about their height, or the lack of it, and therefore bark at the taller ones, or so I overheard. However, I can make out that this man knows his onions and is really a soft, compassionate fellow at heart. He portrays an aggressive nature that is only a front. I suppose he needs it to carry out his responsibilities, but I'm certain he can do with a little less of it. He had one weakness and that was to constantly talk about his initial training days onboard the Royal Naval submarine "HMS Tiptoe". Talking of "Tiptoe", his first request to the Soviets after my commissioning was for a special circular stool to be placed around the Captain's 'Periscope Well' so that he could get on to it and look through the periscope in a more relaxed manner! During the pre-commissioning work up he was always on tiptoes when looking through the periscope.

The Second – in - Command, the Executive Officer, is a stickler for correctness and discipline. He displays no front, and is himself always – stiff! He is a very serious fellow indeed, who rarely smiles or relaxes. He is tall, and a good sportsman. He too knows his onions, and I was to learn later that the Captain leaned on him heavily and confidently for results. He too had a special request immediately after my commissioning. He wanted a square hole cut through the wall at the foot of his bunk so that he could put his feet through when sleeping, and so be able to stretch fully and get some good sleep! His cabin mate, the Engineer Officer, did not mind. The Soviets did one better: not only did they cut that portion of the bulkhead but they also gave it a loose rexine covering so that his feet were not physically exposed outside the cabin. However, every time the No2 High Pressure air bottle had to be charged, a valve near the rexine covering and on its outer side, had to be opened by the Watch keeper of the Second Compartment. His feet would get tickled, and his sleep disturbed!

There go the two of them for their daily walk into town! The taller one takes slow, long, deliberate strides while the shorter one does a hop, skip, and a jump, to keep up with him! The crew with some amusement watches this twice-a-day ritual, executed with singular regularity, once in the mornings and once in the evenings. I must admit that even I look out for these unmatched couple's jaunts with some interest.

I can get myself to feel safe in the hands of the two of them, but what of the rest of the officers and men? Many of the officers were very junior Lieutenants who had shouldered their second stripe in Vladivostok. Were they inexperienced? You can say that again! I was beginning to get to know some of the lower deck crew too. There was Leading Seaman Sagar Nath Chattopadhyaya, otherwise known as 'Jack Rabbity', the sonar man. He had trained in the UK before training here, just like the Captain and the Executive Officer. If anyone was slow, he was. He even spoke slowly unlike, I'm told, others from his home state of Bengal. I wonder how he is going to report an incoming torpedo when he hears one on my sonar sensor? Apart from that one deficiency, he was a thoroughly likeable fellow. Then there was Seaman Second Class Hariram who is reputed to be very good on the football and hockey fields. What 'hockey'? I'm sure there is no ice or snow in their country! This Hariram spends hours under the watchful eyes of Leading Seaman Dabur Kalam trying to grease all my moveable fittings inside the Casing, with thick mittens on. What can he achieve through his mittens? Kalam's expressions tell it all. Petty Officer G Singh was the Torpedo Chief and was the Coxswain of this crew throughout their training period. He wears a turban, and I am told he has striking black tresses of hair all rolled up under it. He displays his professionalism by remaining silent most of the time. Mechanician Second Class Jog Raj was another interesting fellow who appears to be anti-establishment and always getting himself into trouble. But there is something in him I am unable to quite fathom. Something - that will rise to the occasion when the crew needs help. Another tall fellow had a long unusual name that ended with …Vanickam. He handles my torpedoes in the Fore-ends. He appears to be intelligent, but lazy. Greenhorns!! All of them!

Just yesterday, I was subjected to a very funny experience that they referred to as a 'training exercise'. All the Executive officers were lined up inside my Fin, on the Bridge, by the 'Old Man', as the Captain is referred to. He stood next to my Upper Lid, stopwatch in hand, and positioned himself a little away and next to the Bridge Helmsman's position. At his shouting 'Go!' each officer, individually and in turn, had to scramble from the Bridge and charge down the Hatch, shutting the Upper Lid on his way down. The Captain would 'time' them, get them back in the Fin, and express his unhappiness at the timing, and repeat the process over and over again till they got thoroughly exhausted. He vowed to continue with these drills till he got the speeds he was looking for. The crew was put through a somewhat similar Drill. They were lined up on the jetty, and on hearing the word 'Go!' required to charge onboard through the one and only Gangway, fight their way through my one and only Fin Door, enter the Fin, and scramble down the Hatch as fast as they could. Each man going down the Hatch was instructed to literally kick the head of the one below, should the latter impede the process or speed of descent. They were also timed, and the process repeated innumerable times. There were some awkward moments as none of them were as yet familiar with my layout, or how to use the vertical ladder. I overheard some of the officers mumble and discuss these drills in the Ward Room in slow whispers:

"These bloody drills were executed during the Second World War when submarines were surprised by raiding aircraft, while tied up on their berths. It is totally outdated and irrelevant in today's context. What are Daddy-short-legs and Mummy-long-legs up to?"

For the past two days, under the orders of the Captain, the entire bunch of Executive officers had been busy taking Sun and Star sights with sextants, sometimes from the PKZ, and sometimes from my Bridge. Neither the PKZ nor I were moving. I suppose they were familiarizing themselves with using these old and time-tested instruments. On the first day I heard one of them grumble;

These bloody Russian Sextants! Everything in them is reversed. The sea is up and the sky is down! Instead of bringing the 'sun' down to the horizon to read the angle, we are supposed to bring the sea down from top for the horizon to touch the 'sun' which is below. Shit!!"

Are they forgetting that I am a submarine and move mainly underwater at sea? What good will their hand held, portable sextants be? I have a sextant fitted in my Search Periscope. They would have been better off practicing 'shooting' the Sun down through my periscope. That requires some expertise, especially when the artificial horizon has to be used. Who is to tell them? …. Greenhorns!!

I learnt that the Captain is a Navigator by specialization. He constantly nags the actual Navigating Officer about this, that, and the other. He ordered him to plot the passage back to India in three days and show him the Charts. Many chart folios and charts had to be pulled out to work this out. The Navigator's cabin in the PKZ was overflowing with charts strewn all around. That was not so bad. What was odd was that he also wanted him, over the next few days, to work out the exact time of Sunrise, Mer-Pass (when the sun is at its highest altitude), Sunset, and Nautical Twilight, for each day of the three months of passage to India, and show him the finished effort. That put paid to any plans for outings to town the handsome young Navigator had. In the PKZ, he has been working till very late hours in the night these past few days - and all for what? The moment we get out of position on any day at sea, for whatever reason, all his calculations would only be fit for the bin and he would have to re-calculate everything. To add insult to injury, and perhaps with a streak of sadism (?) the Captain burst into the Navigator's cabin one night, just before going to bed, and teased him with,

"You are working too hard, my boy! You must learn to relax and strike a balance between work and play. Work during the day. Go out in the evenings. Go to town and enjoy yourself … but, by God, if you don't show me the final work by the day after tomorrow, I will chop your b…. off!"

The smile that had just begun to light up the Navigator's face quickly disappeared, and with a glum look he hunched over his table and continued with his work.

At last, the day for my first outing with the Indian crew arrived. We were required to sail out for Acceptance Trials of machinery and equipment – a continuation of the three months of acceptance and work up that we were halfway through. It would also be the first independent work-up for the crew, and both Control and Tactical work up were programmed. The Soviets designated the work-up area in the Baltic Sea, and an escort vessel preceded us to show the way.

I was topped up with fuel the previous day, and my batteries were also fully charged. Fresh water, Distilled water, dry rations, fresh vegetables, fruits, chicken, mutton, personal effects of individuals, all documents, stores, and spares were all transferred from the PKZ and embarked the previous day. These puny sized Indians took more time to embark all these items than the big, broad shouldered Russians had before previous outings! Be that as it may, I was ready to take them out. Were they ready to take me out? We would soon find out. At crack of dawn, they closed up to man my insides. It was slowly comforting to see them go about their tasks as if they knew what was required of them. They looked nervous, but most of their actions were familiar and fairly correct. I normally take two hours to get ready to move. The Indians took two and a half hours. My propulsion systems, hull openings, energy sources, juices etc. had all to be checked and flexed before I was ready to move. It takes time, and a set procedure has been laid down that has to be gone through meticulously. I must admit that the Indian crew did this fairly well. They were in the process of changing over from Russian to English words of orders and commands. So they would pass their orders in Russian first and then repeat the same in English before executing the orders, and this contributed towards the extra time they took to get me ready. Some confusion, mumblings, and corrections were there, but it gave me also an opportunity to familiarize myself with the commands and orders in English.

The 'preparation for sea' having been completed successfully, we were ready to cast off and leave harbor. Two tugs were standing by to help if required, but the Captain decided to maneuver me without their help. A smart 'casting off', which was met with approving looks from the watching Soviet Officers and sailors onboard the PKZ, was followed by an equally smart turn seawards by me, and we were off! The escort vessel was waiting at the entrance of the Daugava River, and we followed her into the Gulf of Riga, and to our 'exercise area', on a north - westerly course. We were to stay at sea for the next five days, carry out a work up of the crew, and complete sea trials.

It was a dull, dreary first day. I looked up and saw tiny hesitant patches of blue playing hide and seek and straining to peep through the generally grey overcast sky. The sea was reasonably calm, but a north-westerly wind was blowing, and these chaps from the tropics on the Bridge were taking cover under sheepskin jackets with the hoods over their heads, and large mittens on their hands. I started a gentle corkscrew, rolling motion in rhythm with the slight swell, unnoticeable to seasoned sailors but very noticeable to greenhorns. Slowly but surely the coastline and shore features receded behind us till they disappeared astern over the horizon. We were surrounded by the Gulf of Riga, with only the escort vessel and a few sea gulls for company.

The crew was divided into three 'watches' (Red, White, and Blue). The Red Watch was called upon to man the stations required to be manned. I could hear an announcement about breakfast being served in my innards, and soon the 'off-watch keepers' settled down to their first meal at sea.

A handful of Soviet sailors and two of their officers were onboard too.

Their task was to see that the Indian crew operated the boat correctly, a condition which was a part of the guarantee clauses between the two countries. However, one of them was in my Wireless Cabin (W/T Office) to operate the sets and get necessary approvals from the Soviet shore authorities while passing selected points on our way out and while coming in, to maintain constant communications with the escort ship ahead, and to establish communications with new platforms we encountered at sea on an 'as required' basis – all in Russian language. I guess in true Soviet style, he was armed with a special set of codes he was to use without revealing them to the Indians. He felt important. I guess he was important. With the Cold War on in full swing, these precautions had become second nature to these men in 'Red'.

We were to proceed to our Work-Up Area which was a rectangular 'box' marked by co-ordinates in terms of Latitude and Longitude, that was not far from the island of Ruhnu in the middle of the Gulf of Riga. After each day's work up, we were to anchor off the island for the night to conserve battery power, if the batteries did not require to be charged. I heard the Commanding Officer relating all this to the Navigating Officer. My diesel engines settled down to a gentle staccato beat and with my three propellers giving the ordered thrust, we headed for our destination. As I ploughed through the water, the wisps of sprays from the crests of the waves that the wind blew onto my Casing formed icicles on my guardrails like stalactites, as also a thin layer of ice on the deck that made it dangerously slippery.

"Man over-board! Man over-board!" I heard the Officer of the Watch yell down the broadcast with some urgency, and I felt my insides churn as every man-jack moved about rapidly in all my compartments. In a trice a few seamen had come up the Hatch to my Fin with life jackets on, and with a life buoy and 'heaving lines' in their hands. Another lot brought up a Neil Robertson Stretcher to the Fin in case it was needed. The Captain was up on the Bridge, the Engineer Officer in the Control Room, the Electrical Officer on his way aft to the Motor Room after having tripped and fallen over a sack of potatoes in the corridor in front of the Galley, the Navigating Officer in the Chart House in the Control Room …… . Someone was in the Control Room Heads (WC) and banging the door to come out. He had locked himself in and couldn't open the door from inside. He was allocated the least priority and was largely ignored after being told to stop banging. A series of orders saw me maneuvering away in tight arcs, now to Port and now to Starboard. The Captain was quiet and was listening to all the Orders being passed by the Officer of the Watch on the Bridge down to the Control Room and to the Helmsman in the Fin, and by the Executive Officer over the 'Main Broadcast' to the rest of the submarine crew. He was intently noting the sequence of orders and actions of the Officer of the Watch on the Bridge. He didn't seem to be interested in looking out for the 'man' who had fallen overboard. After some length of time, he called the Executive Officer up to the Bridge and some whispering went on between them. I couldn't hear all of it but snatches told me that the Captain was passing on his observations of the crew's reactions to the Executive Officer. He then turned to the Officer of the Watch and ordered him to call off the search. Leaning over he got on to the Broadcast himself and spoke to the Control Room:

"Man recovered. The evolution is over. This was an 'Exercise'."

This was an exercise conjured up by the Captain, without warning, to test the correctness of the drill and speed of actions on the part of all involved! Obviously he was far from happy about what he had seen and heard because he had called it off prematurely, and the Executive Officer dressed down those involved, later on.

The next task in hand was to get the man in the Heads out! Very patiently, someone from the Control Room yelled the sequence of actions to operate various levers and switches through the door, for him to follow in order to be able to open it. A very sheepish looking sailor emerged, sweating, and very embarrassed! He scurried off towards the Aft Ends before too many questions were asked of him.

We arrived at the exercise area a little after lunch, and the crew prepared me for a "Trim Dive". A "Trim Dive" is carried out onboard a submarine to check and correct the theoretical calculations of placement of moveable weights in my innards, and the compensations made, so that I am finally evenly balanced and neutrally buoyant to maneuver safely under water. The moveable weights include fuel, fresh water, lubricants, rations for the crew, their luggage, weapons, etc., etc., all of which are stored in various tanks and places dispersed inside me. They have to be evenly dispersed forward and aft of my center of gravity in such a manner that when I dive, I am on even keel. I should also be neutrally buoyant under water. Compensations to calculations are made by adjusting the amount of water in my Trim tanks situated in the extremities of my long body for keeping me on even keel, and in my Compensating Tanks situated around the center of my body for attaining neutral buoyancy when under water.

When I am on the surface, I have to be positively buoyant to stay afloat, and keeping my Ballast Tanks empty ensures this. I have ten Ballast tanks, each split in to halves (Port and Starboard), with each half on either side and along the length of my body. These are located outside my Pressure Hull. They are flooded with seawater to gain negative buoyancy and get me down and under water. When I am required to come up, these tanks are pumped with high-pressure air to force the seawater out, thereby making me positively buoyant again. To maneuver me in the horizontal plane, both dived and on the surface, I have one rudder behind me, next to my center propeller (I have three propellers!!). To maneuver me in the vertical plane, which is possible only under water, I have two sets of hydroplanes, one set right in front, and one set right behind. The Helmsman operates the Rudder, and one Planes-man operates both my Forward and Aft Hydro-Planes. All this is done from inside my Pressure Hull by remote control. No one is positioned outside my Pressure Hull when I am dived. When I am on the surface, however, the Officer of the Watch, the Helmsman, and the Look Out man the Bridge, which is located in the upper portion of my Fin and outside the Pressure Hull. The Upper Lid is left open for personnel to come up from inside the Pressure Hull to the Bridge for a breath of fresh air. This movement of personnel up and down is strictly regulated, as simultaneous movement up and down is not possible through the narrow hatch.

The Trim Dive and necessary corrections did not take too long and I remembered to award some marks to the Engineer Officer for this achievement. After all, it is he who is mainly responsible for calculating and putting on the Trim. The Soviet escort ship stood by and watched the whole maneuver. A ceremony of sorts took place at Safe Depth once we got there and settled down. 'Safe Depth' is a depth designated as safe to hang around in without fear of any ship on top running over the submarine. The whole Indian crew drank a glass of seawater each, on orders promulgated over the intercom. I was to learn later that this is a practice each submariner is expected to follow on his first outing, after his first dive, when he qualifies to wear the submarine badge, when he gets to the deepest depth he has ever got to for the first time in his life, and on other similar or auspicious occasions.

Thereafter, I was put through some gentle maneuvers underwater till it was time for supper when I surfaced and was steered to a position off Ruhnu Island and anchored for the night. The sea was not exactly calm. It was turbulent, and I rode my anchor yawing, rolling, and rising and falling, in keeping with the rhythm of the undulating swell. For the crew, eating supper became more of a balancing act with the plate in one hand and a spoon in the other. To retain the gravy in the plate one had to tilt the plate opposite to the side that I was keeling over to. The sea sick ones had no problem as they just skipped supper. Around the beginning of the First Watch, (around 4 AM) the sea got worse and I was moving about so violently that sleep was difficult to come by for the crew. The Captain decided to weigh anchor and ride the sea – a better and more comfortable option to lying at anchor. The 'Special Sea Duty-men and Cable Party' team was woken up for the task.

My cable couldn't be heaved in or veered. It was jammed! The anchor chain cable that was wrapped around the Cable Holder had 'jumped' during the many jerks it had been subjected to, and had jammed itself in the Holder in an awkward position. By now every eighth or ninth wave was sweeping over my Casing and completely immersing it, leaving only the Fin above water. The Fin too was being subjected to a lot of spray. Someone had to go onto that Casing, get to the Cable Holder under it (there is a gap between the Pressure Hull and the Casing where the Cable Holder is housed) and put that cable right soon or we were in for some worse trouble. The Forward Casing Officer and Leading Seaman Dabur Kalam readied themselves in the Fin with ropes, torches, life jackets, a hammer and a long iron rod. The Fin door was opened and they were given permission to go on the Casing. With the Casing all slippery, they had to hook their belts onto the guardrails to prevent themselves from being washed overboard. It was dark, and the water was extremely cold.

Seamanship is an art every sailor imbibes during his initial training days. It is an art evolved and passed down from generation to generation, through books, by word of mouth, and by experience based on the many demands of the rigors of the sea. It is shared by mariners the world over. My opinion of this Indian crew took a new meaning as I saw the way they went about clearing the cable that was jammed in the Cable Holder. Every wave that washed over my Casing had the Forward Casing Officer standing on the Casing in waist deep water, and the sailor under the Casing completely submerged. The one on top would watch the waves and yell to the one inside to take a deep breath and hold his breath as the 'big one' came. Between these waves and while the water had receded, attempts to twist the cable into its right position continued. It took time but finally my cable was set right and could be heaved in. The two of them came in, and we sailed out to ride the waves and counter the rough sea. It was a night to remember.

The following day the crew was programmed to practice carrying out underwater attacks on surface targets. I was dived and quickly caught a good 'Trim' in anticipation of the excitement to follow. The Soviets had retained the escort vessel in the area, as she was to act as the target. This was the first phase and so no torpedoes would be fired. Water shots would be fired instead, from my torpedo tubes. The target ship disappeared over the horizon till she was beyond my sonar range. The crew onboard got ready to commence an attack on her.

When going in for an attack, the crew has to first work out the Course, Speed, and Range of the target from the firing platform, which, in this case, was me. They then have to work out whether I can close the target near enough to get within firing range of the weapons I am able to release. History has many accounts of submarines having worked out targets' details, only to watch them go by safely because they were out of range! If it is possible to get me within firing range, they have to maneuver me into a firing position for me to release my weapons. My fire control system's computers help them. However, they have to maneuver me and put me through certain paces before they can have all the answers. Easier said than done! The targets often sinuate and weave to prevent my fire control computer from working out a solution. On the weave they superimpose a zigzag to further make life difficult. Sometimes sea conditions are so bad that my sonar is not able to hold the target continuously. Sometimes the sonar operator is just not experienced enough to hold the contact on my sonar. All in all, it is not an easy matter to solve the conundrum through my fire control computers and get into a firing position to release my weapons. Practice is what is required, and no opportunity should be allowed to slip by when it comes one's way. There is, however, one saving grace – my sonar equipment detect surface ships well before they can detect me, always and every time. Sometimes, by the time a ship detects me, I am already in position to release my weapons, and she may have time only to take emergency evasive measures.

The silence was broken by the intercom blaring:

"Action Stations! Action Stations! Attack Team Close Up! Attack Team Close Up!"

There was a general scramble and in a few moments the crew was closed up in their respective posts, and reports to this effect made to the Control Room by each compartment. The Fire Control Computer was switched on.

"Sound Room! Sweep ahead from Red 140° to Green 140°. Report all contacts" boomed the Captain. He followed this up with:

"Stop all motors! Half Ahead - Eco. Speed Motor!" The three motors on my three shafts stopped, and so did the three propellers. In a trice, the Economic Speed Motor on my center shaft turned the center propeller, and I silently moved ahead at creep speed. At this speed my sonar equipment performs in an optimum manner without my self-noise creating any disturbance. My main passive sonar, my eyes and ears underwater, was straining to detect any ship within the ordered sector ahead while my other active cum passive sonar kept a good watch all around in the passive mode. Submarine sonar equipment listen passively without transmitting, as greater detection ranges are possible in the passive mode. Active transmissions compromise one's own presence, as ships pick them up early, and that is undesirable. Ships, being noisy platforms find that their passive sonar sets give poor ranges of detection. They use their active sonar sets to detect submarines. Some ships trail a string of sonar transducers behind them, well away from their own noise, to get better passive or even active ranges. This 'tail' behind them somewhat restricts their maneuverability, but sometimes it is the preferred option.

"Control Room this is Sound Room. Carried out passive sweep from Red 140° to Green 140°. No contacts".

The target ship was not detectable on sonar. Perhaps she was beyond my sonar range?

"Sound Room, continue to sweep in the allotted sector, and report when any 'contact' is picked up" ordered the Captain.

"Aye, Aye, sir!" responded Sound Room. The long wait continued.

History is replete with accounts of submarines on patrol during World War II finding nothing and returning with no kills claimed. A submariner has to learn to display a certain raw patience, and yet show remarkable alertness, with not a hint of boredom overtaking him at any time.

The Captain was looking pensive. In this cat and mouse game one has to be ahead of the other all the time. He probably guessed that the target ship was circling around to make an approach from an entirely different direction from the one he disappeared in. Craftily, he ordered me to weave and sinuate, to cover a larger sector with the 140° on either side he had ordered the Sound Room to search. His hunch paid off.

"Control Room, this is Sound Room. A faint sound of propellers can be heard - bearing Red 50°. Attempting to classify it."

Apparently the target was far away. The Captain ordered me to hold my Course, changed over my mode of propulsion from Economic Speed Motor to Center Motor, and then swung me to Port by 50° so that I was pointing in the direction of the noise source. Sound Room confirmed that the sound source was now right ahead. Sound Room was also able to confirm that the contact was indeed our escort vessel, and that she was at some considerable distance from us.

"Stand by to start the watches. Sound Room standby bearing. Standby …. Standby …NOW!" All stations that formed a part of the Attack Team started their Stop Watches at the same time. Sound Room reported the target on a bearing 354°. A minute later, as per drill, came the next requirement for a bearing reading:

"Sound Room stand by .. minute 'one' bearing . now ..now .. NOW!" ordered the Captain.

"Relative bearing .. right ahead. True bearing .. 354.5°." Reported the Sound Room operator. A variation of half a degree in one minute, noted the Captain. I continued on my steady course, propelling on Center Motor.

"Sound Room stand by .. minute 'two' bearing . now ..now .. NOW!" ordered the Captain once again. He wanted to ascertain the target's course after three successive bearings at one-minute intervals, but this was not to be.

"No contact at minute two" reported the Sound Room. Some expletives could be heard in the Control Room from the Captain even though he had said them under his breath. Within moments however, the Sound Room reported regaining contact.

"Sound Room standby minute two and a half bearing .. now ..now ..NOW!"

"True Bearing 355.5°" reported Sound Room. The next reading would obviously be taken at minute four now because of losing contact momentarily at a crucial juncture. Not bad for the Indian crew. They had apparently worked up well in harbor on the Attack Simulator!

"Sound Room, standby minute four bearing .. now .. now .. NOW!"

"True Bearing 357°. Target closing." reported the Sonar Chief from Sound Room.

The Navigating Officer independently plotted and reported an approximate course the target was steering, and the computer showed the computed course. They almost tallied and the Captain was satisfied. He maneuvered me onto a Course where the target bearing was constant and updated the target's speed on the computer. That done, he then turned me around on to the firing course and repeatedly updated the target's range to match the bearings reported by the Sound Room. The target parameters were finally accurate enough for an attack to be carried out. If actual torpedoes were to be fired, my torpedoes with their homing-heads, would have zeroed onto the target without any difficulty.

"Standby to fire water shot from Torpedo Tube No1" ordered the Captain. The tube had been flooded with water earlier. Now the Bow cap of the tube was opened. At the desired range, a water shot was fired and the Bow cap shut. I shuddered for a moment with the sudden and forceful water discharge of around two tons of water from the tube. The attack was over! I was surfaced near the target ship and, on seeing me, the ship stopped. Her actual Course and Speed was passed on to us on wireless to compare with what we had worked out, and then she disappeared over the horizon, her job for the moment done. She was to come later in the day for another run.

The following day, another vessel joined us. She was a specialized Torpedo Recovery Vessel. My bow tubes were loaded with five practice torpedoes from the racks, and the crew carried out actual torpedo firings with the Recovery Vessel picking up the torpedoes at the end of their runs. After a very eventful and successful five days, we returned to harbor with the escort ship leading us in, and our planned work up completed satisfactorily. It had been a good work up and this Indian crew had performed well. All my initial apprehensions about them had been allayed. We were going to be all right."

HOMEWARD BOUND

The big day the crew was looking forward to, had drawn close. The submarine was finally ready to set sail from Riga for the last time – homeward bound! The instructions were to generally move on the surface with the Indian Naval Ensign flying high, and dive on an 'as-required' basis en route without embarrassing anybody. It was going to be a long voyage around Africa and the Cape of Good Hope, as the Suez Canal was closed for shipping. At a modest pace, and spending a few days in harbors on the way, it was going to take around three months! Vanshali was directed to enter four ports en route for rest and recreation - La Pallice (the commercial deep harbor of La Rochelle) on the western seaboard of France, Las Palmas in the Spanish Canary Islands west of the Sahara, Lagos in Nigeria, Diego Suarez in the northern portion of Malagasy off the eastern seaboard of the continent of Africa, and finally enter her home port of Visakhapatnam on the east coast of India. Four days were given in each of the four ports en route, and an extra five days in Lagos, as certain extra routines were to be done there on machinery. Christmas would be in Lagos! The Navigating Officer had prepared the 'Passage Plans' well in advance (sic) and it only remained for the crew to bid farewell to the Soviets, and leave.

Actually, there was more to it than that. Some very good friendships had developed over the preceding two years, and it was hard to leave them all behind and just sail away, for that was what was about to happen. It was an emotional parting with deep, mixed feelings on both sides. While the Indians were eager to shake off all the restrictions they had lived with behind the Iron Curtain, and re-enter the Free World, the Soviets were full of envy to see the submarine depart into a world most of them could not dream of entering. There were also some gloomy faces, as those with 'aching hearts' were facing the moment of truth and trying to come to terms with it! They were bidding farewell to their girlfriends.

There was some confusion on the last day and the departure had to be delayed. The stores from India for the long journey back had arrived only the previous evening, and the Soviet Customs Department was reluctant to clear it for landing ashore for onward transshipment to the submarine. They wanted an officer to come from the boat and explain what certain items were.

"What is this?" asked an imperious Customs Officer, pointing to the gunny bag of yellow turmeric powder. As the officer did not know the Russian word for turmeric powder, he replied, "We eat this. We cook it and eat it". The officer looked at him dubiously and went to the next gunny bag of brown coriander powder.

"And what is this?" he asked again only to get a similar answer. He walked on a little ahead and saw a sack full of red chilly powder.

"Don't tell me, let me guess. You eat this also!" he sneered. "Yes!" was the officer's smug reply. This time he could not resist putting his finger in and tasting it. There was pandemonium to follow as he raced away to wash his tongue with water. With a withering look his assistant passed that consignment. He next went on to a box and asked what was inside. The officer read the tag in English and told him it was a Projector. Actually it was a 16mm film projector that had been sent all the way from India, along with some Indian films to provide some recreation on the way home. All hell broke loose once again, and the Projector was 'confiscated'. This was not acceptable to the submarine crew and some 'influence' through Flag Officer Riga and the Political Officer was necessary before it was released. The word "Projector" in Russian translated to mean a signaling projector that was an 'armament' item, and weapons could not be imported! All this took much of the forenoon and the submarine's departure was delayed considerably.

After embarking all the rations and stores, Vanshali cast off from the PKZ for the last time amidst a rousing send off by a Soviet naval band and a sea of uniformed and non-uniformed friends, all waving forlornly. A slow and seemingly never ending turn around to face seawards, and Vanshali quietly made her way out of Balderai harbor for the last time. A Soviet escort ship was waiting outside to lead the boat out as usual, also for the last time. Gradually, the jetty with its totally barren trees and their branches and trunks now burnt by the cold, receded, and those standing and waving at the end of the pier became blurred figures. Only the physical movement of the bandsmen could be seen, the tune no longer audible.

Mercifully, the sea was calm, although it was bitterly cold – even inside the steel Pressure Hull of the boat. The submarine had been built with an air-conditioning plant for the Tropics and had no heating arrangements, unlike the Soviet boats. Not all those who were shivering would attribute it to the cold. Some were shivering in anticipation of entering the free world, - a world beyond the Iron Curtain that they had not seen for well-nigh three years.

Compared to a merchant ship, a warship is cramped. Compared to a warship, a submarine is even more cramped - and how! All submarines are cramped. That is one of the reasons why most navies ask for volunteers to serve onboard these denizens of the deep. However, Vanshali and her class of ocean-going conventional submarines were more spacious and more comfortable than other conventional submarines, and a delight for submariners to serve on.

There was this problem of only two 'Heads' (WCs) onboard for a crew of a minimum of sixty nine sailors and eleven officers. Members of the crew had to adjust their biorhythmic cycles on sailing out, and revert back to normal on returning to harbor. The Executive Officer decided to address the crew on this issue so as to avoid queues forming up outside the two doors and hindering other normal work.

"All of you have to train yourselves to restrict the time spent, and the timings when you spend it, in the 'Heads' as an act of consideration for others. I require only two minutes, and I don't see why each of you should require more than three minutes. From now on, each of you will be permitted only three minutes at a stretch in the Heads".

The announcement over the broadcast was received by all onboard with great trepidation. There were some onboard who were used to spending up to an hour on the 'throne' before getting off. One of these types, the Navigating Officer, approached the Executive Officer:

"Excuse me, Sir. In addition to my three minutes, can I have your extra minute?"

Even the normally very imperious Executive Officer could not hide his smile!

A word about the very limited bathing facilities (precisely one!) onboard; it could hardly ever be used at sea – perhaps only by a few who badly needed to have a wash after a particularly grimy assignment. Water was a restricted commodity, to be used very sparingly as part of standard submarine practice. With everyone around sharing their personal odors about them in the confined spaces of the submarine, no one had any right to feel guilty about sharing his own with the others! That was it then – no baths at sea!

Once in the Gulf of Riga and away from the coast, the crew settled down to the 'Watch' system and to making themselves comfortable in tucked away corners with their small suitcases and personal belongings, in what was now to be their home for the next three months. It wasn't easy. The already cramped space inside was further cramped with three months of victuals and stores received from India for the passage back. These bags had to be neatly stowed away, in smart naval fashion, in places from where they were easily accessible to the Cook, in proper sequence, for his daily use. All these months the Indian crew had been eating a modified type of Indian food made by their cooks on the PKZ from whatever rations they got from the Soviets. Now, at last, they could eat genuine Indian food with all the right ingredients! Under the supervision of the 'Victualling Officer', it didn't take long for the crew to put everything in place and settle down to a routine.

Those who have read, or are familiar with operations in these regions during World War II, would have heard about the extensive mining operations carried out by both the Allies and the Axis in The Sounds and the Kattegat, between Denmark and Sweden. These are the only waterways available to any vessel proceeding in and out of the Gulf of Riga into the North Sea. The area is generally shallow and ideal for trapping submarines and ships with underwater mines. International rules stipulate that those who lay mines during a conflict must sweep them and clear the waterways after the war, so that others can use them for innocent passage. Very few do this. The Sounds and the Kattegat were so heavily mined that ridding them of the entire lot of mines was not feasible. So, channels were swept and visible marker buoys positioned, to define the width and extent of these cleared channels. Vessels were required to ply only within these swept channels. There were many incidents during post-war years of fishing vessels violating these orders, trawling outside and beyond these swept channels, and coming to grief. There were also incidents of mines being caught in their nets as late as in the late Sixties. These mines had to be detonated with proper safety precautions thereafter. Minesweeping is an immense task, and therefore these miles and miles of channels that had been swept and cleared were fairly narrow, and passing vessels had to maneuver uncomfortably close past each other. These channels also crisscrossed at certain points to afford ferries to ply between the northern and southern ports of the region. One therefore had to be very alert when sailing through The Sounds and the Kattegat.

Vanshali was planned to enter these waters by day, but her late departure resulted in her entering these waters after darkness had set in. Submarines on the surface are very low in the water with most of their hull being underwater, like icebergs. At night only their navigational lights are visible, which are not dissimilar to those of small vessels. They are quite deceptive. Small vessels generally keep clear of larger vessels, as it is easier for them to maneuver and move out of the way of comparatively sluggish huge monsters carrying cargo, fuel, and the likes. Some navies have introduced a blue flashing strobe light on their submarines to distinguish them from other small vessels at night. Vanshali, however, had no such distinguishing feature. In The Sounds and the Kattegat, where there is very little scope for maneuvering out of each other's way, larger vessels also have a tendency to hog the center of the channel and leave it to the smaller vessels to move along the edges, close to the buoys marking the outer, swept, limits. Post World War II submarines, unlike small vessels, are sluggish to handle on the surface because they are designed to move faster and more adeptly underwater than on the surface. In any case, these submarines move generally underwater and surface only for the minimum of periods of time, like when transiting through shallow waters, as in this case.

The night was cold and the Officer of the Watch, standing on the open Bridge, was well clad to battle the icy winds into which they were heading. The Helmsman was comparatively lucky. He was positioned inside the Fin where he was cold, but sheltered from the wind. The well-clad Lookout was behind the Officer, facing the full fury of the winds, with his binoculars straps slung around his neck and his eyes glued to the eye pieces, looking for unlit small vessels lurking in the swept channel. The Officer was concentrating on navigation and ensuring that the submarine remained within the limits of the buoys in the channel. On his Port side, in another almost parallel swept channel not far away, he could see a large ship which looked like a passenger ferry, lit like a 'Christmas tree', proceeding in the same direction as the submarine. The Chart showed that at some point ahead the two swept channels would meet and cross over. He watched the ferry carefully. Bearings showed that it was moving slower than the submarine and therefore would reach the crossover point after the submarine had gone past it. He periodically checked to confirm that his deductions were correct.

"Officer of the Watch, this is the Captain!" the intercom crackled and pierced the silence of the night. The strong head wind made the Officer bend down closer to the intercom to listen to what the Captain had to say.

"Officer of the Watch, Sir!" responded the man on duty on the Bridge.

"Officer of the Watch, pay attention to the Night Orders I am going to read out. You can sign the Night Order Book as having read these Orders, after you come down the hatch at the end of your Watch."

"Aye, Aye, Sir" responded the Officer of the Watch. On warships, all Commanding Officers issue Night Orders every night at sea before going to bed. These are written in a Night Order Book. Every officer, before closing up on night watch, must read these Orders and sign in the book as having read them. There followed a rather long-winded monologue over the intercom, necessitated by the fact that the submarine was maneuvering through restricted waters throughout the night, and extra care and precautions were required to be taken. The Officer of the Watch continued to crouch and listen carefully to every word that was being read out.

At some point in time, while the Officer was crouching, the ferry on the Port side decided to suddenly increase speed to cross ahead of the seemingly "small" vessel on his Starboard side. The Lookout saw the ferry drawing ahead. Ordinarily he would have brought this to the notice of the Officer of the Watch, but this time he decided to keep quiet because the Officer was listening to what the Captain was saying, and he had been taught never to interrupt when two seniors are engaged in conversation! It was the Helmsman, Jack Rabbity, peering out of his limited field of vision inside the sheltered portion of the Bridge, who saved the day. In his slow drawl, and in no hurry whatsoever, he piped up,

"Sir, I ….. can ….. see ….a …. large …. vessel …. right …. in …. front …. of …. us".

The Officer of the Watch looked up and his knees buckled. The ferry looked like a brilliant city of lights almost right up in front of the submarine. It was crossing the submarine's path. There wasn't a moment to lose, and he had been trained to react quickly in such situations before he volunteered for submarine service. He couldn't turn to either side, as he would then take the submarine out of the swept channel into un-swept and, possibly, still mined waters. He could only reverse engines and cross his fingers. Reversing engines is the slowest course of action onboard a submarine as speed and momentum will continue to move her ahead for a while before she stops and begins to move astern. Interrupting the Captain's monologue, he screamed on the intercom,

"Full Astern Three! Full Astern Three! Captain - to the Bridge!"

He also ordered the submarine to assume the highest state of Damage Control Readiness. In seconds, the Captain was on the Bridge, but he could only silently observe, as there was nothing more that he could do in the restricted channel under those circumstances. Both he and the Officer of the Watch died a thousand deaths as the submarine continued to inch closer and closer to the ferry that was still right ahead and slowly moving from left to right. After what seemed like ages, and the submarine closing to just a few tens of meters short of colliding with the ferry, she picked up sternway, and the distance between the two now began to increase. The ferry, blissfully unaware of the size of the vessel low in the water with just three visible lights, cut across the submarine's channel and proceeded northwards in its own channel, totally oblivious of the close encounter. There was total silence on the Bridge; neither the Captain nor the Officer of the Watch spoke. The motors were stopped and the diesels prepared to move ahead again. The submarine once again gathered headway and slipped away under cover of darkness, on her original Course. The Officer of the Watch was thoroughly shaken up. In his mind came the realization that the maiden voyage to India almost got terminated even before it had started. Worse! The lives of around eighty men were on the balance during those seemingly long, dreadful, minutes that had just passed. It would take many weeks for him to get over this incident. Lying asleep in bed during his off Watch hours, he would re-live those moments again and again in his dreams. He would hear someone screaming "Full Astern Three!" and wake up to find that he had jumped out of bed to rush to the Bridge.

There were no more untoward incidents in The Sounds and the Kattegat, and Vanshali finally crossed the area and entered the North Sea. This time of the year, the North Sea was generally rough, and the submarine found to its horror that it was going into a storm. The North Sea, like The Sounds and the Kattegat, was a shallow sea, and the Captain decided not to dive the submarine, but to ride the storm on the surface. Vanshali tossed and turned. She corkscrewed and yawed. She rolled and pitched. It was a grim reminder of Nature's might, and how we mortals are but minions before her. Mariners are repeatedly humbled by this lesson time and again, in some form or the other, and in all parts of the world they sail in. In such weather it is important to ensure that the submarine does not broach, and every effort was to be made to make her head into, or away from, the direction of the sea. In this case, the submarine was heading in a southwesterly direction, towards the English Channel. She had a following sea. Wave upon wave would come from astern, towering over the submarine's Aft Casing for a moment, and then crash down on her - completely submerging the aft portion of the Casing, flooding the Bridge and the Fin, and thoroughly drenching the three stalwarts on watch on the Bridge. One moment, the submarine would be riding the crest of a wave and appear as if she was on a mountain peak with the horizon very low all around, and the next moment she would be crazily yawing her way and fighting to hold course in the trough of the wave, as if in a valley, with the horizon so high that visions of the sea completely immersing the hapless boat appeared to be a distinct possibility. Every seventh or ninth wave appeared to be larger than the rest, and came crashing down on the backs of the Officer of the Watch and the Lookout as if a strong, beefy, giant of a man was giving them a hearty thump on the back. The result was momentary breathlessness, but recovery was quick. Through experience, they learnt to look out for the 'big ones', brace themselves, and hold their breaths till the moment passed and the water drained out from the Fin. They wore belts around their waists that were hooked onto steel railings on the Bridge, and this ensured that they were not washed overboard. To keep the Control Room dry, the Upper Lid was shut. It was opened only when the Watch was to be changed around and quickly shut again. Huge amounts of seawater could gush down the Hatch and flood the Control Room when the Fin was awash under the 'big ones', if the Upper Lid was kept open for long periods.

Periodically the intercom would crackle,

"Officer of the Watch – All Well?" Of course all was NOT well, and the S..O..B...s in the dry environs down below well knew it! They were only reassuring themselves that the wretches on top had not been washed overboard or injured. When the Watch was to be changed around, which was once every three hours, the Hatch would be opened for the next Officer of the Watch and the next Lookout to come up and relieve the thoroughly soaked sods on top, who would hand over the Watch quickly and make a beeline for the Engine Room, where they would strip and lay their wet clothes on top of one of the three flat-topped diesel engines to dry, and lie on top of one of the other two, to get some warmth and circulation through their bodies. The drill was repeated endlessly, and the storm showed no signs of abating till the submarine approached the Dutch coast, when the waves got gentler, and the tossing and yawing reduced.

In all this rough weather, the main High Frequency transmitter packed up, and Vanshali was unable to report her Position, Course and Speed to Naval headquarters, New Delhi, as she was required to do, at 0800hrs Indian Standard Time, every day. Near the Dutch Coast, a patrolling Dutch naval destroyer was spotted, and through her, a message was conveyed to New Delhi via Hague, giving the reason for this prolonged silence, and assuring them that all was well.

By comparison to the North Sea, the busy English Channel was calm, somewhat foggy, and a piece of cake to maneuver through. It was alive with ships passing each other, ferries cutting across their paths from the English to the French Coast and vice versa, and occasional hovercrafts and hydrofoils whizzing past. The rough weather was left behind and the submarine entered the North Atlantic Ocean and shaped a southerly course. Suddenly she was alone and all was quiet. There was nothing in sight, or on the radar, apart from a school of whales that was sighted seaward earlier in the morning, heading away from the Arctic winter on their migratory journey southwards. They are difficult to make out by themselves, and difficult to count. It was the spray from their spouts that drew one's attention, as they lazily moved together in no apparent hurry to go anywhere. Yet these creatures are known to cover great distances during their migration – from the Arctic Seas to the Antarctic Ocean, and back. They parted company as the submarine headed for the Bay of Biscay.

The Bay of Biscay, reputedly a rough patch of sea throughout the year, was unbelievingly calm, and Vanshali used the opportunity to first carry out a 'Trim Dive' and then snort (or 'snorkel' as the Germans called it) her way to her next destination, at Periscope Depth.

The Engineer Officer presented his theoretical calculations for Trim to the Captain who scrutinized it very carefully, asked a few questions, and cleared it.

"Keep her light, Chief. We have all the time in the world to catch a good Trim. We will carry out a slow and deliberate dive " he said. The Engineer Officer made some minor adjustments to the water in the Trim and Compensating Tanks, and reported back to the Captain that he was ready for the Dive.

"Officer of the Watch - Sound Diving Stations" ordered the Captain from his intercom in his cabin, and then wended his way to the Control Room.

"Diving Stations - Diving Stations – Negative access to the Bridge. Radar Room - report all contacts. Sound Room - report all contacts", announced the Officer of the Watch from the Bridge. The last two orders were given to check whether any ships were around who needed to be tracked while the 'Trim Dive' was being executed. The diesel engines were stopped on orders from the Control Room.

There was a flurry of activity inside the behemoth as all off-watch personnel got out of their bunks, or from wherever they were, and rushed to their Diving Stations to relieve the Watch on Deck. Most of the junior sailors slept in the Aft Ends. A few slept in the Fore Ends. The senior sailors slept in the Fourth Compartment, and the Officers in the Second Compartment. All of them – every person onboard – had an Action Post to which they headed on hearing the orders on the intercom. Each compartment was made watertight. Every individual, in each Compartment, went about inspecting his domain to ensure that all valves, hatches, switches and equipment were in the state they should be in. The Executive Officer gathered reports from each compartment to the effect that all personnel had closed up at their stations, and that the Compartments were 'Checked Correct'. Meanwhile, on the Bridge, the Officer of the Watch had sent the Look Out around to check that there was no one else apart from the two of them left in the Fin. It was mandatory for him to peep into the Fin WC to ensure that no one was easing himself there. The Executive Officer and the Engineer Officer then proceeded to the Fore ends from where they worked their way through the compartments to the Aft Ends, checking all vital valves, switches, flaps, indicator lights and the likes en route for 'correctness'. Returning to the Control Room, they made their reports to the Captain that the boat was ready to carry out the dive. The Captain asked the Navigating Officer to report the depth of water in the area, and having satisfied himself that there was adequate water below the keel, took the next step.

"Officer of the Watch - Come down below and shut the Upper Lid" ordered the Captain. The Look Out preceded the Officer who descended down the vertical ladder in the Hatch, and shut the Upper lid.

"Upper Lid Shut - Upper Lid Shut!" yelled the Officer of the Watch down the Hatch, and proceeded to the Conning Tower situated halfway between the Bridge and the Control Room, inside the Pressure Hull. He then raised the Search Periscope and peered through it to continue with the duties he was carrying out on the Bridge.

"Upper Lid Shut - Upper Lid Shut! Diving Now - Diving now!" announced the Executive Officer on the broadcast, and the Engineer officer went about the business of diving the boat and 'catching a good trim'.

"Open End Group Main vents" ordered the Engineer Officer, and the Panel Watch Keeper in the Control Room operated the Buzzer sound signal and hydraulically opened the Vent valves of Ballast tanks 1 to 4, and 7 to 10. As their Kingston Valves in the lower portion of the ballast tanks were already open to the sea, there was a loud hiss heard along the length of the submarine, as air from the Ballast tanks escaped through the Main

Vents, to be replaced by sea water through the Kingstons. The Officer on the Periscope in the Conning Tower saw fine sprays of air and water shoot out through the outer casing vertically up into the atmosphere as the submarine began to settle a little lower in the water, on an even keel.

All eyes in the Control Room were on the 'Bubble Indicator', the 'List Indicator', and on the Depth Gauge. If the Engineer Officer's theoretical calculations for Trim were reasonably accurate, the 'Bubble' – meaning the departure from even keel – would not exceed half a degree on any side, away from zero, the List would remain zero, and the depth Gauge would show that the boat was down by a meter or so. On this occasion, all was well and the crew could go on to the next stage of diving.

On getting the nod from the Captain, the Engineer officer ordered the Fore Planes to be turned out. The Fore Planes were above the water line when the submarine was on the surface, and were always turned in. The Aft planes were below the water line and did not have a turning in and out arrangement. It was always in the usable position. The next sequential order was given:

"Slow Ahead Three Motors! Open Center group Main vents". Ballast Tanks 5 and 6 were now flooded from the Control Room by the Panel Chief, as the motors drew power from the huge batteries onboard, and the boat settled lower in the water and gained speed.

" Dive to Periscope Depth with Three Degrees Aft Bubble" ordered the Captain, which was duly acknowledged and announced over the broadcast by the Executive Officer: The Planes-man put both Fore and Aft Planes to 'Dive' and the boat began to tilt with its bow down. The Depth Gauge needle began to move ….2 meters, ….. 3 meters, …. 4 meters, …… and she began to go down. The bubble in the Bubble Indicator began to move aft and the Planes-man held it at three degrees 'aft' with the help of the Aft Planes. The Planes-man was also the Coxswain of the submarine and the most experienced man on the Planes.

"Diving to Periscope Depth - Diving to Periscope Depth! Inspect Compartments".

Vanshali slipped away from the surface and settled down at Periscope depth. The Engineer Officer made fine adjustments to the Trim by transferring and flooding seawater in the Trim tanks and Compensating tanks. When he had caught a good Trim, he reported to the Captain:

"Boat trimmed at Periscope Depth, Sir!"

Reports came in from all compartments that all was well at Periscope Depth, which was duly reported by the Executive Officer to the Captain.

"Dive to 40 meters", ordered the Captain, and the drill for this maneuver was carried out, which included lowering of all masts and the Periscope. The Officer of the Watch in the Fin lowered his Periscope and came down to the Control Room. The submarine could now see nothing visually, and the sonar sets became the eyes and the ears of the boat. Having then caught a good trim at 40 meters, the Engineer Officer ordered all compartments to record the level of fluids in all tanks. He would eventually compare the 'actual' with his 'theoretical' calculations, and record the differences for future use. This dive was carried out at a leisurely pace, as it was the first dive to be executed after leaving the Soviet Union, and the boat was heavy with equipment for the long passage to India.

An interesting bit of area is the Bay of Biscay, particularly for anti-submarine warfare ships and submarines playing the cat and mouse game. There is a continental shelf that extends westwards from the French coastline that suddenly drops to present a vertical underwater cliff face. Against this cliff, submarines can do a 'stopped trim' and hide in a motionless state so as to confuse ship's active sonar sensor from differentiating between sonar's beams bounced off the submarine's hull from those bounced off the cliff face. French submarines often tactically maneuver into these positions during peacetime exercises, or when wanting to shake off inquisitive, suspicious, or hostile, foreign warships lurking in the area.

Once the boat had settled comfortably at 40 meters, the Captain ordered the boat to be brought up to Periscope Depth again, and 'Snort'. This involves putting out a huge breathing tube (referred to by some as the Snort Mast and by others as the Snorkel), to suck fresh air and run diesel engines for propulsion while at Periscope Depth. By doing this, the motors are not used for propulsion and the batteries are conserved. Now the Periscopes and other masts could be raised once again and visual sight restored. Vanshali remained dived at Periscope Depth for the best part of the day and surfaced later, at dusk.

The first port, La Pallice, was entered the following morning with some difficulty. There was a thick layer of fog over the sea, and even the radar was not proving to be of much assistance. Straining ears finally caught the sounds of the Fairway Buoy bell next to which the Harbor Pilot was waiting to take the submarine in. Mail from India was awaiting the submarine's arrival! There was much excitement as the bag was opened, and the mail distributed. The port serves the city of La Rochelle located just three miles away. It had six German built submarine pens under bomb-proof concrete shelters that served as grim reminders of the Battle of the Atlantic and the many early 'kills' made by German submarines that operated out of this, and other French ports, in 1940 - 41.

Unlike ship's crews who continue to live onboard in harbor, submarine crews, on entering a port, stay ashore with only one Watch on duty retained onboard. Denied comforts out at sea like space, a good bed, fresh air to inhale, and a bath, all of which are taken for granted by those on surface ships, submariners are compensated by being accommodated ashore in harbor. In foreign ports, they are put up in hotels. Submariners do without a bath for days on end at sea, as fresh water is a restricted commodity. At best, a sponge bath is all that is affordable. They need a good hot bath on entering harbor – for other people's sake!

The next few days were spent in relocating in the 'free world', stretching ones legs, sight-seeing, and doing a bit of shopping. There was a sense of discomfort in the slow realization that 'Ivan' was not following you! There is no one on earth that can beat an Indian sailor in shopping. God knows from where, but he steps out with accurate knowledge on what best to buy in the country being visited, where to buy it, and how much to pay for it. All this was achieved those days without the availability of Internet services. The officers are, comparatively, novices in this field. One officer, who was the paymaster of the submarine, had little time to do his shopping, or even to investigate what was available in town. He got a brilliant idea! On the evening of the day he was on duty onboard, he positioned himself at the bottom of the hatch and asked each sailor coming down, to open his packages and display his purchases and wares. If he liked anything, he would give the sailor the money and ask him to go back to the same place and buy one for him. This way, in one go, he got to see what seventy odd men had bought from different corners of the city! Had he gone about by himself, he couldn't have shopped half as much in the time that was available. He wasn't an avid shopper but he had to carry something back for his near and dear ones whom he hadn't seen for ages. He, subsequently, did this in every port, and saved himself the agony of shopping!

There was a station wagon Citreon car parked on the jetty from the moment Vanshali tied up alongside. A demure French lady was the sole occupant in the car. She was selling perfumes and eau-de-toilettes of all brands piled up in her car. One of the officers walked up to the car to inspect her wares. Familiar brands were available – Jean Patou, Ma Griffe, Channel No5, etc, etc. He carefully selected four bottles of various brands.

"I'll take these please," he said. The lady pulled out her pocket calculator and went to work. Her English wasn't too good and so she showed him the total amount on the screen. It was quite a sum and one he could ill afford.

"Please keep them for me. I will go and bring the money from inside the submarine," he said and went down the hatch. He had to wait for hours for her to drive off for lunch before venturing out of the boat to his hotel room.

The sojourn in La Pallice included a trip for some of the crew to the wine growing Champagne district, where they visited and learnt how the family of Baron Otard had perfected the art of making VSOP Cognac over centuries. Some shot off to Paris by train, to enjoy all the sights that famed city had to offer, including the Can-Can girls at the Moulin Rouge! Two of the officers overslept in the train and forgot to get off at Paris at 6AM.

They got off at the next stop – Brussels in Belgium! They had no Visa for Benelux, and could have got into all sorts of trouble. However, they were lucky and managed to get another train back to Paris soon enough, without being discovered. All told, this stopover in France was a welcome one for the crew, and one that they enjoyed thoroughly.

With much pomp and show, and with the Mayor of La Rochelle waving her off from the jetty, the submarine left harbor silently on her motors. Even as the figures on the jetty became mere dots, the order to secure the Casing for sea was given, and all hands on the forward and Aft Casings began to secure bollards and cleats in their housings and reel up the ropes to tuck them away under the Casing.

"Man Overboard! Man Overboard!" froze all aboard momentarily as the intercom disturbed the regular hum of running machinery. Then there was a flurry of activity as the drill for such an event kicked off. There was a series of maneuvers ordered on the propulsion motors as the Captain took the boat near the hapless individual floating in the water. He was not in danger, as he had his life jacket on. He was only the Aft Casing Officer who had leaned over a bit too much to check on the Aft Towing Hook when a wave moved the submarine's stern and caught him off balance. He was recovered and soon made his way down the hatch to change his clothes, looking very embarrassed!

Soon the shore lines of La Pallice and La Rochelle was left behind as Vanshali resumed her now familiar 'sway' and the crew, their sea routine.

WARMER CLIMES

The crew refreshed after the very brief but essential sojourn at La Pallice, Vanshali headed southwards for Las Palmas. Located in the Spanish colony of Canary Islands, situated off the west coast of Sahara Africa, the group of islands promised to be an exciting and interesting place. Although small in size, these islands offer varied landscapes with European, African, and even American vegetation. You name it and the islands have it – mountainous terrain, desert landscapes, tropical forests and lovely beaches. The climate is also tropical, - the type the Indians were very familiar with, and longed for. So said the 'Pilot', which is a book that informs mariners of what to expect when entering an unfamiliar place. The salt water saturated wool-lined sheepskin wind cheaters were discarded by the Bridge teams, not to be used ever again. On passing the Spanish coast and the approaches to the Mediterranean Sea, Vanshali maintained her southerly course and dived. The crew went through various underwater drills to keep themselves in touch with the intricacies of maneuvering a two thousand ton hulk of steel below the surface of the sea. She surfaced twenty-four hours later, and fair warm winds and following seas enabled the submarine to comfortably make her way to her destination, but not without some excitement.

Vanshali was to enter Las Palmas harbor at 0700hrs on a Friday morning. The night before, at about 2200hrs, the Officer of the Watch reported to the Captain that the Islands were visible through his binoculars, but were not 'painting' on the radar. The Navigating Officer got worried. The Navigational radar had an extreme range of about 40 nautical miles at mean sea level. Islands are picked up at greater ranges. The islands should have painted on the radar before they were sighted, and they were not supposed to appear on radar before 0200hrs. Was Vanshali ahead of her intended position? Had the Navigating Officer got her position wrong? According to him, the submarine was supposed to be at least 100 nautical miles away from Las Palmas. A few officers came up to the Bridge to have a last breath of fresh air, and some for a smoke, before turning in for the night. Smoking was not permitted inside the submarine. Seeing the excitement in the Chart House and on the Bridge, they lingered a little longer. The last 'fix' showed that the submarine was indeed 100 nautical miles short of Las Palmas. Yet there was one island clearly visible ahead through binoculars and even through the naked eye. It had to be one of the Canary Islands as there were no other islands around for miles and miles. Nothing is visible to the naked eye that is beyond the horizon, and 100 nautical miles was way, way, beyond the horizon. Suddenly one of the officers looking through the binoculars announced that he could see headlights of vehicles on the hill slopes of the visible island. Further excitement! The Navigating Officer's 'Fix' on the Chart simply had to be wrong! Vanshali plodded on and on ... but nothing still painted on radar. The radar technician was summoned and he got working on tuning up the set. At last, at the appointed time, which was around 0200hrs, the islands started painting on the radar at a distance of 60 nautical miles! It coincided with the position predicted by the Navigating Officer! What was witnessed that night was the effect of refracted light waves or a mirage at sea – an effect influenced by the proximity of the Sahara desert. The north western portion of the African coast was just a hundred odd kilometers away. Such phenomena are not unknown to occur at sea, but such an explanation was the last to appear in the minds of those who saw the island visually that night.

Las Palmas was the capital of the Canary Islands that form an archipelago consisting of seven islands of volcanic origin. The islands are a colony of Spain with bananas and tobacco being grown for export. Las Palmas was also a duty free port with tourism being the main supporter of its economy. Banners all over town read, "You can buy whatever you want here duty free, but will your country allow you to take it in without paying duty?" Once settled in hotels, the officers were engaged in diplomatic commitments for the first two days while the men set out to check the duty free wares on offer and eat exotic but affordable Spanish treats. Vanshali had only three round hatches by way of access into the pressure hull, and all purchases had to be restricted in size so as to go down these hatches. Three of the officers had received 'orders' from their wives to bring back gas-cooking ranges! Naturally they had to be small to be able to go down the hatch! They carried pieces of strings cut to the length of the diameters of the three hatches in their pockets, and went shopping. The shopkeepers were treated to a novel way of arriving at a decision on which model of cooking range to buy, the likes of which they had never seen before. There they were showing different models, shapes, and sizes – all affordable – and extolling the virtues of each of them in broken English, only to be met by seemingly disinterested and stony faces. After they had exhausted their enthusiasm, these officers whipped out strings from their pockets and silently went about the business of measuring the diagonals of various gas ranges, shake their heads in disappointment, and moving on to the next shop! All the salesmen would gather round in wonder and amusement. This exercise proved to be a mammoth one as they moved from shop to shop without finding a suitable one that could be taken down the hatch. They finally gave up and decided to buy something else...... all but the Engineer Officer. He moved in a taxi to the next city, and found a suitable one there! He had the goodness to ring up the other two and tell them to hold on to their money. He bought three gas ranges, one for each. Of course the packing and the casing had to be removed on the jetty before the cooking ranges could be lowered down the torpedo-loading hatch, but they finally got what the wives had asked them to get. These cooking ranges served them in their homes for many years to come, the longest of them lasting for over twenty years!

Some of the officers who were interested in seeing a bullfight bought tickets and headed for witnessing, what they thought was going to be just, one big fight. They were wrong. They got to see at least six different fights with that one ticket. Different matadors took on different bulls. They came back agreeing that it was an experience of a lifetime, but one that was never to be repeated ever again. Seeing bullfights in movies, and seeing them live, are two different experiences altogether. The smell of blood and dust, the presence of hundreds of flies in the arena and spectator stands by the third fight, were very sickening. A typical fight sequence begins with the entrance of a four-year old bull of around 600 kilograms in weight. It runs around the arena snorting and with its head held high, looking for its challenger. Picadors follow the bull on horseback and repeatedly weaken the neck muscles of the bull by piercing the nape with lances. There is no real danger to either of them. Both the horse and the rider are well padded. The bull's head lowers as the muscles are weakened. Then enter the Banderillos into the arena. They dart in and out of the stadium, taunting the bull and taking shelter behind screens the victim cannot get past. They stick banderillas (barbed darts with little streamers attached to them) into the bull's neck and shoulders. When all this is over, the 'bold' Matador finally enters to confront a wounded bull, 'plays' with him, and delivers the 'coup de grace'. It is a one-sided, totally unfair, brutal, barbaric, and tragic Hispanic game. The odd bull with a keen fighting spirit does occasionally catch the Matador unawares in a last ditch effort to torment the tormentor. These are, however, incidents in isolation. Fortunately the popularity of this sport has remained within, and not spread beyond countries influenced by Spanish culture.

A picnic was organized for the crew to the top of the volcano that formed a prominent part of Las Palmas. One bus-load of officers and sailors off-duty set off with a guide. Half way up, the guide stopped the bus and took everyone to see some beetles clinging on to huge cacti plants on the hill slope. She prized one out and squashed it between two sheets of paper. Red liquid copiously flowed from the beetle onto the paper. She explained that it was 'cochineal', and the beetle was the cochineal beetle that could be found in abundance in the Canary Islands. They were exported to the United States by the shiploads, and there the dye was used for food coloring and shading lipsticks! The bus moved on till it reached the edge of the crater where it stopped again. In the basin of this extinct, grassy, crater were two buildings and some cattle grazing. The guide explained that there was no road leading down to the crater. Once in three months or so, the residents of this crater would climb up with the help of ropes and come out to collect their logistics requirements that they lowered through ropes along with themselves. The cattle seen below were lowered as calves and had grown up into large animals in the crater. It was very cool up there at the edge of the crater, and all the trees were of the pine variety. It was an ideal spot for a picnic and flooded with tourists. Vanshali's crew had a sing-song session up there – all Hindi film songs – that caught the fancy of some of the tourists who joined them and chipped in with their own songs. Everyone had a wonderful time.

On the last evening in Las Palmas, all officers off duty, including the 'Old Man' and the Second-in-Command, decided to dine in a reasonably priced restaurant offering a floorshow followed by dancing to a live band till the early hours of the morning. It had a mezzanine floor where seating was arranged, giving a good view of the dance floor and the orchestra below. Two adjacent tables were made available and the submariners sat down to some good elbow bending, to be followed by some adventurous forays into Spanish cuisine. The floorshow was an excellent rendition of the famed Spanish Flamenco by a very professional troupe that drew sincere applause from a packed hall consisting mostly of tourists from Europe. The floor was soon jam packed with couples dancing to some very exhilarating Spanish music. The submariners kept sipping and watching. The waiter who sidled up with the Menu Card was waved away with a "later" followed by an order for another round of drinks that seemed to satisfy him. All eyes were on the dance floor below and very little conversation took place. In any case, it was difficult to be heard over the music. But the Captain got through.

"Pilot!" he addressed the Navigating Officer, "Go and ask one of the girls from the next table for a dance". The young, handsome fellow looked across and found four girls at a table without a male escort. He looked back at his Captain, smiled, and nodded, but did not get up. After awhile the Captain again called out to him and asked him to get on the dance floor. He once again demurred.

"Sir!" he replied, "This is not the Soviet Union where you can go and ask a stranger for a dance. I'll get slapped here." The Captain did not press him further.

A while later, the Captain got up and announced that he was going to see 'a man about a dog'. The "Men's" was pointed out to him and he left. All eyes were still on the dance floor watching a cross section of Europe gyrating on the floor, some expertly and some without having the faintest idea of how to dance or what they were doing. Suddenly the Second-in-Command yelled:

"Oh my God chaps! Action Stations! The Captain is on the dance floor!" There was the Old Man, being pushed and jostled by couples as he worked his way alone to the center of the floor. A tall couple was doing the jive. The man whirled his partner around and did a turn himself. The lady, on turning around, walked slap bang into the outstretched arms of the short Indian submarine Captain. She was not offended and neither was her partner. She danced a few steps with the Captain and returned to dance with her partner. The Captain walked away from the dance floor and the officers on the mezzanine floor relaxed, although a little dumbfounded. Returning to his table, he scoffed at the Navigating Officer:

"You! - Scared, gutless, dumb-wit! You couldn't ask a girl for a dance – I did!" There were no further incidents and the evening passed off well. The food was excellent – or so they all concluded the following morning. Nobody could recall the menu.

A Soviet merchant ship was noticed in Las Palmas harbor, and the Electrical Officer went across with firm intent. He was successful. He got the component that was required to re-activate the High Frequency transmitter in exchange for a bottle of pure spirit that was used onboard to clean electrical contacts. Spirit was drunk 'neat' by the Russians when they ran out of liquor! A lot has to be said for the standardization system of the Soviet Union. The crew was to get further affirmation of this system later on in another incident.

Is Navigation an art or a science? – Mariners often wonder! Vanshali's Navigating Officer was a light-hearted, fun-loving fellow, who was well liked by his superiors, peers, and subordinates alike - an absolute gem of a person. In his own way he was very hard working too. He would get up to the Bridge with his sextant at first light, at odd hours in the forenoon, at noon, in the afternoon, and at sunset, to get the sun's altitude which he would then use in the Chart House to ascertain the position of the submarine. This, in addition to the Bridge Watch he kept, his other duties, and his many visits to the Galley to 'taste' food. Between Las Palmas and Lagos in Nigeria, something went wrong. He 'fixed' the ship's position with the sextant readings he had taken with persistent regularity, on a steady course across the Sahara Desert, heading for Lagos! All onboard swore that the submarine was navigating across water and not sand! Another mirage? Not likely. He never lived it down.

One evening, somewhere west of Dakar, Vanshali was on a southerly course when all of a sudden the Officer of the Watch broke the monotony of ocean sailing and reported sighting a tall column of smoke rising on the horizon, on the starboard bow. This stirred up some activity onboard and personnel off duty headed for the Bridge to see what was up. The Captain ordered the Officer of the Watch to shape course for the smoke. It was dark by the time the submarine reached the spot where a merchant ship was ablaze and three other merchant ships were hovering around like vultures waiting to move in for their 'kill'. No one is allowed to board a distressed vessel till the Captain of that vessel gives permission. The crew was still trying to fight the fire, and had not abandoned the ship. Once they abandon the vessel, any of those standing by could attempt to board her, put out the fire, and take her as their 'prize' – an attractive and fair booty indeed.

Vanshali, with her deceptive three lights showing low in the water, asked the vessel in distress whether they needed any help. There was no response initially, but because of the submarine's persistent questioning, she finally received a curt 'no thank you'. The Captain then had a brilliant idea. Knowing fully well that merchant ships carried no doctors onboard, and Vanshalli having one, he asked whether they wanted any medical help? This time the response was almost immediate:

"Do you have a medical officer onboard?"

"Yes!"

"We have three cases of burns and two cases of fractures," replied the merchant ship. They sent a boat across and the Balzam-loving medical officer went across and did a splendid job of treating those who needed attention. A 'Letter of Appreciation' was received from the shipping company that owned the ship, many months later. The ship managed to survive.

The submarine was now well into tropical waters and conditions were ripe to carry out trials on the air conditioning system. This was the only system that had not been tried out and accepted in the Gulf of Riga. Orders were given, and the system prepared for trials. The plant was switched on. Within a few minutes of running, there was a loud sound, and the machinery came to a grinding halt. That was the end of the trials! Engine Room Artificers got down to investigating the cause of the problem and the extent of damage. The culprit was some rag pieces stuffed into the cooling water circulation system pipe that had blocked all circulation, thereby causing the temperature to soar and over heat the compressor. Who was responsible for this? Certainly not the Indians, as they had not touched this system till now. The damage – three pistons distorted and seized in their respective cylinder chambers. No spare pistons were available onboard. No air conditioning was available, and temperatures inside the hull were rising and getting to be uncomfortable. There was disappointment all round, especially since expectations were high - in anticipation of the system working and cooling the compartments.

It is not that a submarine cannot survive without air conditioning. In fact, during operational sorties out at sea, dived submarines use their air conditioning systems very sparingly in order to restrict draining current from the batteries. The temperatures, the combination of reducing oxygen content and increasing the carbon dioxide content due to eighty odd men breathing the available air inside the steel hull, the effects of the cook chopping onions or frying spices for the next meal, the gases emitted by the batteries, and other such factors make atmospheric conditions onboard very unhealthy when a conventional boat is dived. Of course, attempts are on continuously to maintain as balanced a composition of air inside the hull as possible, but it is never the same as the fresh air that is breathed when the submarine surfaces. The insides of a submarine are always warmer when she is on the surface as compared to when she is dived. But then, what is a submarine designed to move underwater doing on the surface anyway? The Captain decided to take her down for some time, as part of training, and in order to cool the steel hull a bit. The Drills were gone through, and Vanshali 'snorted' through the tropical waters, spending more hours dived over the next two days than on surface.

The submarine had surfaced at night and was displaying her Navigational lights when, like a moth drawn to a light, a small, tiny bird, no bigger than a sparrow, flew in from nowhere and settled down on the bridge, not far from the Officer of the Watch. It had very ordinary looking plumage. It was gasping and looked very tired and exhausted. Where had it come from? There was no land around for miles. What was it doing in the middle of the Ocean all by itself? The Officer of the Watch, a wild life enthusiast, asked for some rice grains to be brought up from the galley and offered it to the bird. It was ravenous and, coming suddenly alive, ate up all the rice in a trice! He reached out gently and caught it. No resistance was offered. It was sent down the hatch and put in a box where it was fed and allowed to rest for a whole day. No books on ornithology were available onboard, but webs between the feet were discernible and it was gathered that this was a land bound migratory bird that grew these webs only for migration. At the end of the journey the webs fall off, till the next migration is due when they grow again. Mother Nature and her wonders! When released the next day, she happily flew off to the north without asking the Navigating Officer for a course to steer.

There is another creature drawn like a moth to the submarine's navigational lights. Flying fish! At dawn, everyday in the Tropics and the Equatorial belt, a whole lot of them could be seen lying around on the Forward and Aft Casings. The fish-eaters onboard, who thrive on sea fish as their staple diet, would literally drool at the sight of them lying around on the Casing. Quite often, the fish would be collected and brought to the Galley where this 'clan' would prepare and eat them for lunch.

Vanshali's crew continued to follow the three-watch system onboard with the whole crew divided into the Red, White, and Blue, Watches. This was a good system to follow when transiting great distances on surface. Each Watch would close up at their duty stations for three hours at a time in succession, round the clock. That meant that an individual did three hours of Watch and then was off-watch for six hours between Watches. Some of these six off-watch hours were utilized in carrying out routines on the equipment each of the crew had been charged with. So, in addition to the Watch system, there was the Daily Routine that began at 9 AM and went on till 12 AM in the forenoon, and continued from 3 PM to 6 PM after lunch. That still gave an individual a lot of spare time with nowhere to go!

Life was getting monotonous, and the Executive Officer knew this was dangerous. Carelessness and a lackadaisical approach to work follows, and such a state was definitely not desirable onboard a submarine. When a submarine is dived, everyone is very busy with his professional work, but when she is on passage, on surface, between two ports widely spaced apart, with no operational role assigned, the off watch crew can get terribly bored. All forms of distractions have to be thought of and conducted in the very restricted spaces available. Traditionally, and for very good reasons, entertainment has to be of the physically and mentally non-exertive type. On conventional submarines, every care is taken to see that personnel inhale minimum amounts of oxygen and exhale minimum amounts of carbon dioxide while dived. When 'off-watch', sleep or simply lying down in the bunk is what is recommended. As a standard practice, this is followed while the boat is on surface passage also. But for how long, and for how many days, can an individual keep on sleeping? So, other forms of activities and entertainment have to be thought of that do not physically or mentally tire them out during 'off-watch'. 'Chess' is mentally tiring and not recommended. 'Uckers' or 'Ludo', or 'Snakes & Ladders' are silly games but not tiring, and therefore recommended. Here, the ingenuity of the crew to think of various types of games is called for, and it is amazing what all they come up with. Competitions and tournaments between compartments were launched by the Executive officer, and off-watch keepers sat up and competed with great interest.

Vanshali had also been sent a 16mm cine-projector and some Indian movies from India, along with their victuals. These were seen over and over again till the dialogue was almost learnt by-heart by almost all onboard! The officers would see the movies in the Ward Room, sitting on both sides of the Dining Table, in the space between the Cine Projector and the Screen, which was around 14 feet. One lot had their heads turned sharply to the right, and the other lot sharply to the left. When a reel finished and had to be replaced, the officers would also change sides to avoid a crick in the neck! Around eight to ten officers could see a movie at a time. The men saw movies in the Aft Ends, lying on their bunks, with the Screen hanging between the Aft Torpedo Tubes. About twenty-two of them could see a movie at a time.

Library books were available onboard for those who preferred to avoid movies and just lie down and read between their Watches and during off working hours. However, this luxury was not available to all without some inconveniences. Barring a handful of Officers and Senior Sailors, the submarine did not have fixed bunks for every single person onboard. In fact, there were bunks for only around two-thirds of the crew. One-third was expected to be on Watch at any given time. So, an individual coming off Watch had to find a bunk left by someone just gone on Watch, and settle into it. This system is called the 'hot bunking' system, as the bunk is always 'hot' with the previous person's warmth. Some sailors avoided this hassle by making their own modified beds in inconceivable spaces – like between two spare torpedoes on the three-tiered racks in the Fore Ends on the Port and Starboard sides, or next to the air conditioning plant on the deck, or on big diameter pipes laid out in a cluster.

Apart from indoor games, hobbies, quiz games, movies, etc, the Captain and the Executive Officer worked out a training program between the two, to keep the men busy and well trained. This sometimes took the form of what is referred to in the Navy as 'General Drills'. All personnel were closed up at their Action Stations for General Drills.

" For Exercise (meaning not the real thing), Fire in Galley" announced the Executive Officer, and everyone in IV Compartment went about the business of 'putting out the fire' while personnel in the adjacent compartments stood by the access hatches to IV Compartment to pass on whatever they wanted by way of equipment, to put out the fire.

"Seaman Raja Manian has fallen from the uppermost torpedo racks onto the deck and has been injured. Medical Officer to render assistance" went on the Executive Officer even while the Galley fire was being fought. That would keep the Medical Department busy for some time.

"A cup of hot tea to be rushed up to the Bridge for the Captain!" Chief Steward in the Ward room got cracking with his kettle ………. .

Such Drills are light hearted, fun, and interesting. The aim is to use them to break the monotony, prevent boredom from setting in, and to liven up the crew. BBC news was down loaded from the W/T office and read out over the intercom so that all compartments got to know what the outside world was up to. This was generally done in the evenings. Sometimes after dinner, a quiz competition between compartments would be conducted and the topic would generally be 'submarine knowledge' or the country that was to be visited next. Vanshali's crew was put through all these activities as she made her lonely way to Lagos. It helped to pass time.

LAGOS & CHRISTMAS

The Biafran War was in full swing when Vanshali entered the Port of Lagos in Nigeria and tied up alongside the Nigerian navy's flagship. A British colony till 1963, Nigeria gained independence and became a republic with four regional governments. The ruling party consisted of mainly northerners. Trouble began between the regional governments within a year, and between the Ibo tribe (Western Region) and the Hausa tribe (Northern Region). Elections failed, military rule was imposed, an attempt to revert to civil rule failed, and finally a Federal Government was formed which divided the country into 12 states. Peace didn't last for long. The Eastern Region decided to secede, and declared the area as the independent Republic of Biafra. The war that followed between this seceded state and the rest of the Federal States was termed the Biafran War.

Vanshali had ten days in Lagos, and in the prevailing situation the crew did not know what to expect. Fortunately, at that time, there were some Indian naval officers present who were training the Nigerian navy, and some of them were known to some of the officers onboard Vanshali. Those days the Nigerian navy and the Indian Navy had a very successful exchange program underway. Nigerian naval officers were training onboard Indian naval ships in India, and an Indian naval team was in their academy, training their junior officers. On the submarine's arrival, they met the crew and assured all onboard that as long as they moved around in a military area, or with defense services people, they would be safe.

The Pay Officer went to the Indian High Commission with a naval escort to collect money to be disbursed to the crew. A bachelor officer from South India, he immediately caught the attention of the High Commissioner who himself was a South Indian and had a daughter of marriageable age. Unaware of the High Commissioner's interests he sat through an unusually long meeting with him, then collected the money and returned to Vanshali to disburse the allowances to the crew. That meeting was more of an interview than a meeting. The hapless Pay Officer realized this only much later.

Enquiries were made if there were any Russian merchant ships around, as the air conditioning plant onboard had to be attended to, and new pistons were required. There was disappointment all round when the answer came in the negative. The repair yard that repaired Nigerian warships was approached with a sample of a piston. They said they would machine a similar one in size, but of different material specifications, to finally achieve the same weight and balance specifications. The 'go ahead' was given as the submarine had time in hand to get the system going. On the third day or so, some Russian trucks were sighted lugging long wooden logs from the neighboring forests of Ghana, to the docks in Lagos. Russians were driving the trucks! One of them was approached and asked where pistons of the type required by the submarine would be available in Nigeria. He surprised the questioner by answering that he had some with him! Apparently the same pistons were used in the air compressor of the Russian truck. So, three were acquired (in exchange for cleaning spirit, of course) and soon the air conditioning plant of Vanshali was made operational. Oh, what a relief! The morale of the crew rose many times over and life onboard became very comfortable. Here was another example of the advantages of Russian standardization.

The Main diesels and other auxiliary machinery had to be subjected to oil changes and other routines, so the Engine Room crew got busy with that. The Electrical chaps got down to cleaning electrical equipment with their depleted stock of cleaning spirit, the weapons department got down to routines on their torpedo tubes and the weapons control systems, the ... . in short, the whole crew got down to attending to what they had to, and for which the extra five days in harbor were given.

The Indian community in Lagos decided to give Vanshali's crew a big lunch; the 'white man's club' decided to have a number of friendly squash matches between them and the officers; and the Nigerian navy organized friendly football and volleyball matches between the sailors of the two navies.

The Indian community in Lagos consisted mainly of people from the Gujarat and Saurashtra coast of pre-independent India. They were largely vegetarians. When the officers from Vanshali arrived at the Chinese restaurant where they were invited to lunch, the Indian High Commissioner sought out the Pay officer, and introduced him to his wife. The wife invited the completely unsuspecting Pay officer to sit next to her at one of the many circular tables, and he gallantly agreed. It took him awhile to realize that he was one of only two males at that table, surrounded by eight ladies. When the first course – the soup – arrived, there were loud protests from the ladies on his table, and the soup was immediately withdrawn. It was a table for vegetarians only, and one of the ladies had discovered probably the only bit of chicken the cooks had overlooked when removing pieces from the non-vegetarian sweet corn and chicken soup, to serve it as vegetarian corn soup! All the other tables went on to their second and third non-vegetarian courses while the non-vegetarian Pay officer waited for freshly prepared vegetarian corn soup to arrive at his table! It took a long while coming. The others had finished, the vegetarian ladies were scowling, and after lunch speeches were made. The Executive Officer asked the hosts to excuse the squash players, as they had to leave for the European club immediately. The Pay officer got up, without lunch, and joined the rest of the squash players. There were two more receptions for Vanshali's crew after that – one by the High Commissioner, and one by the Nigerian navy. During one of those receptions the now suspicious and worried Pay Officer spent a good part of the evening playing 'hide and seek' with the Indian High Commissioner and his wife! He skipped the other one.

It was apparent that, in the prevailing conditions of unrest, the Nigerian defense personnel had the run of the country. They moved into whichever houses they fancied, acquired and drove whichever cars they liked, and drove on the wrong side of the road with impunity whenever there were traffic hold ups. They ruled the roost. One of Vanshali's officers – the Sonar officer - met up with a Nigerian naval officer who had served with him on one of the Indian naval cruisers back in India some years ago. They had developed a good rapport then. The Nigerian was a tribal leader of sorts, which was obvious from the permanently etched three, long and broad scratched marks on his face, on either cheek. He was thrilled to revive old contacts and decided to take the Sonar officer under his wing for the duration of Vanshali's stay in Lagos. He begged the Captain to relieve the Sonar officer of harbor duties, and asked permission to take him home for the next few days. This was granted, and away went the Sonar Officer with his Nigerian friend, to his home. The Nigerian officer was a bachelor. His sister lived with him, but was away on duty with the Nigerian Railways in another town. The two of them had a big house all to themselves.

"Normally, every Christmas, I have a big party in my house", he explained,

"This Christmas, however, I had decided to go party hopping to all my friends' places. Now, I have you with me and so let me see if I can organize something in my place at short notice" he said.

The two went to the homes of many of his friends, only to be disappointed. An obviously popular fellow, everyone was thrilled to see him but had already committed to going elsewhere, and it was too late to cancel their programs.

In one of the houses they visited, the Sonar officer had a strange experience. The two of them entered the house, were warmly received by the male member of the house, and were asked to sit down. Within minutes of their arrival, even while introductions and pleasantries were being exchanged, the doorbell rang again. The host said something to the Nigerian officer in a language unfamiliar to the Sonar officer, and went to answer the door. The Nigerian Officer turned to the Sonar officer and explained,

"Now just observe what you see, carefully. Don't ask questions, keep sitting, and don't move! I will explain later."

The host walked in with a witch doctor holding a leafy branch in one hand and a bell in the other. He could only have been a witch doctor – his body and face was painted up and he was dressed like one, complete with feathered headgear and grass skirt. Without talking to anyone, this witch doctor walked to the four corners of the room, shook the branch he was holding and rang the bell vigorously each time, chanting in a low monotonous tone all the while. There were screams of women heard from upstairs. Ignoring the two officers who were seated, the witch doctor then proceeded to the next room, escorted by the host. They did not come back for a long time and the two officers got up and left.

"This witch doctor should not be seen by women while they are in their child bearing ages," explained the Nigerian officer " or else they will remain barren for the rest of their lives". He went on "Witch doctors everyday route and the approximate time of passing that route, is published in the local papers. Women take note and keep out of the way".

"What is he doing in your friend's house?" asked the Sonar officer.

"Something must be weighing heavily in his mind that he wants to discuss with the witch doctor. He will offload it, and the other will give a patient hearing and follow it up with some advice" he explained wryly.

"Then?" prodded the submarine Sonar officer.

"Then he will drink a lot of the host's 'Star' beer and go home!" he said, 'Star' being the brand name of Nigeria's famous beer.

The Sonar officer and the unsuccessful Nigerian officer abandoned their plans of hosting a party in the latter's house and went party hopping over Christmas. From all accounts, the two of them had a rollicking time.

The Nigerians loved their 'Star' beer and could literally drink gallons of it, without even once exercising their bladders over two, maybe three, hours. Even so, they met their match during the Christmas Eve celebrations in the Naval Mess, in Vanshali's officers. Games and competitions were organized throughout the evening. One of them was a beer drinking competition. Four teams with four participants in each team were formed up some distance away from a table that had sixteen tankards of beer arranged in rows of four each. The first member of each team had to run up to the row of four tankards in front of him, gulp down one tankard of beer, and run back to the second member of his team and touch him. The second, third, and fourth members of the team were to follow the same drill. The team to finish drinking all four tankards first, would be declared winners. These were no ordinary tankards. They were huge and, in capacity, equal to large water jugs. The Nigerian army, navy, and air force formed three teams. Vanshali's team formed the fourth. A word about Vanshali's team; they were all hardcore vodka drinkers who had taken easily to Balzam while in Riga. Their drinking prowess had been somewhat affected by the many 'dry' days at sea, and they were very thirsty indeed! The Indian Navy does not drink at sea. The competition began, and loyal supporters boisterously cheered their respective teams. Vanshali's Assistant Navigating Officer was the last participant from their team, but the first to finish the remaining tankard of beer. He then proceeded to pick up the Nigerian Air Force team's last tankard and downed it before their last participant could get to the table! The prize was a crate of 'Star' beer that was taken to the submarine's Ward Room for all to share at an opportune time.

The party went on till well after midnight. Dinner was served at a decent hour, and decent people went and helped themselves. The table looked grand, and there was a large, generous, spread. Two officers from Vanshali were at the bar, and having a wonderful evening. They were in no hurry to get to the dining table, and took their time. When they did finally get to the table, the food had run out! Not upset, they went back to the bar and carried on with their liquid diet. Ultimately, they went back to the submarine without a meal and turned in.

It hit everyone in the wee hours of the morning. Food poisoning! With only two toilets onboard the submarine, the officers ran to the Nigerian navy's flagship alongside, to use their toilets. The scene was the same on the flagship. Gradually, an evacuation process to the hospital began, and ambulances were charging up and down the roads to get near-dehydrated officers to doctors for urgent medical attention. The hospital beds were full by first light, and beds overflowed onto the verandahs. The Nigerian Naval Chief was in one of those beds! A calamity of gigantic proportions, and an embarrassing one at that, had struck the naval base. In all this chaos, the two officers onboard Vanshali, who hadn't had dinner, slept peacefully! Some party!

On Christmas Day, there was much activity on the jetty where the Nigerian flagship was tied. The Chief of the Naval Staff had presented his flagship with a buffalo as a Christmas gift. It was hacked and portioned on the jetty, next to the ship's gangway, for each crewmember to take his share on his way home. The jetty wasn't too welcome a sight to Vanshali's crew, some of who were vegetarians. Many of the crew spent that day onboard, and stepped out only after the jetty was washed.

The Indian High Commissioner hosted his party on the last day of the submarine's stay in Lagos. The Pay officer opted to stand duty onboard that day! It was another late party that finished in the wee hours of the morning. The Officers returned onboard just a few hours before Vanshali was due to sail. When she did cast off and maneuver her way out of harbor, the Captain ordered a South Westerly course that took the boat out of the shipping lane and well clear of the coast, and which, if persisted with, would have taken the boat to South America! All off-watch officers hit the sack to catch up on sleep. Late in the evening, after a good sleep, the course was altered to head for the Cape of Good Hope. Vanshali was on her way to crossing the Equator and entering the South Atlantic Ocean. Christmas was now well behind her and there was the New Year's Day to look forward to, at sea.

Mariners the world over have great respect for King Neptune, the King of the Oceans. Legend has it that he and his courtiers look after the safety and well-being of all seafarers who have been welcomed by him into his domain, and this is traditionally done when they cross the equator. Ships, crossing the equator, have a simple ceremony full of humor and light-hearted revelry, wherein someone dressed like Neptune, accompanied by his mermaids and members of the court, makes an appearance onboard, and all those crossing the equator for the first time are summoned before him. The 'sins & offences' committed by each one is then read out by a courtier, and the King awards a punishment which is carried out before all present. After that, the individual is 'cleansed' and welcomed by the King into his domain and protection. A certificate is awarded to him that gives the date, time, and year, when the individual crossed the equator, and at what longitude he was pardoned and subsequently welcomed by Neptune into his domain. In Indian mythology, 'King Neptune' is 'Lord Varuna', and so Lord Varuna makes his appearance on Indian vessels, and the rest of the revelries are much the same.

Two days out from Lagos, and there was much activity onboard in preparation for Lord Varuna's expected visit. The Chief Bos'n mate, referred to as the Coxswain onboard submarines, had a long discussion with the Executive Officer followed by another discussion with the Navigating Officer. The scope and extent of celebrations, and the time of crossing the equator, were both defined. Now he got on with the preparations. It requires a lot of ingenuity to produce suitable costumes onboard a submarine for the event. Basic materials are lacking and one has to find agreeable substitutes. One way out was to dress the troupe scantily so that the needs were limited – and that goes for the two mermaids as well! Coconut shells were produced out of nowhere for the mermaids; beards and skirts were made from bits of rope and cordage; grease and paints were used to give the necessary color to the bodies and 'costumes'!

At the equator, the submarine was stopped. With only essential personnel on duty, the rest of the crew mustered on the Aft Casing. Those crossing the equator for the first time were singled out and mustered ahead of the rest. Finally, to the sound of drums (read – empty kitchen vessels), Bos'n pipes, and other indefinable noises, out from the Fin popped Lord Varuna and his entourage. The mermaids looked bashful with mascara, lipstick, coconut bras and hemp skirts, and very little else on, and were the cynosure of all eyes and wolf whistles. With them came a few tins of grease, some tins of different oils, some soap solution, and what not. Swords and shields and an enviable crown for King Neptune were cut out from cardboard cartons, and given a menacing look with paint from the Bos'n Store. Soon the ceremonies began.

"I, Lord Varuna, ruler of the Oceans and all who dwell in them, welcome Vanshali and her crew into my domain. I understand there are some amongst you who have committed certain crimes and who are not a part of my Kingdom. No one, I repeat, - no one -, can sail the oceans without being a member of my Kingdom. I request the Captain of this submarine to produce all such individuals before me so that I can examine their crimes, mete out punishments, and see them carried out before all here present. On properly carrying out the punishments before you all, the individual will re-appear before me and make a promise that he will be my faithful subject always. I will then decide whether I want him in my kingdom or not, and act accordingly. Bring on the first offender".

One of the courtiers announces a name and lists out his crimes;

"Your Lordship, Leading Seaman Francis is guilty of an act prejudicial to good order and maritime discipline in that he stole a whole bowl of pudding from the galley and ate it all by himself in the Sonar Office, with no one else present, the day after we sailed from Lagos. He thus deprived other members of your kingdom and many of the crew onboard of their rightful share. He needs to be severely punished for this despicable act onboard a submarine".

Leading Seaman Francis is then led by two members of the court with swords and shield before Lord Varuna who announces;

"You have committed a dastardly act. You need to be banished from my kingdom for this awful behavior. However, I will give you a chance. Firstly, apologize to the crew and promise you will eat only your rightful share onboard in future."

He apologizes.

"Now! You are to wash your mouth with soap water, drink a glass of seawater, stick cello tape over your mouth, and not eat for the next three minutes!"

This action is then carried out after which he is brought before Lord Varuna for the final time.

"I, Lord Varuna, am a considerate king, and quite humane. I welcome you into my kingdom as a full-fledged member. Henceforth, you will have full freedom to sail the seven seas with impunity. But be careful and share what you are supposed to share with your shipmates. Bring on the next offender!"

One by one, each novice was brought before him and similar charges read out. Light-hearted punishments were awarded, and carried out. The whole ceremony lasted for an hour, after which the submarine got underway again. The certificates – all printed in India, and brought by the crew when they came for initial training – were handed over to the 'first timers' that night after entering the date, Latitude, and Longitude in ink in the appropriate places that were left blank when the Certificates were printed. New Year's Day came and went – just like any ordinary day at sea.

SOUTH ATLANTIC & THE HORN OF AFRICA

The surface of the equatorial sea in nil wind conditions is to be seen, to be believed. It is like a pliable glassy surface. Not a ripple! No signs of breaking waves. Even the wake of the submarine, or her masts when dived, and the propeller 'wash', all seemed to simply disappear below a pliable glassy surface within moments of forming. It is as if oil has been spilt over the sea to calm it. Not for nothing is the area referred to, in geographical terminology, as the 'Doldrums' or the 'Equatorial Calm'.

A few days after she had crossed the equator, the Captain decided to dive Vanshali and put her through the paces again. Fresh stores and victuals had been embarked from Lagos, and the Engineer Officer had to re-work the 'Trim'. This done, he took his calculations across to the 'Old Man' who went through the book and cleared it. On orders from the Captain, the Control Room Officer of the Watch got onto the intercom:

"Diving Stations - Diving Stations!" he announced, and the Panel watch-keeper sounded the appropriate Buzzer signals. Every order is accompanied by sound signals on the Bell or the Buzzer, which is heard, understood, and obeyed by all onboard for what they are meant to be. A flurry of activity and movement followed, as the crew scampered between compartments to get to their Diving Stations. Soon everyone was at his post and confirmation was received by the Executive Officer by way of reports from each compartment that this was so.

"Stop Engines" was the Captain's next order, and the Engine Order Telegraphs were put to 'Stop'. The Engine Room, having received these orders, shut down all three diesels, and the boat slowed down till it came to a stop.

A word about who is 'in command', and at what stage. The Officer of the Watch on the bridge is always in command of the boat when she is on surface. All orders are promulgated after obtaining his approval. The officer on the Periscope is in command when the boat is at Periscope Depth. When deep, the Control Room Officer is the officer in command. In all these eventualities, if the Captain gives a direct order to con the boat, it is assumed that he has taken over command. If he wants the officer in command to continue in command, he will ask him to execute an order instead of directly giving one.

The sea was calm, and there was no need to select a particular diving course. In a heavy swell, the course is altered to take it on the beam. The Officer of the Watch on the Bridge confirmed that there were no ships or boats or sailing vessels around. A 'sounding' was taken and there was adequate water below keel to carry out a safe dive.

"Officer of the Watch, come down below and shut the Upper Lid", ordered the Captain. After going through the drill on the Bridge, the Look Out and the Officer of the Watch came down the hatch with the latter shutting the Upper Lid and yelling down the hatch to the Control room,

"Upper Lid shut - Upper Lid shut!" He then went into the Conning Tower and raised the Search periscope to keep an 'all round Periscope Watch'. He could see the bows of the boat with its shining, stainless steel sonar dome reflecting the sun's rays. He put the filter on to reduce the glare through the monocular eyepiece of the Search Periscope. Swinging it around, he now looked aft. There was no propeller wash or wake, which meant Vanshali was stopped with little or no way on. He searched the skies. No birds in sight. No aircraft. All was calm.

"Take her down to Periscope Depth, Number One" said the Captain, addressing the Executive Officer who was in the Control Room. These were old terminologies inherited from the Royal Navy. The 'Old Man' was the Captain of the ship, the Executive Officer was the 'Number One', the Engineer Officer was 'Chief', the Electrical Officer – 'Sparks', and so on.

"Conning Tower - this is Control Room. Request permission to dive to Periscope Depth" asked the Executive Officer on the intercom.

"Dive to Periscope Depth with three degrees aft bubble" said the Officer of the Watch, from the Conning Tower. This was repeated by the Control Room and then promulgated to the whole boat:

"Diving now - Diving now!"

"Open End Group Main vents" ordered the Executive Officer to the Panel Chief standing not far from him. All eyes went automatically to the 'Bubble' and the Depth Gauge. The buzzer signal was followed by hydraulically opening Main Vents of Ballast tanks 1 to 4 and 7 to 10. The Fore Planes were turned out.

"Open Center Group Main Vents. Slow Ahead three motors".

The now familiar sound of air hissing out of the Ballast tanks was heard in two lots. Everyone waited for the boat to start going down, as the Ballast Tanks were fully flooded. This was to be a gentle, deliberate, dive and not one of those crash dives normally executed during training exercises and operations. For a long time nothing happened. She wouldn't go down. A look at the Hydroplanes showed that the helmsman had put both the Fore and Aft Planes to maximum angles of 'Dive'. The Engine Order telegraphs showed all three motors propelling the boat. The Log showed a speed of three knots that was slowly increasing. Everything seemed to be OK, but she wouldn't go down.

"You've kept her very light, Chief" remarked the Old Man. "Take in some water in the Compensating Tanks to get her heavier, so that she goes down".

"But, Sir," mumbled the Engineer Officer, "I've only kept her as light as we did the last time". He ordered the Ballast Pump to run and flood

Compensating Tank No2.

Everyone waited …. and …. waited. Compensating Tank No 2 was almost full and still Vanshali wouldn't go down.

"May I flood Compensating Tank No1, Sir?" asked the Engineer Officer. There was no reply from the Captain. He looked distinctly uneasy. Compensating Tank No1 was already half flooded as a part of Trim calculations. Something was not all right here. The tonnage of water taken in was far more than normal. It wasn't prudent to carry on taking in more and more water.

"Stop all motors! Blow Center group" ordered the Captain. High Pressure air was blown into Ballast tanks 5 and 6 and the water expelled from it.

"Shut Center Group Kingstons! Chief, bring your Trim Book to the Ward Room," said the Captain as he wended his way through the hatch into the Second Compartment. Some minutes passed while the rest of the crew waited curiously for the next set of orders.

From the Ward Room, on the intercom, the Captain asked the Navigating Officer to bring the Chart to him with an updated position of the boat. The Navigating Officer disappeared into his cabin and soon came out with the Chart and joined the group. Further discussions took place. Some time later, they all wended their way back into the Control Room. The Captain took the microphone and addressed the crew over the intercom:

"This is the Captain speaking. We will not be carrying out a dive now. We shall do it later in the day. That's all".

The End Group Ballast tanks were blown, the Upper Lid opened, the diesels prepared, and Vanshali continued with her surfaced passage. The Engineer Officer got down to re-calculating his Trim. He also checked the density of the seawater.

When Trim calculations are worked out, the density of seawater in the area is an important factor that is taken into consideration. During earlier dives, the Engineer Officer had taken the value of seawater density in the Baltic Sea and temperate latitudes and worked out the Trim. The salinity and density of water there is far less than in the Tropics. For this dive he should have taken the density of the Tropics in his calculations, which he had forgotten to do.

Late in the evening, Vanshali attempted a dive again with a corrected Trim and modified values for the density of seawater in the region. This time everything went off well. Another lesson was learnt that day.

The following day, the submarine began to experience a sudden strong current pushing it from eastwards. A look at the Chart explained this. The Mighty Congo River was flowing out into the Atlantic Ocean, and the effects of the current were being experienced far out at sea. Adjustments to the Course to steer had to be made to counter this, which the Navigating Officer promptly did.

An encounter took place a few days later that brought back nostalgic memories of the Soviet Union to the crew. They had already been away from that country for quite awhile but could not help reminiscing about their days there. That very morning, the officers in the Ward Room were discussing the various long queues they had stood in for basic items of food and clothing. The long drawn out queues of men, women, and children, to buy something rare in erstwhile Soviet Union, is now legendary. Like a flash of lightening, word would spread that in so-and-so place, at so-and-so time, on so-and-so day, some attractive item would be available. 'Raedka Bivaeth' means 'rarely found'. It could be anything from cauliflower in winter months to boiled prawns or even Jeans made in India. At daybreak on the appointed day, the queue would begin to grow ... and grow ... and grow, till it wound its way around pillars and posts, round the corners of buildings, and onto pavements that seemingly stretched endlessly. Not everyone in the queue got to the front to get what was being sold. Suddenly a shout would announce that the item was all sold out. The queue would break up and a lot of woefully faced people would rue the waste of time and disperse. Maybe next time ..... . This was true of even mundane stuff like daily food requirements. The Indians sometimes felt that the authorities, to keep the populace busy and away from mischief, intentionally created these sorts of situations! Today, in the shop in front of your house, bread would be available - but not butter. Butter was available in the shop 200 meters down the road. Tomorrow, butter may be available in the shop in front - but no bread. Bread was available in the next street. And so, like a colony of ants, the Soviets would hunt daily - both for their everyday requirements and for items which 'Raedka Bivaeth'. ...., except for tinned sea food which was always available in plenty. At any time you could walk into a shop and be sure that you would get a variety of tinned fish, squid, whale meat etc, that you could choose from, and Vanshali's crew was reminded of all this in the Southern Atlantic Ocean that day.

The Soviets had the concept of operating huge fishing fleets all over the globe. Each fleet was capable of staying out at sea for nine months at a time, without having to enter any port. A Fleet consisted of a huge 'factory ship' or 'mother ship', with seven to eight ocean going trawlers accompanying it. The 'factory' or 'mother' ship had a variety of functions. It would carry enough fuel for herself and her trawlers. It had workshops onboard with sufficient spares to look after the needs of the whole trawler fleet, and sustain them at sea. It carried the families of all the men in the trawlers and its own crew, who were kept busy during the nine months at sea. A school functioned onboard for little children, with sufficient teachers to impart instructions as per the common syllabus followed along the entire length and breadth of the Soviet Union. Most of the teachers were wives of the men in the fleet.

The smaller ocean-going trawlers would net seafood of every type in their trawls that would be brought to the stern part of the 'factory' ship and transferred to 'mother'. A powerful winch would haul the trawl / net up the sloped cutaway in the stern. Furious activity would follow onboard by way of washing the catch down, sorting them out - first by 'type' and then by 'size'. Then the cleaning would begin. Slowly and methodically every step or process that was required to be followed before canning the fish would be gone through. They would finally be canned, sealed, labeled, and stowed away. One cycle was thus completed. Over the nine months out at sea, many such cycles would be completed. Periodically, a Soviet freighter would come and take away the products already canned, and take them back to 'fatherland'.

There were slack periods as well as hectic periods. There were periods when the mother ship would lie adrift with two or more trawlers lying alongside - for the trawler crews to spend some time with their families, or to carry out urgent repairs. Each fishing fleet was given its own area of functioning. It was, thus, no surprise to suddenly come across Soviet fishing fleets in the southern latitudes of any of the oceans.

Mail - letters, Soviet magazines, literature etc - were regularly flown to sea and dropped onboard the mother ship. Mail from the crew was also regularly picked up. The Soviet radio had one Short Wave channel exclusively for messages to and from family members ashore and onboard. Anyone who understood the Russian language could listen in.

The fleet would enter harbor for a ninety-day's rest and recuperation period once a year - with nine month's unspent salary! In the port, a warning on the radio and TV would go out one month in advance, with daily reminders, that the fleet would be entering harbor on so-and-so day. Everyone was advised to stock up before the fleet entered harbor, or face the consequences! At last the 'day' would arrive. The jetties and piers would be packed with relatives and friends, and even, sometimes, a band. A very warm welcome would be accorded to the crews, with the whole event beamed 'live' on TV. A festive air could be discerned all round.

That would be Day 1. From Day 2 onwards you could see them everywhere - walking unsteadily on the streets with a bottle in each hand and in their overcoat pockets too, shopping in huge quantities, and buying up just about anything and everything. Shop shelves, and liquor in particular, ran dry. Basic requirements were hard to come by. Lucky were those locals who heeded the advice and stocked up.

Tons and tons of tinned fish would be unloaded - non-stop - for a week and more. They would be transported by road and rail across the Soviet Union. Of tinned fish, there was no short supply - ever.

In the South Atlantic, that very morning, Vanshali espied a Soviet fishing fleet. Having spent over two years in that country, the crew was overjoyed and the Officer of the Watch, with the Captain's permission, signaled Vanshali's identification to them in Russian - a language every one onboard was familiar with. The factory ship closed the submarine and the latter stopped in anticipation of getting some good, fresh, fish. At a reasonable distance from the submarine she also stopped and lowered a boat. All those on the submarine's Bridge could count six oarsmen rowing in unison as the boat speedily closed the boat. Did anyone say 'oarsMEN'? They were all women - big and powerful, and of the Soviet variety. They came alongside with plenty of fish. Much conversation was exchanged in Russian while the fish was taken onboard the submarine. The Captain sent down a bottle of Scotch, all properly wrapped up and tagged, and requested them to give it to the Master of the Factory ship. They happily took it and laughingly promised to hand it over to their Master. As they cast off, and the submarine got underway, to the horror of all on the submarine's Bridge the women in the boat were found tearing off the wrapper from the bottle. It was opened and passed around! They finished the bottle then and there and toss it overboard! They then STEADILY rowed back to their ship!

That evening there was an overpowering smell of fried fish throughout the submarine which lingered well past dinner, through the night, and through much of the forenoon the following day, despite all efforts to ventilate the boat and expel the 'fishy' air! The cooked fish, however, tasted super, and the crew thoroughly enjoyed it.

Vanshali was soon approaching the southern tip of Africa. She closed the coast and got into the shipping lane. Two Albatrosses with extremely wide wingspans, for which they are known, took up position on the bows of Vanshali, and led the way to the Cape of Good Hope! Normally gulls, terns, and albatrosses take up positions astern of ships to see if they could pick up any food discarded overboard by the crew. These two showed no such inclination and the Officers of the Watches named them Vasco and Pedro. Tirelessly, they escorted the submarine right up to the Cape, and then vanished.

The submarine passed umpteen seals bobbing up and down in the water, resting on their backs, and looking curiously at this grey, steel, fish-like vessel going past them. Some of them barked at the submarine and sounded like dogs. Soon the Table Mountain of South Africa was visible on the horizon on the port bow, with a huge cloud seemingly resting on top of it. The passage across the Atlantic Ocean was almost over. Vanshali was now struggling to make good the speed she was supposed to, as she had run into the famed Benguela Current that was flowing along the coast and directly against her. This was expected, but never experienced before. From now on, she would have strong currents constantly against her till she rounded the Cape and went halfway up to Malagasy. The three diesels were ordered at 'half ahead' and the submarine barely made good a speed of seven knots against a normal thirteen to fourteen knots at these diesel revolutions. From now on, the consumption of fuel was going to be higher than normal.

The strong current, and the slow progress made by Vanshali reminded the Assistant Torpedo Officer of one of the ships of the Indian navy he had served on that had been de-commissioned subsequently. It was a store ship, and one of those second hand ones procured cheaply from the merchant navy. It met the navy's requirements of yesteryears. On the submarine's Bridge, he narrated this story to some of the other officers around him. He had served on INS Dharini only for a brief period. The store ship was entering Bombay harbor at her top speed of three knots! With the flooding tide, she would make good five knots. With the ebb tide, she would slowly drop astern by a mile every hour! With the change in tide taking place at six hourly intervals, the ship took over a day to enter harbor from the Floating Light at the entrance to the harbor, and tie up on her berth. The Officers of the Watches would hand over their duties to their relievers with very little changes in 'bearings' of Khanderi Light House, used for determining the position of the ship, and which was on an island by that name located on the starboard side when entering harbor. The situation here was almost similar. The bearing of Table Mountain hardly changed from the time the Officer of the Watch took over his watch, till the time he handed over to his reliever!

The Benguela Current moves up from the south, and brings with it a sudden drop in temperature. Off the Cape of Good Hope, it is a cold current. Bridge watch keeping, especially at night, became a chilly affair! Out came the windcheaters and coats for Bridge watch keeping!

The South African Navy is the largest navy in this particular region, and one cannot round the Cape without their noticing your presence. In fact, they keep an eye on all shipping in the area. With the Suez Canal shut, they were busier than ever. Most of the shipping otherwise consisted of giant super tankers carrying oil, and other vessels too deep in draught to transit through the Suez Canal. It was not surprising, therefore, for Vanshali to be 'buzzed' by Maritime Reconnaissance aircraft, followed by a frigate, and finally by a submarine! Diplomatic relations were estranged between India and South Africa due to their 'apartheid' policies, and so the greetings exchanged between Vanshali and their ships were cold and very civil. The South African submarine dropped behind and took station on the 'Quarter' of Vanshali. The intention was obvious. She was going to dive and record the propeller signature of Vanshali. This is known in naval parlance as 'fingerprinting' Vanshali. Once recorded, she can be identified at any future date by the recorded values. Anticipating such an eventuality, the Captain had ordered 'masking' propeller sounds. As Vanshali had three propellers, by ordering different revolutions on each of the propellers, the ensuing combined noise would be too confusing to get a proper signature. Having done that, he signaled to the South African submarine;

"Are you ready to record my signatures? - Or should we send you some recordings on tape and spare you the effort?"

Cheeky? Of course it was! But she got the message. She altered course away, and disappeared over the horizon. She was not seen or heard thereafter.

The sky was clear and peppered with stars. The configuration of stars known as the Southern Cross was prominent in the sky. There was a light headwind inviting wisps of spray over the bulbous stainless steel sonar dome in the bows, onto the Forward Casing, and wetting the deck. The moon appeared to be dancing through the reflections on the wet deck. Vanshali was twelve nautical miles off Cape Town, still struggling to make decent headway against the currents. On Watch, on the Bridge, was the Assistant Torpedo Officer. He was not alone. The Sonar officer had come up to the Bridge for a smoke before turning in for the night. Fine on the Starboard bow, some distance away, was what appeared to be a trawler. From the lights she was displaying, and which were visible at that time from the submarine's Bridge, she was certainly a small vessel. Broad on the Port bow, also some distance away, was what looked like a static offshore oilrig. She was brilliantly lit, like a Christmas tree. The two officers were chatting on the Bridge, but both were periodically looking at those two, lit, objects, as seamen are wont to do. Finally, the Sonar officer asked the man on Watch what he was going to do. The latter replied that he would continue on the present course and pass between them. Some sixth sense told the Sonar Officer that it was best that they both be passed on the same side, and he voiced his opinion. His friendly advice was taken, and the Assistant Torpedo officer boldly altered the course of the submarine to Port so as to get both of them well clear on her Starboard side. It was just as well. When the submarine got closer, the static oilrig turned into a floating dry dock, and the trawler turned out to be a powerful tug towing it, without displaying proper towing lights! One can only imagine the disaster that could have followed had the submarine continued on its original course. A thick, steel wire rope between the towing vessel and the vessel being towed would have created damage of unimaginable proportions to the three propellers, and other underwater fittings of the boat. The rest of the night was serene.

THE COMING OF AGE

Vanshali and the crew had got used to each other by now, after all these days together at sea and in harbor. The Grey Lady could not resist reflecting on these past many weeks with the Indian crew onboard. While most of the days were spent on the surface and not underwater where she was really at home, it did not greatly alter her impressions. With her bow slicing through the water, and her engines purring with a healthy sound, she looked back at these past few weeks and reminisced.

"Pushing against the Benguela Current, with very little else happening, I had time to look back and take stock of all that had happened since I was christened. In a short period of a little under three months, I have sailed from Latitude 60° North, across the Equator, down to Latitude 35° South, almost spanning the entire Atlantic Ocean from north to south, and visiting three ports en route. I have also sailed through two Seas – the Baltic and the North Seas. Very few warships would have matched this, and I am quite complacent about it! Warships of most nations don't sail far and wide like merchantmen. They generally venture beyond their territorial waters only with a specific purpose, and that too, occasionally. In my case, it is to head to my new home. True, I am a submarine and should have done the passage dived. However, the speed of advance I was required to maintain was too high for a dived transit on motors. Such a voyage, dived, would have consumed a number of operating cycles of my batteries, which are required to be preserved for operations in India after we get there. I carry enough diesel oil to go halfway around the world without the need to re-fuel on the way. It is not for nothing that my design has been acknowledged as one of the most successful in conventional submarine designs the world over. I use diesel oil only when propelling on the surface, or while snorting at Periscope depth. So, the directive to remain on the surface and dive only for training en route was a right one.

That incident on my Air Conditioning system hurt. It was standard practice among the Russians to stuff rag pieces at both ends of any pipeline removed from any system, as also to stuff rags in the openings of the portion of the system left in place. This is to ensure that no dust or foreign particles went in. It is a good practice, but one must remember to remove the rags when re-assembling the system again. Obviously, 'Sasha' forgot, and the consequences were what my Air Conditioning system had to face.

As a consequence of all that I have just explained, my story so far has been mostly about little incidents that occurred at sea while on passage, and in harbor. It could be the story of any ocean going vessel, barring a few incidents when we went through the process of diving. So what's so special about it?

I have been observing this crew these past few months, ever since they first embarked onboard. I have seen them as a nervous, inexperienced lot. I have seen them going through the process of learning and confidence building. I have seen them commit, and learn from, mistakes. I have seen their behavior onboard, and in foreign ports. Their sincerity, their cohesiveness, their discipline, their ability to learn and understand quickly, and their eagerness to learn from their juniors and seniors alike, all convince me that they are from a mature navy, and that I should be proud to have them exploit and handle me. They certainly do not behave like the conscripts of the Soviet Navy and I am certainly looking forward to joining this navy and serving as an important part of their third dimension. Can you believe it? – Two and a half months inside my restrictive confines, and not a single fight onboard? No signs of claustrophobia either! Quite a few of them have even managed to side-step the 'hot bunking' system by making permanent, comfortable, sleeping places for themselves where no bunks or mattresses exist.

Some of them have developed selective friendships, but these, I find, are based on the commonality in the languages they speak, and the part of India they come from. They speak many regional languages in small groups, but one language on matters 'navy'. They are all eating the same food, and I must confess that their food is aromatic, very spicy, but greasy compared to what the Russians ate. These chaps stock up bread, eggs, mutton, chicken, vegetables and fruits in each port and, for the first ten days at sea, eat well. After that, as fresh victuals run out, they eat more and more tinned stuff, rice, and lentils disguised by the cook to make them appear as if their origin wasn't from cans. That takes some ingenuity. When they cooked flying fish, and after the Soviet fishing fleet gave them all that fish which they ate for days, my insides stank! Their food preparations seem to be quite complicated! Onions, shallots, and those colored powders in just about every food dish!! They seem to enjoy eating tons of it. The whole crew is in tears when the onions are chopped or ground to fine paste while the air inside is being circulated to ventilate my insides. That poor cook keeps slogging day and night. It's not that the crew is not considerate – I have observed that he is provided with a helper from the many volunteers who are readily available. Why can't they eat food prepared simply? As we approached South Africa, some of the sailors put in formal requests to change their diet from non-vegetarian food to vegetarian food! At the Executive Officer's 'Requestmen & Defaulter's Table', they were reminded by the Executive Officer that he had seen them eating beef in the Soviet Union. Why, then this sudden request to change over? Pat came the answer from one:

"Sir - We will be entering the Indian Ocean soon. In India I, and my family, - we are all vegetarians. What I ate in the Soviet Union were Russian cows, and not Indian cows. I believe that the Gods won't castigate me for eating Russian cows. The Indian cow is sacred, and that is another matter."

I have learnt a lot about these Indians these past few months, and I am sure there is more to learn about them.

Water was scarce and restricted but we were consuming more per day than the average Russian, in an effort to maintain some standard of personnel hygiene. The other day, in the Tropics, the Executive Officer, while on Afternoon Watch, and with the permission of the Captain of course, sent me romping all over the Ocean chasing rain squalls, while some of the crew members came up with soap and towel to have a 'rain bath'. The aim was to stay under a precipitating rain cloud as long as one could, and then catch up with another and follow the same process. This led me away from my course I was steering, but who cared? All they wanted was to have a bath - even at the risk of having to wipe the soap off the body with a towel should the rain cloud leave them with an incomplete bath! On another occasion, just before entering Lagos, I was stopped at sea for a 'sea water bath' that involved rigging up a hose on the Aft Casing through which salt water was pumped. The entire crew lined up in their jocks and walked from the Fin to the suspended hose, paused under it for a few seconds to get wet, and moved on to the Aft portion of the Casing where they lathered themselves with a special 'sea water soap'. Then they turned around and walked back, under the hose once again, to get the soap off, and to the Fin where they had their towels to dry themselves. When all of them finished, I was also hosed down!

I have observed that they change their personal wear once every week. They have what they seem to refer to as 'disposable clothing'. They are all identical and available in three sizes, and worn at sea (only) from the Captain down to the Cook. They use the old, worn and used clothes as scrubbing cloth for keeping me clean, after which they dispose of them. That is good submarine practice. From a safety angle, 'stringed, waste jute' which is freely used on board ships, is not a good thing to use on submarines for cleaning, or any work.

I like the way they keep themselves busy after the day's work is done, with evening quiz competitions and other programs that result in increasing their knowledge and awareness about me and the ports they have visited or are going to visit. The Torpedo Officer pulled out a toy 'chain stitch' sewing machine he had purchased in the Soviet Union for one of his nieces from his belongings, and went about stitching himself a pair of shorts from the waste rags available onboard for cleaning! He wore it and paraded along the length of the submarine to the amazement of all. The Communications Officer was charged with the duty of tuning on to BBC and taking down salient features of the daily news. He makes two versions of it – in English, and in Hindi – and reads out his versions after dinner, daily. In this way, they keep abreast of what is happening in the outside world. Everyone listens attentively. This was also a practice followed by the Russians, but it was their Political Officer who hogged the intercom, and there was disinterest all round in whatever he read.

Most of us are very young and that is a good thing. Youthfulness contributes in large measures towards quick learning, quick understanding, and good reactions that are required onboard vessels the likes of me. Youthfulness also contributes towards that extra daring that is required onboard. An over cautious attitude is seen in middle aged humans and the older lot, which is a trait not desirable in submarines, particularly during battle, where calculated risks enable one to put one across the opponent. Of course there is a subtle difference between a calculated risk and a careless or thoughtless one. The way I see this crew training, they are on the right tracks. I overheard the Captain make a statement in the Ward Room one day, over a meal:

"I don't mind having a 'keen' fellow onboard; I don't mind having a 'dope' onboard. What I don't want is a 'keen dope' onboard. He will surely sink the boat and all of us!"

They have also, over this long trans-Atlantic passage, learnt to economize on the use of fuel. Initially, they ran all three diesels of mine at 'Slow Ahead', to turn all three propellers. Now they have learnt to turn two propellers at 'Slow Ahead' with two diesels, coupling generators on to them, and using the motor on the third shaft, with the current drawn from the generators, to turn the third propeller at the same revolutions per minute as the diesels on the other two. This is possible when doing 'Slow Ahead' only, and they were quick to work this out. In this way they saved diesel consumption of one diesel, and battery current from being used by the motor on the third shaft. That diesel saved is now coming in handy with them having to move me at 'Half Ahead' on all three diesels, to counter the Benguela Current. Clever!

They are meticulous in carrying out routines on all my equipment and more thorough than the Russians. Is it a case of 'new brooms sweep clean'? Or is it out of a sense of belonging that the Russians lacked? I wonder. Anyway, I hope this practice continues. Their paper work is something I am amazed at. They abound in Journals, Log Books, Registers and the likes, which was something the Russians hardly used. There was no paperwork onboard in the Soviet Union. They probably did it all ashore. These fellows are doing it onboard. One could argue that they were on their way home and so did not have access to any shore office where they could carry out their paper work. True! – but the way they are going about it, I think they will still have to do a major part of it onboard even with an office ashore. I hope I'm proved wrong when we reach our Base port.

Like the Russians, they are not too upset with the tough and cramped conditions onboard. I mean, they do not seem to be the types who were born in the lap of luxury. However, when compared to the Russians whom I watched when they spent days out at sea with me in the early days, these blokes do not seem to have any inclination towards exercising their bodies and keeping their muscles in fine condition. This seems odd because they are not as hugely built as the Russians, and should therefore work harder at attaining physical fitness. Some of them are really very puny! I'll hold my judgment on this till we reach the Base port, and see if they do any work out ashore.

Their Victualling Officer is a scream. He embarked some grapes at Lagos and put them in the Cool Room after personally counting the total number of grapes he had onboard. He then locked the Cool Room and kept the key under his pillow. Every time any item was required from the Cool or Cold Rooms, he would go there and personally supervise the quantities being taken out and cross check that the balance as per the book tallied with the 'actuals' on ground. He actually worked out how many grapes he could issue per head! Every time he slept, the Engineer Officer would gently sneak up and steal the key from under his pillow, raid the Cool Room, and return the key to its place along with a telltale sign like, for example, one grape or a few seeds! When discovered, he would get furious, go and count the grapes again and rework out the reduced number of grapes he could issue per head, much to the amusement of all the officers in the Ward Room! Such activities kept him quite busy at sea when he was not on Watch.

There was one officer with a strange English accent. The way he pronounced some words often led to confusion or amusement. He was on his way up to the Bridge to take over the Watch one day when he happened to peep into the Ward Room only to find the Executive Officer thoroughly embroiled in a game of Chess with the Engineer Officer. Knowing a bit about the game himself, he paused to see how the game was going. At one stage he thought that the Second – in – Command had possibly over looked the fact that he was going to lose his 'Horse'. He couldn't help shouting,

"Watch it 'Saar': He is after your 'arse'!" He was told to beat it and close up on Watch, but there were many such attempts at murdering the Queen's language that resulted in misunderstandings, or hilarity.

A change in the engine regime suddenly broke Vanshali's thoughts. What was up?

"Captain Sir, this is the Officer of the Watch. Request permission to chase a rain cloud and permit the crew to come up to the Bridge for a wash."

They were at it again! – trying to get a free bath. Quite a few went up the hatch through the Control Room, clutching a towel in one hand.

P.R. Franklin

THE INDIAN OCEAN – AT LAST!

In a confined space like a submarine, falling ill with a contagious disease has disastrous consequences on the whole crew. Just before entering the Indian Ocean, off the South African West Coast, the Engineer Officer got chicken pox! It must have been dormant for a while, but manifested itself clearly that morning. After a lengthy discussion with the Medical Officer, the Captain decided that the patient would have to be landed ashore. The Navigating Officer was summoned and directed to make his plans for entering Walvis Bay. The Communications Officer was summoned with his signal pad, and a number of signals were made – the first one to Naval Headquarters, India, reporting the incident and requesting for diplomatic clearance to enter Walvis Bay to off load the patient. This was going to be tricky, as India did not have proper diplomatic relations with South Africa because of their apartheid policies. Another signal was made to the Walvis Bay Port Authorities, asking for permission to enter and offload the patient on humanitarian grounds. Merchant ships often land up in such situations and offload patients by affecting unscheduled stops en route. Warships, having their own sick bays, opt for keeping such patients isolated in their bays. Warships in company without sick bays transfer the patient to a bigger warship having the facility. Submarines have no choice but to offload or risk the high probability of more members of the crew catching the infection. With one more foreign port to enter, this would have meant being placed under quarantine there, with no member of the crew permitted to step ashore. The approval eventually came from both sides, and a miserable Engineer Officer was offloaded. The Assistant Engineer Officer, a quiet, short man who loved his bunk by day and by night, now had to reduce his sleeping hours and shoulder the Department's responsibilities. The patient, after recovery, was driven to Windhoek by road by an army Major, and then flown to Johannesburg. Then he was flown across the length of Africa to Alexandria, on to Rome, and onwards to India to rejoin Vanshali after she had entered her homeport.

Having struggled against the Benguela current up to the southern tip of Africa, Vanshali found herself heading right into the Agulhas current which flows in a southerly direction along the East African coast. There was nothing to choose between the two except that the former was a cold current as it moved from south to north, while the latter was comparatively warmer as it moved from north to south. Both were equally strong, and, as it happened, flowing against the submarine. By now, barring the few hours she spent in Walvis Bay, Vanshali had spent over 20 days at sea since leaving her last port, and there were a few more days ahead before she would sail up the Mozambique Channel, pass between Malagasy and the eastern coast of Africa, and enter Diego Suarez on the northern tip of this massive island.

There was an exuberant, scraggly bearded Sikh officer onboard who was expecting his promotion. Promotions up to the rank of Lieutenant Commander were by time. A young officer spent fixed years in each rank and got promoted. After the rank of Lieutenant Commander, however, he got into the 'pyramidical' phase of the hierarchical structure of ranks and had to be selected by a Board of officers to be placed on the 'select list', to be promoted eventually against a vacancy. The Sikh officer, being a bright man and having done well in Service, was expecting to be placed on the Select List. He was disappointed when the mail from India, which arrived in Lagos, did not have a copy of the Select List issued after the recently held Promotion Board back home. He would now have to wait till the mail was received in the next port of call. His colleagues onboard decided to play a prank on him. One morning, the signalman came to the Ward Room with his usual pack of routine radio signals received during the previous twenty-four hours. In that pack was a seemingly innocuous signal that stated that the Sikh officer had been placed on the Select List and was to be promoted on the day the submarine arrived in India. There was a loud whoop when he read it, and everyone congratulated him with a straight face. A promise to host a champagne party on entering Diego Suarez was extracted from him. The Indian Navy does not drink at sea.

Malagasy was the old island of Madagascar, and Diego Suarez was the old name for the capital of the island's northernmost province, since named Antsiranana. A French colony, it had, and still has, one of the world's most beautiful deep-water harbors. A ring of mountains surrounded the sparsely populated French Garrison town. A very weary crew arrived only to find the place quite primitive, with no shore accommodation available in the scanty town. They spent four days onboard in harbor, and very few of the crew ventured ashore, as the place had nothing to offer and no one spoke the French language. A French Naval canteen had some 'goodies' and a few did some shopping there. Some others – naturalists – went to see the gigantic turtles the island was famous for. One of the evenings was spent by the officers in the Wardroom, drinking the Sikh officer's champagne with a vengeance! The Indian mail that arrived did not have the genuine Select List once again!

There was one interesting, very old, islander of Asian origin who visited the submarine, stepping onboard very gingerly and hesitatingly. He spoke fluent French but only a smattering of English. He claimed to belong to 'Hindosthan' with his roots in Bhawalpur. He hadn't heard of the partition of India, nor of Pakistan! On the island they lived in, it probably didn't matter. The crew updated his knowledge on peninsular India, and it was all a bit too much for this man whose great-grandparents had moved bag and baggage to Madagascar decades ago. He had a story to tell. Apparently, he had visited another submarine, in another era, when he was younger. It was during World War II. A British submarine had entered Diego Suarez for replenishment. A strapping young lad at that time, he went onboard to sell silks and cottons from the Orient. Even while he was onboard selling his wares, the submarine slipped her ropes and left harbor in pursuit of a German man-of-war that they were suddenly told was in the vicinity. They forgot to offload this young man from 'Hindosthan', and it would have been suicidal to break radio silence to inform the port that he was onboard. So they took him along and he went through the experiences of a war patrol. They did not find the German light cruiser and returned eventually to Diego Suarez, to complete the replenishment. The reactions of his next of kin on his return can be well imagined. The old man was pleased to visit the submarine, and the crew made much of him.

Now only the last leg separated the crew from their near and dear ones they had left behind some two years ago when they had gone for their submarine training. The last bit of any journey always appears to drag on and on, especially when expectations are high and there is a lot to look forward to. Vanshali seemed to leap out of the water, eagerly competing with the accompanying, frolicking, dolphins for speed. Unknown to the Navigating Officer, the Engine Room had decided to crack on 'home revs' on the engines. This expression is well known in the navy. When a certain speed in the form of 'revolutions per minute' is ordered on the propeller shaft from the Bridge, the Engine Room unofficially cracks on a few revolutions more when heading home, thereby getting the ship to her port a little earlier than planned. The course was set to get to the southern tip of Sri Lanka, as Vanshali's homeport was going to be Visakhapatnam.

Bottle-nosed dolphins were aplenty in the Indian Ocean. Known to be very intelligent creatures – the next most intelligent creature to man – schools of them would race up to the bulbous bows of the submarine and give a spectacular display of leaping out of the water at speed and hitting it with a resounding slapping sound on re-entry. One would start and the rest would follow. This would go on for quite some time before they shot off in another direction, looking for the next ship. They are fast in the water – very fast. Mariner's tales are replete with accounts of dolphins having saved seamen from drowning on innumerous occasions. All mariners look at the dolphin as man's best friend at sea. They are not hunted or netted for meat.

The crew kept busy with the type of entertainment described earlier. The Captain and the Executive Officer had decided to repaint the submarine black before entering Visakhapatnam harbor, and to do this she would anchor off the port of Kakinada for a few hours. So, there was no time to dive and slow down the speed of advance. The Equator had to be re-crossed, this time from the Southern to the Northern Hemisphere, and Lord Varuna had to be appeased once again. Another ceremony was conducted, and this was a definite improvement on the previous one, but a shorter one. Crossing-the-line certificates with the new longitude were issued to the crew.

The glorious tropical sunsets at sea are to be seen, to be believed. The different hues of the sky that Mother Nature conjures up; if they were to be put down on canvas and shown to land lubbers, the efforts would be condemned as unnatural. Hues ranging from golden brown, to shades of yellow, to shades of purple, and then pink, all blending with each other, edged by silver lined clouds projecting the rays beyond them only to fade away into a dusky darkness overhead. Almost the entire off-watch crew would come up around sunset time to the Bridge to watch this play of colors on the western horizon. Sunsets at sea are constant reminders of nature and all its wonders.

Vanshali was now once again in the shipping lane between India and Africa, and the Officers of the Watches had to be more alert about the movements of ships being passed. Normally, there would have been fewer ships plying on these lanes, but with the Suez Canal closed down, the traffic was considerable. If one looked at in another way, it helped to ease the boredom. The density of traffic increased on arriving off the southern tip of Sri Lanka as ships from the Persian Gulf to the Malacca Straits, or vice versa, joined those making a Sri Lankan landfall from the African coast. They were soon left behind as the submarine broke away and headed north along the eastern coast of Sri Lanka, up to and off the eastern seaboard of India.

Late one morning, Vanshali anchored off the port of Kakinada, just south of Visakhapatnam, and out came buckets, paintbrushes, paints, grease, lubricants, and what have you. "Paint Ship" is an evolution in the navy that includes personnel from all departments. Lower decks are cleared, which means all junior sailors onboard are ordered out of their bunks or stations, to come up on the upper deck to join this combined evolution. The Grey lady slowly turned black, and black she would remain for the rest of her life. By sunset the evolution was over, but the submarine stayed at anchor overnight for the paint to dry, leaving Kakinada and heading for her home – Visakhapatnam, or 'Vizag' as it is better known – the following morning.

There was a radio message received to say that the Commander–in–Chief at Visakhapatnam would be present at the jetty on the submarine's arrival, and the ceremonial procedures to be followed were listed out. To the crew's horror, they found that they were to fall-in on the jetty in 'No2s'! 'No2s' was a ceremonial uniform worn in summers. It consisted of Peak

Caps, white tunics with closed Chinese collars, white long pants, white shoes, and medals. The crew hadn't worn this uniform for over two years while they were away in the Soviet Union. Russian food had made almost all of them stouter. There were serious doubts of whether they would fit into their tunics. Worse still, most of them had put this uniform away at the bottom of their respective suitcases, where it was lying in a crushed state. There was a flurry of activity as suitcases were pulled out of bilges, and various, almost unreachable, parts of the submarine. To get at some of them, bags of rations, toolboxes, and other boxes had to be removed. There was complete chaos onboard the submarine for a couple of hours. Finally they were pulled out. Then there was a massive exchange of tunics to see who would fit into whose tunic. Then they had to be ironed! There were no arrangements onboard for ironing clothes. Mess tables made way for ironing. Torpedo tops, wooden boards of all dimensions, and anything flat were converted to iron the tunics. Even the Navigator's chart table became a make shift ironing board! It wasn't all that easy. There were limited number of irons onboard, and flat surfaces had to be selected only in the vicinity of plug points that had 220 volts AC. These were rare onboard a DC, battery operated, submarine.

That day the navy witnessed what was probably the worst dressed crew east of the Suez Canal in ill-fitting No2s, formed up on the jetty to receive their C-in-C. He arrived and stared at them for a moment, but did not remark on their attire. The ceremonies were gone through perfunctorily, and he left. In the car, while returning, he turned around to his accompanying Flag Lieutenant and asked him:

"Flags - What do you think of their turn-out?"

"I think it was awful, Sir. – The worst I've ever seen. They need to be taken to task for daring to stand before you in the 'costumes' they wore."

The Admiral heaved a deep sigh as he looked out of the window, and replied:

"You know 'Flags', my son grew up with very neat habits and always took pride in dressing up immaculately - till he joined this newly formed submarine arm of the navy. Now something seems to have happened to him, and he is not the same chap he was earlier. I have noticed that he has become untidier. What's more, he has even stopped cleaning his Royal Enfield motorbike daily – a task he used to execute unfailingly, as a matter of pride."

Vanshali had come home! One more submarine had joined the Indian Navy to give her more punch. She would tie up alongside for some weeks while the crew went on leave to meet their near and dear ones. Some of the families were present on the jetty when the submarine arrived. Others were spread all over the length and breadth of the massive subcontinent of India. The crew dispersed for some well-earned leave.

COMPLEXITIES OF UNDERSEA WARFARE

It was Jules Verne who was one of the first to successfully draw the attention of the world at large to the undersea space, with exciting descriptions of offensive submarine operations in his epic book 'Twenty Thousand Leagues Beneath the Sea', which was subsequently made into a movie. Propelling submerged, ramming wooden hulled ships, being held by giant squids rising from the depths of the oceans, all portrayed on the big screen, whetted the curiosity about the many mysteries the oceans have to offer. Scientists have been trying to understand these mysteries of the deep ever since man was born. However, if any progress has been made in this direction, it has largely been in the twentieth century, thanks to rapid advances in science and technology in that millennium.

Man's inability to breathe underwater, the lack of appropriate technology to provide a solution to overcome the problem, the realization of the negative effects of pressure on the human body, all deterred human beings from venturing deep into the oceans to uncover its mysteries. It has been easier for man to venture into outer space and come to terms with 'zero gravity' conditions than to explore the deep oceans, where tremendous gravitational forces and its negative side effects are experienced. The human body is most suited to exist around sea level. It can survive at lesser than sea level pressures up in the mountains up to a point, but only after some acclimatization. Man is able to breathe manageably, and his lungs are able to function at those heights. He has been able to go into outer space with the help of technology to equip and be able to withstand the absence of external pressure by donning special protective suits. His success in withstanding and sustaining higher pressures that exist below the oceans has, however, been limited. He hasn't stopped trying. The search for solutions goes on. Mammals like whales and dolphins, which need to periodically breathe air from the surface of the sea and yet are capable of going deep into the ocean for lengths of time, are being studied to see if their methods can be utilized by man to explore ocean depths better.

The many varied suits and breathing apparatus that divers wear permit man to descend underwater to very limited depths. Pressurized cylinders hold oxygen to breathe freely up to depths of 33 feet below sea level. Beyond that depth, pure oxygen is poisonous to breathe, and so atmospheric air is carried in tanks for the diver to breathe. However, beyond 120 feet or so, even atmospheric air is unsuitable, and helium is inhaled. Partial pressures of gases come into play at depths, and affect the human body. There is a limit to how deep a human being can venture with, and without, diving gear and proper gases for inhaling. Attempts have been made to go deeper through a process known as 'saturation diving', which involves living in submerged diving chambers under pressure for some lengths of time till the human body gets used to that depth and pressure, and then stepping out into the water to explore at that depth or go slightly deeper. However, man is still a far cry away from freely swimming underwater and venturing deep like marine mammals.

The other option available to man was to go underwater in an enclosed chamber that can sustain external seawater pressure but hold one atmospheric pressure of normal air inside. Scientifically, material for material and volume for volume, a spherically shaped body is what can go deepest, and it withstands the most pressure as compared to other shapes. As to 'how deep' is decided by the material used in making that sphere withstand external pressure. Man hasn't found the perfect material that is economically affordable to make these spheres that can go deep, in large numbers. Only a few exist, and they are exorbitantly expensive. They are largely used for marine research or salvage work.

Submarines used in the business of war require being able to dive and surface, carry underwater detection equipment, carry missiles and torpedoes to destroy the enemy, carry the fire control system that can use the detection equipment and home weapons onto the target, and carry personnel to operate all this. To sustain the personnel for any length of time at sea, boarding and lodging arrangements are also required. A spherical shape to accommodate all this would be enormous in size and quite unsuitable. The shape to house all this evolved eventually into a cigar shaped hull or a teardrop hull. For a given material, a cigar shaped or teardropped hull cannot go as deep as a sphere. So there are limitations on how deep a submarine can go, and this information is held close to the chest and never disclosed by a submariner about his boat. It would suffice to say that with the present knowledge and available material, it is still not possible to go down to any meaningful depths and return safely. The external pressure exerted on the hull, as the boat goes deeper, is considerable and can best be explained by the fact that a small pin-hole in the hull at a depth of just a hundred meters will let in water with a force that can amputate a human being's hand with ease. The rate of flooding into the hull through a hole increases with increase in depth, and so every care must be taken to see that the submarine is leak proof, so as to ensure safety. From all this, and in a comparative sense, it can be deduced that there are very limited forays to the greater depths of the oceans, and the depths to which naval submarines dive are sufficient for them to sneak up to a target, destroy it, and quietly get away.

Above water, the electronic spectrum has been largely used in warfare for detection, classification, tracking, gathering the required information and homing weapons of destruction onto targets. Electronic beams dissipate with such rapidity underwater that it had been discarded in favor of 'sound' as a replacement in the business of undersea warfare. Sound travels further underwater than electromagnetic waves. Sound, however, presents a large problem in the oceans to the user when attempting to trap a target. The underwater target is not sighted physically. Its presence is detected by sound and then localized. There are umpteen creatures underwater whose presence complicates the process of classification. The homogeneity of seawater medium is never assured. It varies in an irregular manner and sound rays end up refracting up or down, based on the fluctuations encountered. Seawater medium is identified by salinity, density, temperature, and pressure. All these have a direct bearing on the velocity of sound. Changes in any or all these parameters result in changes in speeds of sound, and bending of sound beams away from their intended path. The theory is well known, but accurate prediction of behavior patterns is a skilled business, and ships operating 'sonars' to detect submarines often find that they are unable to affect a 'kill' because the submarine is not where they thought the submarine was. The latter, on the other hand, moves in the vertical medium underwater, and this enables it to have up to date information of the seawater medium more readily and gauge more accurately as to how a sound beam will bend, and which is the optimum depth to be in for an attack, and which for evasion. It, therefore, has an advantage over surface ships in this respect, and exploits the medium to come out favorably in most of these 'cat and mouse' games.

The story is different when an aircraft, equipped with anti-submarine warfare gear, is pitted against a conventional diesel submarine. The submarine is hardly equipped to attack airborne platforms and can therefore only resort to evasive action. In a general sense, she has one factor in her favor – aircraft have limited endurance on task, and have to return to base to refuel and get back. Submarine batteries have a longer endurance and so can keep her down for longer durations – long enough to outlast the aircraft on task. These loopholes can be plugged to some extent, but the fact remains that aircraft can pursue submarines with relative immunity. The final outcome depends on how skilled the submarine is in evading the aircraft sensors and weapons with the help of the environment, and who wears out whom first

Anti-submarine warfare envelops a host of offensive as well as defensive actions. As part of defensive actions, vulnerable ships are protected and screened by a group of anti-submarine warfare equipped warships, with airborne elements integral to the ships, and/or supported by shore based anti-submarine warfare aircraft. A single submarine attacking a vital target that is protected in such a manner faces formidable opposition and considerable challenge. So long as she is discreet, she has the odds in her favor. Sometimes, however, she can become indiscreet out of carelessness, overconfidence, underestimating the opposing forces' capabilities, or plainly because she is not in a favorable position to carry out an attack and has to shed 'discreetness' in favor of 'indiscreetness (do noisy high speeds)' to get into a firing position. That is the challenge for a submarine Captain, and that is the art that he strives to perfect so as to be able to fight, kill, and live to fight again. Apart from the submarine's own capabilities, he must use the vagaries of the ocean environment to his advantage to outwit his enemy, get his target, and get away. Of all forms of maritime warfare, undersea warfare is the most complex of them all, both for the hunter and the hunted, no matter who is in which role.

Ships plying on the surface of the sea move about with the help of Maritime Charts to navigate, and localize one's position at any given time. They also use satellites to assist them in locating their position, but the position has to be plotted on the same Maritime Chart. Submarines move underwater and use the vertical plane to change depths. They, therefore use special submarine charts that give them the necessary additional information to move safely along the ocean floor and use its undulations to advantage. Just as helicopters maneuver through mountainous regions, submarines use submarine charts to maneuver underwater. That is, of course, provided the depths of water are shallow enough to encompass the submarine's range of diving.

The warm Tropical waters of the Northern Indian Ocean include the Arabian Sea and the Bay of Bengal. The former adjoins the western seaboard of India while the latter has India's eastern seaboard as its western limits. The subterranean profiles of the two vary distinctly. The western seaboard of India extends into the Arabian Sea in the form of a continental shelf that gently slopes westwards at the rate of one fathom for every six nautical miles, roughly speaking. Closer to the coast, the shallow water effects of the sea are very prominent, and play a disturbing part in undersea warfare. The reverberation effect is more prominent in shallow waters and hence the increase in disturbances. To get deep waters, one has to go some distance away from the coastline.

Between 8° and 11° N, and not too far away from the southwestern seaboard, lie the many coral islands of Lakshwadeep that enables one to play hide and seek with an opponent and strike when the time is ripe. The considerable flow of fresh water from the five rivers of Punjab into the Arabian Sea also brings with it a large amount of sediments and a turbulent medium in as far as density and salinity of water is concerned. That flow is contained on the westward side by the subterranean Murray ridge just off the Gulf of Oman but heads southwards into the central part of the Arabian Sea. Then there is the flow into the Arabian Sea from the Red Sea (not really red but blue for the most part of the year, and turns red only when marine life in the form of algae die and rot). The Red Sea is more saline than the Arabian Sea and empties a significant amount of 'extra' saline water into the neighboring seas. All in all, the Arabian Sea is a 'nasty sea' for undersea warfare with the use of sonar for detection, classification, and destruction of one platform by another. It is also very favorable towards submarines for evasion and attack.

The Bay of Bengal has a few commonalities but is largely different to the Arabian Sea. The group of Andaman and Nicobar Islands exist, but they are further away from the Eastern mainland of the sub-continent than the Lakshadweep Islands are off the West Coast, and are a result of subterranean volcanic upheavals rather than coral formations. The islands are nearer to the Indonesian and Myanmar coasts. There is no continental shelf off the eastern mainland and therefore a few miles off the eastern seaboard one comes across very deep waters that are deeper than the submarines' maximum diving depths. Right down the center of the Bay, on the sea floor, is a huge ridge formed as a result of the flow of the mighty Brahmaputra River into the sea. Sediments and varying densities are faced again albeit less noticeable at the depths submarines operate in. Good sonar ranges are possible in these waters. The Bay of Bengal is, however, frequented by depressions that change into Tropical Cyclones, especially after the South West Monsoons, making it difficult for surface and airborne craft to hunt for submarines that may be lurking in that area. Submarines go deep and escape much of the fury of the sea, but conventional submarines have a rough time when they come up to charge their batteries, which they have to do frequently.

The Tropical waters around India present an environmental challenge that far exceeds that presented in the temperate latitudes and this makes very significant contributions to undersea warfare in the region. Vanshali would be operating in such an environment for the rest of her life. Those operating her had much to learn.

P.R. Franklin

A NEW WAY OF LIFE

By now the crew onboard Vanshali had settled down to a new way of life, far removed from what they were introduced to in the Soviet Union when they first got into the submarine world, or what they had experienced on the long and arduous passage to India. They were in Visakhapatnam – their base port – where facilities for exploiting, maintaining, and repairing Vanshali were coming up slowly but surely. The bachelor officers and crew all lived ashore in Officer's Messes and in sailor's shore barracks. The married crew members lived in married quarters located far from the jetty where the submarine was tied up – a far cry from the 'PKZ' or the hotels they had lived in when in foreign ports! The Duty Watch – those on duty onboard the submarine in harbor during off-working hours – got hot meals from the galley ashore. The crew could step ashore for a bath and change after a days' work onboard in harbor, and the off-watch crew could look forward to stretching their legs and toning up their muscles in the playing fields next to the barracks. The married lot, or the 'brown baggers' as they are famously referred to in naval parlance, also joined the rest of the bachelors for games in the evenings.

A standard uniform was introduced for use onboard at sea, and officers and sailors wore identical gear. These were identical to the samples for trial that the commissioning crew wore on the passage to India. They were referred to as 'disposable clothing', and consisted of a pair of shorts with an elastic waist, and a collar-less, loose fitting, short-sleeved shirt of fairly thin material. When dirty or soiled, they would be handed over to a common pool in exchange for a new set. The soiled set was then used to clean the insides of Vanshali, and finally disposed of. Sandals with back-straps were worn at sea and special non-skid soled shoes in harbor. At sea, one didn't have to shave – a ritual that was embarked upon only just before entering harbor. A new submarine badge was awarded to all those who had qualified for submarine service which they wore on their normal uniforms, setting them apart from the rest of the navy.

The crew was given extra rations to compensate for the unhealthy and unnatural breathing environment onboard and to ensure that the lack of vitamins and fresh greens and the likes during long sailing periods were compensated for.

Soon a spirit of bonhomie and camaraderie developed among the submariners that became the envy of the rest of the Navy around. Submariners were soon excelling in sports and team events in the Command and walking away with most of the trophies on offer. There was this 'Esprit de Corps' amongst them that others found hard to match. It attracted younger ones to volunteer.

Training in the Soviet Union was expensive but unavoidable in the initial stages. However, now with trained manpower available in India, indigenous training was initiated. Visakhapatnam was chosen as the site, as the submarines had already been based there. It was a poorly developed city and had a port with poor infrastructure facilities those days. By way of inhabitants, it had the very rich, the very poor, and no middle class to speak of. It therefore held no promise for any prosperity with its existing set up. It was in the interest of the very rich to keep it that way. The Indian Navy had plenty of land but only a small Base there and everyone dreaded being posted to that one-horse town. Those posted there kept very much to themselves and did not mingle with the civilian population. Everyone resisted being posted to Visakhapatnam.

The following story, related by a Sikh naval officer, on his being posted out from Visakhapatnam after a reasonable tenure as the Chief of Staff of the Command, tells it all.

A few years earlier, he was strolling along in Flora Fountain area in Bombay one evening when he saw a crowd gathered around a man and his monkey who were entertaining them. He ambled his way in and heard the man shout:

"Ten Rupees for anyone who can make this monkey cry!"

The Sikh officer, seeing no one responding, decided to take up the challenge. He walked up to the monkey and whispered something in his ear. At once the monkey started bawling, to the amazement of the crowd. He got his ten rupees and as he was walking away the owner of the monkey challenged him directly once again and in full hearing of the crowd:

"Double or quits – if you can make the monkey laugh"

The officer thought for a moment and walked up to the monkey and again whispered something in his ear. The monkey burst out into laughter immediately. Triumphantly, the officer collected his prize and walked away. The crowd stopped him and wanted to know what he had said on each occasion.

"The first time I only told him that he was being sent to Visakhapatnam. The second time I told him that I was being sent there too!"

Despite the dismal picture the town presented, Visakhapatnam had some very pretty beaches north and south of the city. Blue waters, white sands bordered on the landward side by casuarinas trees, and a shoreline that was irregular with alternating headlands and inlets fringing the hillocks that sloped down to the sea made a pretty picture. A narrow but metal coastal road completed the scene. It was difficult to choose a good picnic site from the many scenic options available.

Not far from the town, adjoining nearby villages, were a number of lakes that invited migrating ducks annually in the months of December to February. Those interested in 'shikhar' would venture out during those months and return with green – blue headed mallards with that very prominent white ring round their necks, or red-headed pochards, or short-necked teals, etc for the 'memsahib' to rustle up a good duck 'vindaloo'. The frustrated among them would shoot down some almost tame moorhens that had a very 'fishy' taste. (How could they come back empty-handed?). This practice ceased in later years with restrictions imposed on hunting, but those interested in outdoor life enjoyed the place and its surroundings tremendously.

The infrastructure for training had to be set up in Visakhapatnam from scratch, and this was an enormous challenge those trained in the Soviet Union had to take on. It was hard work. A visionary approach was required as these were going to be permanent assets of a lasting nature that would be used for decades to come. Perhaps, in later years, new classes and types of submarines would be inducted? The crews for those would also have to be trained with the help of the infrastructure being created now. Statements of Cases to the Government had to be prepared very carefully with foresight. Buildings, classrooms, and simulator rooms had to be constructed and preparations towards these ends had to be initiated and executed. Training dockets, charts, models, etc had to be made as teaching aids. No time was wasted and the work began in right earnest. On a parallel track, plans were afoot to create a large Dockyard and a number of jetties to support all the Soviet acquisitions. A large marshy area speckled with a few hillocks was selected as the spot for all these to come up! Land reclamation became the first task.

Soon the first batch of officers to be trained in India arrived. They completed their theoretical training and proceeded to sea onboard Vanshali. One portly and very religious officer, who had volunteered for submarine service, suddenly had some misgivings on his course of action, and decided to pull out. He came up to the Commanding Officer during breakfast at sea one day, and asked to see him privately. This was after three days of particularly rough seas when he had difficulty in getting up on time to close up on Watch. As related by the Captain in the Wardroom later, the conversation went something like this:

"Sir, God has been repeatedly appearing to me in my dreams and telling me that by opting for submarine service, I have done a wrong thing. So I would like to withdraw."

"Funny thing that you mention this" replied the Captain, "You know, I was talking to God only this morning, and He didn't mention anything to me about you. When I talk to Him next, I shall seek clarifications."

Over the next week, the Captain proceeded to give this officer a very rough time at the end of which he came up to the Captain and said:

"Sir, He came to me in my dream again, but this time He said all was well and that I could stay on in the cadre"!

He stayed on and served well for many years thereafter.

In the navy of old in Visakhapatnam, the Officer's Club or Institute was situated next to the residence of the Commanding officer of INS Circars, and the old Naval Mess. INS Circars was the boys training establishment that trained and churned out seamen for the navy. The club had a spreading tree in the middle of a dance floor, just outside the bar. The club was big enough for the small navy that was based there those days. It was a popular haunt, especially since the town had little to offer by way of entertainment or distraction from the daily routine. The tree was involuntarily known to one and all as the 'Yum-Yum' tree. Under the 'Yum-Yum' tree one late evening, soon after Vanshali's arrival, sat six young, hot-blooded, officers in a group. Most of them were course-mates and old chums. The favorite pastime of imbibing liquor had gone on to well beyond the shutting time of the bar, as these veterans had lined up enough glasses of reserves in front of them after "Last Drink" was announced. Somehow the topic drifted to the newly created Submarine Arm. The first effort to train submariners in India had been announced, and these officers, individually, were wavering in their minds about volunteering for the course. However, in their inebriated condition, and in a spirit of careless camaraderie, they resolved that the decision, whether to volunteer or not, would be taken by a toss of the coin. All join or no one joins. They ended up volunteering for the course!

Many hilarious incidents took place during Vanshali's 'work-ups' with trainees onboard. Once she was carrying out a 'bottoming' exercise when a difference of opinion cropped up between the Captain and an officer under training who was tasked with bottoming the submarine on the sea floor, on how it should be done. This discussion initially took place in the Control Room in full view and hearing of all present. As both the gentlemen were adamant on holding their grounds, the volume got somewhat loud, and they both withdrew to the Officer's Wardroom in the IInd Compartment for a few moments. All this, while the submarine was making her approach to the area marked for bottoming, at slow speed. On the planes was one of the submarine arm's most experienced planes-man – the Coxswain of the boat. Just as the two senior-most officers returned to the Control Room, the Coxswain bottomed the boat, and she settled down nicely.

"See Sir? I told you this is how it should be done! She has settled down beautifully." said the Officer under training.

The Captain, very angry and at a loss for words, just shook his head and retired to the Ward Room.

On another occasion, the crew was practicing 'General Drills' at sea before presenting themselves for inspection by the Squadron Staff. Vanshali was on the surface, and the Captain was conducting the exercise, sitting on the Bridge. In the Control Room was the Sikh officer who had earlier celebrated his anticipated promotion in Diego Suarez on the submarine's passage home. He was expecting the crafty Captain to suddenly make an 'enemy' aircraft appear over the horizon, and see how an 'Urgent Dive' was executed by him. He listened intently for the orders to come over the main broadcast and was on tenterhooks.

"Man Overboard" announced the Captain, which really warranted remaining on the surface and executing a series of quick maneuvers to recover the man in the shortest possible time.

"Dive – Dive - Dive!" ordered the Sikh officer, and to the Captain's horror, the Upper Lid was shut and the End group Ballast tanks flooded, leaving him and the Officer of the Watch on the Bridge. Soon the center group ballast tanks would also be flooded and the submarine would go down leaving the two holding onto the two periscopes or swimming in the sea! Fortunately, others around in the Control Room drew the attention of the very busy Sikh officer to the fact that he was carrying out the wrong drill and the maneuver was cancelled, end group ballast tanks blown, and the Upper Lid opened. A thoroughly shaken up Captain came down the hatch. The rest is left to the imagination to figure out, but the sounds that followed could be heard all over the Control Room, and in both adjacent compartments.

There was an occasion when a very bright and enthusiastic Officer of the Watch locked a part of his upper clothing with the Upper Lid during an 'Urgent Dive', too late for him to open it and release his clothes. The Captain let him 'hang' around there till the maneuver was completed and the submarine surfaced.

Training was a continuous process and extended from the classrooms to onboard a submarine. Even the so-called veterans had something new to assimilate every time they went out on a sortie to sea. No two 'dives' or no two 'surfacings' were ever the same, there being so many variables confronted at sea, and that is what made evolutions and life onboard all the more interesting.

Being a very forgiving submarine with a plethora of back-ups and safety devices, none of the goof – ups that took place during training led to any serious mishaps. Fortunately!

Soon, Vanshali found herself carrying out two different roles. The first was one of training the Fleet in Anti-Submarine Warfare. Week after week she would go to sea with anti-submarine warfare ships and work them up in detecting, classifying, tracking, and attacking submarines. Her other role was the one she is designed for and which the crew preferred any day – to roam the high seas and patrol on intelligence gathering and other missions.

Visakhapatnam also began to change. With the installation of a major steel plant on the outskirts of the city, the population of middle class grew manifold. A number of ancillary units for the steel plant sprang up, and other industries followed. In a matter of a few decades, Visakhapatnam grew to become the second largest city in the State. It is now no longer the one-horse town it used to be. The Naval Base had also grown in leaps and bounds, and boasts of one of the largest Dockyards in Asia. Vanshali saw it all.

Meanwhile, some good news was received by the submarine world – a submarine depot ship and a submarine rescue vessel were soon to join the force. The former would be based on the west coast of India to support submarines deployed off that coast. The latter would be based and operate off the east coast where the waters were deeper. Both acquisitions would contribute positively to the morale of the submariner. The depot ship could be placed anywhere to support a submarine – even at a prearranged spot at sea. Not only the crew, but also the boat could be supported materially. The submarine rescue vessel may never be used for rescue work during its lifetime, and that's a good thing. It may not get to the spot to rescue a submarine in distress on time if the place was too remote. However, the very fact that it was there was a morale booster. Submariners eagerly awaited the arrival of these two ships.

P.R. Franklin

A TRIP TO THE ANDAMAN ISLANDS

A very interesting outing that Vanshali had, within months of her arriving in India, and after the crew had returned from some well-earned leave, was a sortie to the Andaman Islands where the Eastern Fleet was exercising, carrying out amphibious operations. The crew surmised that this was going to be a long detachment away from base port from the quantum of rations they had embarked onboard! Submarine outings are generally treated as restricted information and so the crew is informed of the exact nature of the mission only after leaving harbor. It is difficult to keep the duration of the outing a secret because the crew observes the quantum of victuals being embarked and makes a fairly accurate guess of how long they are going to be away. However, on this occasion they were slightly off track. Quite a bit of the dry rations embarked were meant to be offloaded at Port Blair for the naval detachments there that mostly depended on supplies from the mainland for sustenance.

It became standard practice for Vanshali to leave harbor under cover of darkness as part of an effort to keep her departure time a matter of guesswork. In accordance with that practice, she slipped from her moorings well after supper, when the world around her was asleep. There was one difference. It was a moonlit night and the black silhouette was easily discernible against the shimmering reflections of the moon playing on the water surface. Normally her departures were planned during pitch dark nights but this time she had to get to the Andaman Islands by a particular date and hence this compromise. Leaving Visakhapatnam outer harbor channel, the Navigating officer took a 'departure fix' with the help of radar ranges and Dolphin Nose and East Point lighthouses. Once he had accurately plotted the position of the submarine on the Chart with this data, he adjusted the course to head for Pygmalion Point, which is also known as Indira Point. It was the southern-most tip of the group of islands known as the Nicobar Islands. Dolphin Nose was a fairly high piece of headland with a powerful lighthouse on top. On a clear night, the light could be seen some forty nautical miles out at sea because of its height and candlepower. Some weaving and maneuvering was necessary to wend one's way past the hundreds of fishing boats just outside the harbor. They were more intent on fishing than avoiding being hit by a submarine. In all probability, many of them were fast asleep in their catamarans! The time was 0015h.

Once well clear of the fishing vessels, Vanshali carried out a customary Trim Dive to fine tune the compromises required for the variable weights embarked. This done, she could now dive at any time without worrying too much about her trim. That night the Captain decided that she would propel on surface so as to be able to do higher speeds, conserve battery power, and get to her destination by the ordered time. He also wanted some spare time up his sleeve so as to dive and practice attack maneuvers before joining the Fleet.

Surfacing after her Trim Dive, Vanshali's crew got onto the Three-Watch system so that two Watches could get some sleep. The Torpedo Officer was on Watch on the Bridge, with a sailor behind him as the 'Look Out'. The sea was calm and lonely, but for a gentle beam on swell, and soon there was peace and quiet onboard with only the familiar hum of healthy machinery audible inside the hull. On the Bridge, the gentle sound of water lapping against the moving bulbous bows, and the gargling sound of the wake was all that was audible. Astern of the submarine, Dolphin light was flashing intermittently. The radar was on.

The Torpedo Officer, who was the Officer of the Watch, decided it was a good time to send the Look Out down the hatch to fetch a cup of hot coffee. The Look Out promptly went down and got the cook to make two cups of coffee in the galley – one for himself, that he would drink then and there, and the second one for the Officer of the Watch. He took awhile. Meanwhile, the Electrical Officer decided to come up to the Bridge for a cigarette before turning in for the night. He lit his cigarette, and took a deep drag and then turned to speak to the Officer of the Watch. The Officer of the Watch was not there on the Bridge or anywhere inside the Fin! The Electrical Officer then called up the Chart House and asked if the Torpedo Officer was there. He was told that he wasn't there. While this was going on, the Look Out, having downed his coffee, maneuvered his way up the vertical hatch from the Control Room to the Bridge, holding a mug in one hand and grasping the railing on one side with the other. On reaching the Bridge he looked around for the Officer of the Watch to hand over the mug, but couldn't find him anywhere. He saw the Electrical Officer there instead, which confused him because Technical Officers do not do Bridge Watch-keeping. Where was the Officer of the Watch? He couldn't have gone down looking for a toilet because that facility was available in the Fin. A cryptic reply came up the hatch to say that no one had come down the hatch but him. The Look Out searched around the Fin once more and then announced that the Officer of the Watch was missing. Ridiculous! How could he be missing? Such a thing had never happened before.

The Captain and Executive Officer were woken up even as a general search was quietly conducted through the length and breadth of the submarine. It was done quietly so as to not spread any panic throughout the boat. The Torpedo Officer had simply vanished into thin air!

By now, the Captain was on the Bridge. He presumed that the man had fallen overboard. He turned Vanshali around to her reciprocal course and the Executive Officer got a few extra Look Outs up on the Bridge. Unknown to the Captain, the helmsman down in the Control Room did not settle on the right Course but steered five degrees off and did not realize that he was not on the ordered Course. Nobody did! Fortunately, the moon was full and there was enough moonlight all around to make any search meaningful. There was tension in the air. Where could he have gone? Surely, he couldn't have fallen overboard, as such things happen only in rough seas, and here was the sea as calm as a tabletop but for the gentle swell. By altering course to retrace our path, what was the Captain hoping to find?

Half an hour into the search and the silence in the air was broken by the Intercom:

"Bridge – this is Radar Office. There is a small intermittent contact that keeps painting on the radar screen, very fine on the Port Bow, at a distance of one nautical mile."

Such a report at this time sounded irrelevant because all eyes on the Bridge were looking out for the Officer of the Watch swimming in the water. Human beings do not reflect radar waves and paint on the radar screen. Even so, the Captain altered course slightly to Port to get the radar contact directly in front of him. Vanshali kept making headway, apparently on a hopeless mission, as the odds of finding a man in the water, whose time of falling in the water (if at all!) and the position of the submarine at that time were not known, was pretty grim.

The first shouts were made from the Bridge across the dark silent sea.

"Ahoy there - If you can hear us, shout in response!".

Roughly a mile on, and suddenly the silence in the air was broken by a faint sound from right ahead:

"Help – Help - I'm here. Help – Help - I'm here".

A searchlight pointed in that direction revealed the Officer of the Watch paddling in the water. Maneuvering Vanshali professionally, the Captain got her alongside the Torpedo Officer who was then pulled out of the water onto the Fore planes turned out for the purpose, and then taken down the hatch.

This was some miracle! A meaningless disappearing spot on the radar screen, a five-degree error on the Course steered, the exact spot and time when he had fallen overboard not known, and desperate shouts across the sea on a dark night, had all led the submarine to the man! The 'story' eventually came out. Yes, he had sent the Look Out down for some coffee. After he had gone down, he leaned over the side to see if the navigational sidelights were burning brightly, as they could not be seen easily from the Bridge. He checked the Starboard (Green) light and then leaned over the Port side to check the Red light. At that moment, the submarine gently rolled to Port. It was a gentle roll, but enough for him to lose balance and fall overboard, clear of the Casing and into the water. He yelled, but soon realized that no one would hear him. Being a good swimmer, he turned towards Dolphin Nose light and began to swim. He swam for awhile and then realized that land was quite far away and it would be better to conserve his strength by just trying to stay afloat till daybreak and then hope to be found during a search effort by the navy. After awhile, to his amazement, he saw Vanshali coming back and heading straight for him. He yelled ...... and the rest is history. The officers congratulated him and told him he was on his second life now. Nothing more was said about the incident and normal life onboard was resumed. A few years later, another incident would occur in another place, on another occasion, involving the same officer, which would remind submariners about this incident and leave them in a state of wonderment.

The Bay of Bengal is quite a lonely stretch of water with mostly the Bangladesh and Indian navies using it for their work up. The Australian navy sends its maritime reconnaissance aircraft to snoop around as a matter of course, and the three navies bump into each other on occasions. The US Navy comes and goes when they please, just as they are wont to do all over the world. Merchant shipping prefer to sail parallel to the coastline and only cross the Bay when they have to, along well-charted shipping routes. The Eight and Ten Degrees (Latitude) Channels to the south are extremely busy with shipping plying between the southern tip of Sri Lanka and Singapore, through the southern Nicobar islands and the Malacca Straits. The Bay of Bengal also faces the fury of the Southwest and Northeast monsoons, with the latter having a more prominent effect than the former. Between the monsoons, a series of depressions form in the Bay, most of which end up as cyclones that eventually move in a northwesterly direction and lash the eastern seaboard of India, or Bangladesh, and peter out after crossing the coast, creating havoc along the coastal land belt. It is a lonely sea, but a restless one. Vanshali's direct passage from Visakhapatnam to Indira Point was not a common shipping route but one that would intersect quite a few shipping routes from the Malacca Straits to the southern tip of Sri Lanka.

It was noon when the Captain walked into the Charthouse with the Navigating officer to see how Vanshali was doing with respect to time. He found that he had some time to put to useful use and decided to 'snort' and let the crew have lunch while snorting at Periscope depth. The evolution was executed to finesse, and lunch was served. Even while lunch was being eaten, the Conning Tower microphone hooter shrilled sharply and the Periscope Officer of the Watch could be heard:

"Stop Snorting! Stop Snorting! Dive – Dive - Dive!"

The Captain, Executive Officer, Engineer Officer and the Electrical Officer dropped their spoons and forks and charged to the Control Room in time to see the Officer of the Watch come down the Conning Tower hatch into the Control Room.

"What happened?" queried the Captain.

"An Australian maritime reconnaissance aircraft was heading straight for us, Sir" replied the young officer.

"I saw something fall out of it into the water right in front of us" he continued.

"Those were probably sonobuoys dropped in the water to help him track us" said the Captain. "Let's pick them up and upset his plans. Surface!" ordered the Captain, and Vanshali aborted her dive and surfaced.

"Some of these sonobuoys are booby trapped to explode if someone tries to take them out of water. Get our bomb squad ready", said the Captain, and the Executive Officer got down to arranging things for the recovery evolution.

Vanshali surfaced, and the Captain maneuvered her upto a sonobuoy floating in the water after masking his propeller signature. The bomb squad slipped into the water with the required equipment and soon had the sonobuoy onboard after de-activating it.

"A good toy for our scientists to play around with" smirked the Captain. The maritime aircraft flew around the submarine during the recovery evolution and then headed southwest, disappearing over the horizon, not to appear again that day. Vanshali proceeded on surface once again, heading for Indira Point.

The Andaman and Nicobar Islands are one of the last vestiges of ancient tribal presence found in the Indian subcontinent. There are six dwindling, very primitive, tribes found in this archipelago consisting of around four hundred islands of all shapes and sizes. Four tribes are of Negrito descent with dark skins and curly hair. They are the Jarawas, the Onges, the Andamanese, and the Sentinelese. The remaining two are comparatively fairer with straight hair, and of the mongoloid race. They are the Nicobarese and the Shompens. For decades they have defied attempts by civilized people to draw them into their fold and have chosen to live an isolated life by themselves with the bare necessities the islands have to offer. Around 1789, Lord Cornwallis, the British Governor General in India, commissioned a survey of the islands by Lt Archibald Blair, and the settlement of Port Cornwallis was created. In 1857, after the first Indian war of Independence, the British established a penal colony in Port Blair to which the freedom fighters were banished. During the WW II, the Japanese occupied these islands only to be driven out by the British. After independence, India began to take slow steps to develop these islands, as they are very strategically located at the entrance to the Malacca Straits. The six tribes opted to stay aloof and not be a part of this development. The navy played a big role in supporting the civil administration with logistic support from the mainland. Of volcanic origin, and densely forested with paddock and other trees, the waterfront of the Andaman Islands is thick with mangroves. The Nicobar groups of islands on the other hand are bereft of tropical rain forests and have coconut trees, sunny beaches peppered with Nicobarese villages, and emerald waters surrounding them..

Early the next morning, radar painted the first outlines of the larger of the Nicobar Islands, as Vanshali got ready to join the Fleet. The Fleet was exercising in the Andaman Sea, which is on the eastern part of these islands. Vanshali was approaching the islands from the west. Hard work lay ahead and the eager crew was ready for it. Soon, she rounded Indira Point and entered the Andaman Sea. She was greeted with a signal from the Fleet Commander to say that they were heading her way in a screened formation, protecting three amphibious craft simulating an amphibious landing force. Vanshali was directed to act freely and try and penetrate the screening ships and attack the amphibious craft. The Attack Team had practiced this for many hours in the simulator ashore, and had worked up to a good level of competence. The challenge was taken up!

"Dive – Dive - Dive!" the Officer of the Watch ordered, as he scrambled down from the Bridge with the Look Out preceding him. This was no ordinary dive carried out sedately when time and conditions permitted such a luxury. This was an 'Urgent Dive' that carried with it a certain measure of urgency demanding a high degree of alertness and speed of actions. The Control Room buzzed with activity.

"Upper lid shut! Upper lid shut!" yelled the Officer of the Watch down the well, as he scrambled down to the Control room.

"Attack Team close up! Attack Team close up!" the Executive Officer boomed on the main broadcast. The well-oiled combination of men and machines got into full swing as Vanshali slipped from the surface to the environs she was designed for.

Suddenly all activity slowed down to unnoticeable levels and an eerie silence pervaded throughout the boat. Now it was a game of wait and listen – listen for those noisy ships approaching her.

"Sound Room - carry out all round sweep in passive mode and report all contacts" ordered the Executive Officer.

There was further silence as Sound Room went about her task. A few minutes later came Sound Room's report: "Carried out all round sonar sweep. No contacts."

The Captain and the Navigating Officer were hunched over the Chart in the Chart House. A moment later the Captain asked Control Room to take Vanshali down to a greater depth and Sound Room to report the Bathy profile. The Bathy profile gives the variations in sound ray paths underwater as a result of changes in seawater temperature and salinity, and pressure variations with changes in depth. This then enables the Captain to decide which depth was most suited for the submarine to remain at from the point of view of listening out for the ships, and denying them optimum detection performance at the same time. The Bathy profile for a given area changes diurnally and seasonally. It changes continuously and must therefore be constantly monitored.

The Bathy profile is reported to the Captain. Vanshali is taken down to her most favorable depth for listening out for the ships. Since the ships are obviously still out of sonar range, the Captain orders an increase in speed to close the ships faster. As the boat picks up speed, the Cavitation Meter warns all in the Control Room that the propellers are making noise that can be picked up by someone listening out for it. At this stage it did not matter as whoever was listening was too far away to pick it up. However, later on, this indiscreetness would require attention. Own cavitation noise also degrades the quality of performance of one's own sonar sets.

"Ping! …… Ping! ……. Ping!" There it was! Active Sonar of ships faintly discernable! They were still far away. The Captain ordered Vanshali's speed to be reduced and decided to get the Fire Control Computer onto tracking the target through information fed to it from Sound Room. Pretty soon the landing crafts would also reveal themselves. The Computer could track six targets simultaneously while preparing to attack two at the same time. The Screen Penetration Sensor would suggest which two ships to select and slip past, in order to get to the targets. The Captain altered Vanshali's course to the one recommended by the Sensor and the Attack Team. The hunter and the hunted were closing each other! The former had the advantage in that it had already located the 'enemy' while the latter had not! Ships being at a disadvantage in this cat and mouse game would resort to adopting every possible measure that would delay a Fire Control Solution being arrived at by the submarine. This would include weaving, zigzagging, altering base course, altering speeds and the likes. They would send anti-submarine warfare helicopters up ahead of their formation to detect the submarine and extend the period of warning. If and when possible, they would give the helicopters the freedom to attack the submarine. Vanshali's Captain was fully aware of all this, as not only was he a submariner, but a specialist in anti-submarine warfare too! Earlier, he had ordered the Sound Room to report the presence of helicopter sonars, as and when detected. The helicopter was a potent threat as it could launch an attack without any fear of retaliation. Vanshali could only resort to evasive action when confronted by a helicopter, as she had no weapons to attack airborne objects except for a shoulder fired missile launcher that could only be used after surfacing..

Now the propeller noises of all the ships were clearly audible. Each ship had its own peculiar propeller noise and could therefore be fingerprinted and identified by the Screen Penetration Sensor. Even a well-trained Sound Room operator could differentiate them. Propellers driven by steam turbines made a particular noise: those driven by reciprocating engines made another type of noise: others driven by gas turbines made a third type of noise, so on and so forth. Chipped propeller blades helped in differentiating between two ships being driven by the same type of engines. Submarines could gather a whole lot of information by just listening to propeller noises. Ships did not have this luxury because they made so much of self-noise as compared to a submarine that this noise swamped their own sonars and fine sounds escaped their attention. To get over this problem, some anti-submarine warfare ships began to tow sonar arrays away from them to eliminate their own noise when listening out for submarines, but this resulted in restricting their own abilities to maneuver freely.

They were definitely weaving as a formation. The Navigating Officer and the Fire Control Computer were plotting their paths and working out their base course along which they were weaving. Ping! Ping! Ping! Ping! … All of them were pinging away on their active sonars in a desperate attempt to locate the submarine lying in wait somewhere ahead. Vanshali was now committed! She had selected the two ships between whom she would pass, and all efforts were now directed towards ensuring not being detected while slipping through. This time she was lucky. For some obscure reason, no helicopters had been deployed ahead of the screening ships. That was one worry less. This gave her some time to listen out for the three Landing craft that were in the center of the formation – her targets! It was difficult to locate her 'kill' with the noise of all the other ships around her. She would have to be quick in locating them and attacking them once she penetrated the 'screen' because there would be very little time available for action. If they go past the submarine, the chances of getting them in a tail chase would be very remote indeed.

Got one of them! There was another one …. And the last one! The twin propellers driven landing craft were now located. Vanshali had gone very deep and slipped past the screening ships at a speed that would not let her propellers cavitate. Now all attention was on carrying out her attack. A few quick maneuvers later, she solved her fire control solution and fired one of her torpedo tubes with a 'water shot' to simulate firing a torpedo on one of them. The Fire Control solution for the second target was also solved and presented by the Computer, and Vanshali fired her second water shot. The third target was slipping away, and getting her involved firing a shot up her behind! This had to be done quickly before she got out of Torpedo range. The Computer operator worked at a furious pace to give the necessary inputs to the machine to get a firing solution quickly. As the solution presented itself, the Captain fired a third water shot at the receding target. She then surfaced astern of the three of them triumphantly, and informed the Fleet commander that it was all over! Data was then exchanged between the submarine and the Fleet Staff for plotting tracks in preparation for a debrief that would take place in a few days in the Operations Room in Port Blair to decide whether the attacks were successful, and to learn lessons for future such exercises.

Vanshali was then asked to proceed to a designated Submarine Exercise Area not far away, and wait for two ships to join her for anti-submarine work up. She did not have much to do except to follow courses and change depth as ordered by the ships as they 'pinged' their way on a course parallel to, and on either side of, the submarine. This was a part of her duties; working up ships to track submarines competently. Exercises of this nature went on for two to three hours with each pair of ships.

After the training phase was over, actual amphibious landings to be affected under opposed conditions. Vanshali was detached to proceed and act as part of the 'Red Force' that was to affect an amphibious landing against opposition offered by the 'Blue Force' from land, sea, and air. She was required to land a Special Boat Section Team that normally preceded an amphibious landing. The timing and place of landing was a closely guarded secret known to very few, apart from Vanshali's Captain. It would be under cover of darkness, in conditions suitable for a successful landing, and unsuitable for the opposing forces. The submarine would have to close the coast as near as possible and disembark her forces without being detected. Thereafter, she would have to withdraw and leave the area so that other Red Force units, including the Landing Craft, could move in. The Blue Force was to be kept guessing as to where the landing was likely to take place, and when. The exercise was completed after a few days and the ships and the submarine entered Port Blair.

The two days in Port Blair were very busy without shore accommodation. We visited Ross Island, the historic Cellular jail, the museum, and other places of interest. At the museum, some of the officers saw a letter put up on display, written post-independence by an old lady from the United Kingdom who had lived in Port Blair in the early part of the twentieth century as a very young girl. Her father was posted there. It told of an attempt by a British officer to get the prisoners in the Cellular jail to form a brass band for entertainment. Prisoners were selected and each handed over an instrument, which the officer thought would be appropriate for him. He got frustrated when he found that they lacked the lungpower required to blow air into the wind instruments effectively, and concluded that it was because they were all vegetarians. The unwitting officer ordered the cook to serve beef to these selected few so that they would gain strength and blow into their instruments effectively. A few days later, they found him dead with his head cleaved in two by the cook's cleaver! Serving beef to Hindus – worse! Forcing them to eat it – is just not done. That ended all efforts to get the prisoners in the Cellular jail to form a band.

A further week was spent exercising in the Andaman Sea. All of them returned to Visakhapatnam thereafter, exercising all the way back.

GIRIJA !

Thomson was a junior sailor onboard Vanshali. His Action Post was in the Engine Room. He was also an athlete in his own right, and brought many laurels to the submarine cadre in Inter - Command and Intra - Command Athletic Meets. Being a married man, he was allotted married quarters in Visakhapatnam town some distance away from the naval base. He was a thoroughly popular fellow.

Late one night, while the submarine was in harbor, Thompson was relaxing in his home, after dinner, and about to go to bed, when there was a knock on his front door.

He peeped through the eyehole on the door but could see no one. Opening the door just a wee bit, he heard receding footsteps and saw the shadows of someone running away into the darkness. He opened the door wider and stepped in the middle of the doorway to have a good look around. There was no one about. As he turned to go in, and shut the door, some movement not far from his feet, and low in the ground, caught his eye. He stooped to take a closer look and was surprised to see a black round fluffy creature wriggling about. It appeared to be harmless and so he picked it up and took it in to have a good look in brighter light. He couldn't believe his eyes! First total confusion; and then worry gripped him.

What would he do with this creature? He couldn't keep it at home. To reaffirm his thoughts, his wife came into the room at that moment, and saw what he was holding. She wanted him to get rid of it quickly. He calmed her down and promised to get rid of it the following day. They had an uncomfortable night's sleep.

The following morning, while carrying out his ablutions, a possible solution to the problem occurred to him. He would take it to the Submarine Base and give it to the Officer in Charge there. It would be off his hands and their problem thereafter. He followed up this idea without delay, and the fluffy creature was handed over to the Officer in Charge of the Submarine Base, with a whole lot of curious onlookers trailing behind him. All they who saw the creature took to it at once. The Commanding Officer called a meeting of all Heads of Departments to decide on the fate of this small creature.

"Let's keep her as our Mascot" suggested one of them and this was met with whole-hearted support. She was also given a name – Girija!

The dictionary defines the word 'mascot' as 'any person, animal, or thing supposed to bring good luck by being present'! Submariners always needed good luck. So Girija came to stay. One sailor was even detailed off to be with her all the time, to feed her, exercise her, and be her foster mother and father.

She was a very friendly creature. She was gentle and playful and neither timid nor bad-tempered. In fact she was quite at home with homo-sapiens. She quickly settled down to life within the boundaries of the Submarine Base. In the beginning, during her growing years, she was allowed to roam about freely without a leash and without being penned in. Since she had the run of the place, just about everyone in the Naval Area got to know her, or of her existence, and her popularity increased by leaps and bounds. Servicemen from neighboring establishments came over to look at this unusual pet, and the bolder ones even ventured to play with her.

She was growing up well on the diet being given to her – milk, rice, and sugar interspersed with lots of fruits. In a matter of months she grew up to an average man's height when pulled up and made to stand on her hind legs, and weighed around eighty kilograms. She was also running faster than the sailor looking after her, and there were many occasions when he was found panting and chasing her, asking others to help him catch her so that he could take her to her food plate or back to wherever she had run away from. Looking after her was becoming a bit of a problem. It was at this stage that the first restrictions were put on her. She was provided with a leash and collar, and that curbed her exuberance to manageable proportions.

She grew stronger and stronger. Her claws were also growing to lengths too long for comfort. She would not let anyone clip them. There was no one strong enough to hold her back on her leash when she decided she wanted to go off in a particular direction. She was now a very playful, overgrown baby, who did not know her own strength. One day she ran into the ground floor offices of the Submarine Base during working hours and went about disposing paperwork faster than the most adept of staff officers. That was it! A cage was made for her and 'in' she went to spend most of the days, to be taken out only for walks early in the mornings and late in the evenings.

It was about this time that someone taught her how to smoke. Through her beady eyes she would watch smokers puffing away and blowing out smoke. Seeing her interest, someone gave her a cigarette at the end of a rubber hose. She took the other end and with two deep puffs finished the entire cigarette! She became an addict and would plead and plead with smokers to part with a cigarette for her whenever she got an opportunity.

One day, one of the submarine engineer officers was returning from Vanshali when the Officer in Charge of the Naval Base admonished him for wearing a dirty, oily beret and moving about ashore. He had worked extremely hard that day, and a 'ticking off' was the last thing he wanted. On the spur of the moment, he removed his beret and flung it. It went into Girija's cage. Girija promptly picked it up, sniffed it, chewed on it, and ate up the beret! There were many similar incidents that occurred – too many to recount. She was a fascinating creature who kept everyone spellbound with her antics.

Soon the day arrived when the Submarine Base was to be commissioned as a full-fledged naval establishment. The usual flurry of activities preceded this event, one of them being a proper parade. Girija the Mascot was also readied for the event and positioned next to the Quarter Deck with a chain and collar round her neck. She was not brought for the rehearsals, but only on the final day. That, unfortunately, proved to be a very wrong move. There was utter confusion in giving the order "Eyes Right" at the right time on the final day as both Girija and the VIP on the Quarter Deck looked remarkably alike. Sic!

She lived for only about two years, which was far short of her life span. It is said she died pining for a companion from her own kind. She was buried in the Submarine Base where her gravestone is still carefully preserved to this day. You don't get mascots like her very often. She was a handsome, black, gentle, Sloth Bear.

FLEET EXERCISES

"I tell you, Sir, the submarine Captain – and I hate to use this word – is lying! He was where I was holding him on my sonar as a firm, positively identified, submarine contact, and not where he is claiming to have been!" boomed the rather pompous Commanding Officer of the anti-submarine frigate, addressing the Fleet Commander during a particular debrief after ten days of fleet exercises at sea. They were sitting in the auditorium of the Tactical Trainer ashore. A debrief on all the exercises that were conducted at sea over the previous fortnight was being conducted, serial by serial. On the massive screen in front of everyone was a projection of the area, where two ships and the submarine had exercised just a few days ago. The two frigate's tracks were clearly visible in blue color as Track 1 and Track 2. Also visible was the position where the submarine was alleged to have been when it was 'caught' by the frigate, as plotted by the frigate's operations team. It was in the center of the exercise area. The submarine's track and position, as claimed by the submarine, was shown in red color. At the alleged time when she was 'caught', she was showing herself to be in the north-western corner of the exercise area.

Vanshali's Captain did not get up to defend himself. He was way junior in naval seniority to the Captain of the frigate. He was also certain that the man was speaking with conviction. Of course the Captain of the frigate was wrong. Why, then, would he make a strong statement like this in front of everyone? He was certainly not out to belittle or humiliate the submarine Captain. Should the matter be ignored so that the incident is forgotten, and let the 'debrief' continue? No! He would investigate this further during the lunch break that was to follow any minute now.

During the lunch break, Vanshali's Captain called his Navigating Officer and the Sonar Officer to another room, and went over the exercise records once again, with the help of the Chart. The story did not change. Their version was absolutely correct. Then, staring at the chart, suddenly, he got it! There it was, screaming silently to gain his attention. He was now ready to give an explanation to the Fleet Commander, the Captain of the frigate, and to all who were going to be present in the hall after lunch.

"Excuse me Sir! May I take this audience back to the incident when I was accused of lying? I have something of interest to show everyone" said the submarine commanding officer, addressing the Fleet Commander.

"Go ahead and make it snappy" said the Admiral, his curiosity aroused. "We haven't got too much time to waste over one exercise serial. There are many more to be covered. You have two minutes! Make sure you say something sensible. Otherwise, don't waste everybody's time". The Admiral sat back to listen. The same projection was called for and once again projected on the big screen in front of everyone.

"The submarine was where I had stated it was. It is also true that the Frigate had 'held' a firm contact in the position claimed by them."

Whipping out the Chart from behind his back where he had half hidden it all this while, he continued:

"If one were to look at the Chart carefully, and look at the area where the frigate was holding a firm contact on sonar, one can see that there is an underwater pinnacle at that very spot. It was that underwater hillock that the frigate was bouncing its sonar beams off, and getting a firm contact. Yes, she had a firm contact – but it wasn't the submarine! The classification by the ship's Sonar operator was wrong."

He took the Chart across to the Fleet Commander and the Captain of the frigate and showed them the pinnacle. There was silence! No protests from any quarter. Vanshali's Captain had made his point. He sat down. In a few moments, the next point on the agenda was taken up.

Undersea warfare involves a battle of the minds between the hunter and the hunted. During peacetime, it ends after debrief in harbor. Debriefs have to be fought as keenly as the efforts at sea. During wartime it ends with one or the other, and sometimes even both, going down to Davy Jones's locker, there to rest forever, …. frozen in time, …… while time and the world moves on. In this cat and mouse game between the king of the waves and the denizen of the deep, the hardware, the environmental conditions, and the likes available to each may well be known to the other, and consequently the strengths and weaknesses to some extent. However, to be one step ahead of the adversary it is important to know his tactics, his level of knowledge and training, his character, his state of mind, guess his next move, and then outthink and outmaneuver him. Easier said than done! But that is the difference between winning and losing, between killing and being killed, and every navy knows that it has to work during peace towards these ends. During peacetime it is essential to work up basic skills that become second nature, and at the back of the subconscious mind during war, so that the mind can concentrate on other more pressing and immediate matters. For this very same reason, drills and procedures must also come as second nature to the fighting man. This comes only with constant exercising at sea. Peacetime work up is as important as getting the best equipment for one's inventory that money can buy.

It is not easy to locate and corner a dived submarine in tropical waters, no matter how sophisticated the submarine detecting equipment onboard an anti-submarine warship or aircraft is. The tropical waters are more complex than the temperate waters influenced by melting ice from the polar region that gives the latter a less saline composition. In temperate waters it is relatively easier to catch and track a submarine. In the Tropics, all possible skills, gut feelings, and even hunches must be used to advantage to catch a submarine, and on the latter's part, to evade a hunter. The complexities are mind-boggling.

Till Vanshali's arrival, the anti-submarine ships of the navy were trained or worked up for a few weeks annually by an arrangement with foreign navies providing their submarines for this purpose, while transiting Indian waters. Needless to say their more sophisticated submarines were never provided for such training, and the costs were exorbitant. The training was also hardly worth the money as the effects lasted only for a few weeks, what with ship's crews changing around and new crews having to wait for up to a year to get a submarine to bounce their sonar beams off. Now that Vanshali, a Foxtrot Class submarine had arrived, Fleet Commanders could work up their anti-submarine forces and maintain high standards throughout the year by constantly working up with these boats. Work up of the fleet became Vanshali's foremost task for most parts of the year. In return, the ships would give opportunities for Vanshali to hone her skills at outmaneuvering and attacking surface and airborne units. Structured exercises with graduated increase in complexities had been devised to work up ships, submarines, and aircraft in undersea warfare. It must be remembered that the technology of the Sixties was what was being exploited in the days when Vanshali was working up the fleet. The approach to work up and the tactics in use were also those of the Sixties and somewhat overtaken in later years with the introduction of submarine fired missiles. Vanshali carried no missiles and only resorted to torpedo firings. Later, submarines all carried missiles and the ensuing requirements for work up and development of tactics were of an entirely different nature.

Fleet exercises were always fun for Vanshali, although they involved a lot of hard work and a very rigorous routine from morning to evening, with very little respite. Sometimes there were night serials too. One could make out the character of each of the ships coming in for anti-submarine work up by their attitudes towards the training. Both were equally bent upon ensuring that they got the better of the exchanges in the unstructured, free-for-all cat and mouse games. The submarine invariably did, so long as there were no anti-submarine helicopters around. Structured, pro-ship exercises were sometimes boring but used by the submarine to train new planes-men, new sonar operators, or young officers on maintaining Trim and depth during maneuvers, even as the ships worked up their anti-submarine teams. Some of the ships showed very good understanding of undersea warfare, while others appeared to be totally clueless. Onboard the submarine, one could make out if an officer with anti submarine warfare specialization was in command of the ship, or one with navigation or communications or other specializations. One could also make out the caliber of the Anti Submarine Warfare Specialist officer onboard each ship, by the way the ship was put through the paces to corner the submarine.

An exercise week began with Vanshali leaving harbor the evening before the fleet's departure, after charging her batteries and topping up High Pressure air. She would head out to the assigned Submarine Exercise Area, and reach there by the following morning. She would catch a good Trim en route and await the arrival of the Fleet, and the work up would then begin.

Sometimes she would be asked to lie in wait just outside the harbor and try and attack Fleet units as they left harbor for their work up areas. Fleet units would try to intercept or sidestep the waiting submarine on their way out. This called for the submarine to operate in shallow waters with commercial craft and shipping also milling around in the area. She would have to skillfully evade the merchantmen and maneuver to get her assigned targets without being detected. This also called for some very tricky and competent maneuvering skills on the part of the submarine, especially at night. Fleet ships had the option of trying to locate the submarine with the help of active or passive sonar, and then sidestepping or prosecuting her. During one of these exercises, one of the more advanced anti-submarine destroyers decided to use high speeds, and no sonar, to get past the submarine. It did not work. She, very unfortunately, ran over the submarine, scraping the top of Vanshali's Fin and damaging one of her own propeller shafts in the process. The Fin was quickly repaired and Vanshali was back at sea soon enough. The destroyer limped about with one propeller shaft removed for many years. It was only replaced during her next major refit.

While on transit to the Submarine Exercise Area, sometimes a Maritime Reconnaissance Aircraft would be assigned to locate and 'destroy' the submarine, in which case she would have to transit to the Submarine Exercise Area undetected and dived. A high speed of advance would be assigned to the boat to make her task of reaching her destination that much more difficult. She would have to maintain that high speed of advance by resorting to a combination of snorting at Periscope Depth when the aircraft is looking for her elsewhere, and propelling deep when the aircraft is too close for comfort. This cat and mouse game was beneficial to both the aircraft and the submarine, as it provided good training value. The latter would be asked to ensure that she reached her destination without being detected by a certain time, and with a certain percentage of battery power still remaining. A well worked up submarine stood a high chance of reaching her destination undetected. A badly worked up, or careless crew, often got 'caught', or did not make it on time. A lot also depended on how well worked up the aircrew was.

After the Fleet arrived in the vicinity of the widely promulgated Submarine Exercise Area, the Fleet Commander would assign ships, two at a time, to exercise with the submarine, while the rest of the surface units worked up other aspects of maritime warfare elsewhere on the high seas.

These ships would come to exercise with the submarine in pairs. Depending on their standard of work up, they would be programmed by the Fleet Staff to carry out training with the submarine with selected exercises of varying degrees of difficulty. Such exercises gave the submarine no benefit and were really meant solely for the benefit of ships. In between such serials, Vanshali would be left alone periodically, to top up her batteries and be ready for the next sequence of anti-submarine work-up serials.

These exercises and work up would see the ships and submarine at sea for many days after which the ships would then race at 'home revs' back to harbor, to enjoy a weekend with their families. The submarine would chug along at her best economical speed, which was always much slower than that of the ships, and get in the following day. First to leave harbor and last to get back – that was the lot for Vanshali and her tribe when exercising with the Fleet!

Some interesting incidents sometimes took place during fleet exercises. There was this new super-duper ship that was acquired by the navy from abroad that had completed an extremely successful work up in temperate latitudes, and was coming home for the first time. Vanshali was asked to give her a 'warm reception', and the ship was told to expect this. In other words, the ship could expect to be 'attacked' by the submarine. After establishing radio contact with the ship, Vanshali dived. She then proceeded to carry out a series of maneuvers at depth to outfox the super-duper, well worked up, ship. She dived on one side of her, and then proceeded to go under her, and finally surfaced on the other side while the ship was looking for her on the wrong side. It deflated the recently built up ego of the ship's Captain. Not for a moment could he detect the submarine. His ego was hyped up in the temperate latitudes. It was deflated in tropical waters.

It is part of naval practice for frigates and destroyers to screen or shield a bigger but more vulnerable ship or ships from an external threat by forming a defensive ring around her or them, and thereby providing a protective cover. The threat could be from incoming missiles, attacking aircraft, attacking ships, or from submarines. While the general principle for protection was the same, the type of screen varied for each type of threat. When more than one type of threat was expected, a compromising screen formation would be adopted.

There were many occasions when Vanshali was asked to attempt to penetrate a protective 'screen' of ships, and attack the ship being screened. The latter could be posing as a merchantman with 'vital cargo', or a troop carrier, or even an aircraft carrier. Here the skills of the submarine crew would be really put to test. During one such serial, Vanshali was given a free hand and asked to penetrate the screen of fleet ships protecting an oil tanker, and attack the defenseless oiler. It was a night exercise. Two British

Whitby class frigates, four Soviet Petya class corvettes, and two British Blackwood class frigates formed the screen. They were all transmitting on their sonar sets in search of a probable submarine lurking in their path. They were also weaving and zigzagging while maintaining their base course to their destination. Vanshali picked them up at some distance on her sonar and identified each one of them and their position on the screen. The Captain decided to penetrate the screen between two Petya class corvettes and proceeded with his maneuvers. He moved swiftly and silently to a position ahead of the formation and then adjusted himself to slip between the two Petya class corvettes. Having got through undetected, he looked around for the tanker, but suddenly found he could not locate it. He, however, picked up a ship on his sonar that appeared to be stationary. He maneuvered Vanshali to take up position under the ship, and stopped her. There, under the unsuspecting ship, he stayed till the end of the serial, while the rest of the formation moved on, none the wiser of the submarine's whereabouts. After the serial, when the submarine surfaced, she found that the crafty Fleet Staff had placed the oil tanker on the defending screen while a Whitby class frigate was made to act as the one to be protected. This was deliberately done by the Fleet Staff to confuse the submarine Commanding Officer, and fool him. What was not planned was the machinery breakdown that the Whitby class frigate suddenly confronted them with! Unfortunately, the machinery breakdown forced the ship to stop. It was this ship under which Vanshali had placed herself. In defense of the submarine Captain, it must be stated that a stopped ship is difficult to identify without coming up to Periscope depth. This was a night serial and the submarine Captain had decided to stay deep throughout the serial. There were always lessons to be learnt from these types of exercises

On another occasion, Vanshali was in her Submarine Exercise Area, left alone to 'top up' her batteries while all the ships of the Fleet had gone some distance away for a Missile Firing Serial. During peacetime, Regulations demanded that the selected area be cleared of trawlers and other ships before missile firing was carried out. For this purpose, some ships were assigned the task of 'range clearance'. Even while Vanshali was on the surface, charging her batteries, one of the frigates appeared on the horizon and closed her at top speed. When within hailing distance, a voice from the Bridge of the frigate frantically yelled:

"Vanshali! You are in the Missile Firing Cone. Get out quickly! You are delaying the Missile Firing serial."

Now, the Captain of Vanshali was quite certain that he was in the Submarine Exercise Area that was at a safe distance away from the missile firing area. He quickly reconfirmed this from the Satellite Navigation System onboard which gave accurate positions at sea. However, since the frigate was quite sure that Vanshali was in the 'Firing Cone', this was no time to argue. She asked the frigate for the best course to steer to get out of the cone, in the shortest possible time. This was duly given, and the frigate sped away. Breaking battery charging, Vanshali headed out on the course suggested, at her fastest speed. The Captain went down to the Control Room to make a note of this incident with a view to discussing it during debrief in harbor.

"WHOOMP!" a loud sound was heard in the Control Room through the open hatch, quickly followed by a very shaken and nervous voice on the broadcast from the Officer of the Watch:

"Captain Sir! Bridge! A missile just went past our Stern. It .. it .. it was very c-c-c-close."

The Captain jumped out of his seat in the Chart House and scrambled up the hatch to the Fin. Reaching his 'perch' on the Bridge, he asked the Officer of the Watch as to where the missile had come from, and where had it disappeared? This was pointed out by the ashen - faced man.

The Captain turned his binoculars to the direction from where the missile had supposedly come, and scanned that part of the horizon. Then he saw an unbelievable sight! What looked like a total solar eclipse was sighted on the horizon, and the black ball surrounded by an orange flame was getting bigger and bigger, coming straight for Vanshali! In a trice it had gone past the stern with another "WHOOMP", with searing heat following it. A second missile had been fired! Fortunately, the submarine was too low in the water for the missile to hit it, and the missile homing head had been deactivated. A deathly silence followed on the Bridge as those present realized that they had just gone through an experience of a lifetime. The Captain was furious! Someone's pants had to be taken off for this, he promised himself.

It turned out that for this particular Missile Firing Serial, two missile corvettes were to come from harbor and join the rest of the Fleet ships. They were late in arriving, and rather than prolong the delay, the Fleet Staff had decided to move the assigned missile firing area closer to the approaching ships. In the process they forgot that the Submarine Exercise Area would fall within the newly assigned missile firing area. Nobody told Vanshali, as she was not a part of this serial! Such mistakes are extremely rare occurrences, borne out by the fact that it never happened again.

Working with anti – submarine helicopters presented a different form of challenge. Both operated in different mediums. The submarine had no weapon to hit the helicopter with, while the latter carried either torpedoes or depth charges to attack the submarine at will and with impunity. Till the helicopter hovered in one spot and lowered its dunking sonar and transmitted, the submarine was oblivious of its whereabouts. It was also none the wiser about where the next 'dunk' would be, and this complicated the selection of direction in which to get away. While a single helicopter prosecuting a submarine gave the latter some chance to escape, two helicopters working in tandem were extremely difficult to get away from. They could easily 'box' the submarine between themselves – provided detection had taken place. The initial detection was the tricky part. To be hit and not be able to hit was another very frustrating situation to be in, and submariners dreaded helicopters in their area of operations. Vanshali was once deployed to work up the entire lot of Sea King helicopters of the Indian Fleet in anti-submarine operations over a period of two months, by night and by day. After passing a tough inspection ashore, the helicopters were declared technically fit to fly over the sea and work up with the submarine. They were sent in pairs from a shore airbase to 'ping' on the submarine with their Dunking Sonars, lowered by a winch into the water. They worked up well and progressively started to 'hold contact' with the submarine at longer and longer ranges very comfortably. However, at the end of this work up, when a few 'free for all' serials were organized, it is to the credit of Vanshali's crew that she managed to evade detection every time, despite having to confine her evasive measures to staying within the boundaries of the Submarine Exercise Area.

"What is 'Gross Ignorance'?" asked the Engineer Officer in the Wardroom one day just before the submarine was putting out to sea. Various answers were given and he kept scoffing at each of them. Finally he was asked for his version.

"A Hundred and Forty Four Pongos" was his answer! One gross amounted to one hundred and forty four, and 'Pongos' was the term for army personnel given by the British. During one particular fleet work up, Vanshali had to carry a bunch of army 'para-commandos' onboard, to land them clandestinely during a peacetime exercise. They were accommodated in the Fore-Ends, and instructions were passed down the line that these 'Senior Service' members were to be looked after as best as possible. The cooks turned out mouthwatering non-vegetarian fare and puddings rarely seen onboard submarines. Extra mattresses, feathered pillows, and blankets were given out to them. They settled down, and at the first opportunity, the Captain went to the Fore Ends to see how they were faring. He saw them lying on the spare torpedoes, all knotted up and sprawled over each other in various forms of clinches, with their arms and legs entwined – fast asleep. The mattresses, pillows and blankets were discarded and not in use, and were lying on the deck. Later it was learnt that they were all vegetarians who did not even eat eggs! They, however, looked very tough and had a reputation of being very tough even in the army. As part of the exercise, they were landed at night at a particular spot off the coast, at a particular time. The operation was executed very smoothly, and Vanshali withdrew into deeper waters, her job done. The submarine crew eventually ate the specially prepared fare.

Then there were these 'food transfers' that fleet ships loved to execute when working with submarines. Someone had firmly entrenched into the minds of the surface navy that the food cooked onboard submarines leaves much to be desired. If not 'someone', then they were carrying these impressions forward from their readings of Second World War episodes. The Galley was the most frequented place onboard Vanshali, and the cook played a very important role in keeping up the crew's morale. Working under very trying circumstances and challenging conditions, he would prepare vegetarian and non-vegetarian dishes in a very confined space in the IVth Compartment that were equally palatable to the northerner, the southerner, the easterner, and the westerner. At one time, the navy supplied Vanshali with pre-cooked, tinned, food to make life supposedly easier all round. However, the rustic Indian sailor found the stuff unpalatable, what with preservatives and the likes giving it an unusual taste. It was left to the cooks to skillfully disguise the tinned food by adding their own ingredients to make it appear like authentic dishes cooked from fresh ingredients. They did this with aplomb, and the crew was more than satisfied with what they were getting to eat.

The surface navy, however, had it in their heads that it was difficult to cook underwater, and the 'poor' submariners were being deprived of normal food. During fleet exercises, rather unexpectedly and between work up serials, a hapless submarine would be transferred what they called 'hot' food. This was invariably done with the Fleet Commander in the know but without any prior warning to the submarine, and after the submarine cook had already made his fare! It resulted in one or the other being kept aside for the next meal and eaten cold. On one occasion, after receiving one such transfer, Vanshali's Captain decided that enough was enough! The submarine cook was directed to make 'gulab jamuns' – a well-liked Indian sweet - at the rate of three per head for the frigate's crew. After the next fleet serial, the ship was asked to close the submarine and the 'G-jams' were transferred. That ship got the message and never bothered Vanshali with a 'hot transfer' thereafter.

Returning home from fleet exercises one late Friday evening, the Torpedo Officer came up the hatch to the Captain on the Bridge with a signal in his hands. It read:

> From: Flag Officer Commanding in Chief
> Western Naval Command
> To: Vanshali

British Airways Flight No …. Proceeding from Bombay to London ditched at sea off Bombay in position Latitude ..° N .. Longitude …° E at …hours. Proceed with dispatch to the position and render assistance. You will be relieved by INS ……., detached from the Fleet and directed to head for the area.

The Captain called for the Navigating Officer and asked him to plot the position on the Chart and give a Course to steer for the area. On the broadcast, this information was passed on to the whole crew. The Executive Officer was summoned and directed to make all arrangements to pick up survivors and accommodate them onboard. The Medical Officer was directed to convert the Officer's Ward Room in the Second Compartment into an Operation Theatre and make all arrangements to treat survivors who may need urgent medical attention. The Chief Steward was directed to have bottles of Brandy readily available (for medicinal purposes, ofcourse). The Engine Room was ordered to have all three diesels available for maximum speed, which was ordered subsequently.

There was frenzied activity onboard for the next twenty minutes. The Fore Ends was cleared and made ready to accommodate survivors. Blankets were pulled out from storage spaces, and improvised beds made wherever there was space. Extra Lookouts were called up to the Bridge with binoculars to be ready to spot survivors in the water. A cash prize was declared for every person who spotted a survivor. The Navigating Officer had given the Course to steer and it involved only a five degrees deviation from Vanshali's original Course. By now the sun had set and it was dark.

"Bridge – Lookout! A small light in the water on the Port beam about a mile away!"

The Captain swung the submarine around to Port and headed for the spot. Even as the submarine was coming around, there was another cry:

"Bridge – Starboard Look Out! A dark object bobbing in the water on bearing Green 40°. Distance half a mile" …..

"Bridge – Lookout! Someone is shouting in the water!!"…

Reports came in one after another and the Captain weaved the submarine all across the area, to pick up survivors. However, on closing the spots where the survivors were supposedly floating, there were none. This went on for quite awhile.

The Torpedo Officer came up the hatch with yet another signal. This time he looked nervous and uncomfortable. It read:

"In view of it being April Fool's Day, cancel my signal regarding the crash of British Airways flight."

The Captain stared at him.

"Are you responsible for this?"

"Y-y -yes Sir!"

The Captain looked away for a brief moment and then turned back to address him:

"Well done! If nothing else, the crew has been exercised to meet such an eventuality if, God forbid, it ever occurs."

On the intercom he called up the Executive Officer and directed him to call off all preparations. A perspiring and curious Executive Officer soon huffed and puffed his way up the hatch and asked the Captain why he had called off the search. He was told! From that day onwards, a silent war was waged between the Executive Officer and the Torpedo Officer that lasted till one of them left Vanshali.

The Torpedo Officer was a bachelor and a good man, both professionally and as an individual. He had been screened for a special mission and rejected by the medicos who declared him unfit on the grounds that he had suicidal tendencies. This report was confidential in nature, and therefore didn't get around. A few years later, he shot himself, leaving behind a note that stated that he alone was responsible for his actions, and no blame was to be attributed to anyone else. It was only after that that the contents of the medical report got around. It was a probable explanation for his near drowning a few years earlier on a diving mission even though he was a qualified diver and a good swimmer, and his almost getting lost when he fell off the submarine's Bridge one dark night after sending the Lookout down the hatch for some coffee. This had happened on Vanshali's way to Port Blair. The Submarine Arm sorely missed him for many years to come.

In the system of submarine training initiated in India, two very strict courses were introduced that were called the Principal Officer's Course (PCO) and the Commanding Officer's Qualifying Course (COQC). Without making the grade in the PCO's Course, an officer could not be appointed as the second in command of the submarine. The second in command was required to be competent enough to take over command and operate the submarine, should the captain be incapacitated. This included maneuvering the boat safely, carrying out attacks on designated targets, and ensuring safety through evasion from an aggressive opponent. There were many who did not qualify to be appointed as the second in command. Perhaps tougher was the COQC. Very few got through this course to command submarines eventually. Yet, after qualifying in such grueling courses, there were vast differences discernible in qualified commanding officers. Those who had higher promotions in their career in mind were found to be overcautious, not prepared to take chances, and never take chances. One commanding officer who commanded Vanshali never used the diesels at periscope depth to propel, as this involved putting the schnorkel up (a pipe with a very large diameter through which air was sucked in from the surface of the sea into the submarine for the diesels, and for ventilation) and opening a hull valve. During fleet exercises, when he was required to propel at periscope depth in a snorting regime, he would simply put the schnorkel up, keep the hull valve shut, and propel on the submarine's motors (they did not require air as they used battery current for propulsion). He never took the submarine deep, and never indulged in 'crash dives' that involved taking extra water in the Quick Diving Tank initially to make the boat heavier so that she would go down faster, and then blowing out this extra water at the appropriate depth to level her off at the desired depth. His tenure of command came to be called the 'tenure of the virgin 'Q'' (it was never used). He went on to get promoted to a very high rank in later years. He was one of those trained in the Soviet Union, and had not undergone the strict Indian COQC. There was another who tried every trick in the book to avoid fleet exercise (where his competency could be judged by the surface navy) and to operate alone where only his subsequent reports would form the basis for an assessment of his performance. There was another who would come up with some defect in the submarine or the other, at the last minute, to avoid putting out to sea when it could have been rectified if it had been reported earlier. There were those who opted for evasion and not being detected rather than attempting to penetrate a screen of ships and attack, and risk the chance of being 'caught'. Fortunately, there were very few of these types of commanding officers. On the plus side, there were many daring commanding officers who took calculated risks and ensured safety of the boat and crew at the same time. Younger commanding officers proved to be the more daring ones. The older ones were more cautious. In the final analysis, if a true report on the competency of the commanding officer was to be called for, it was the eighty odd men in the boat serving under him and watching his every action who could give a true and accurate assessment. The reporting system did not provide for such an assessment, but a reputation developed and that did the rounds in the wardroom (officers' mess) and the sailors' mess decks and barracks that followed the commanding officer for the rest of his career in the navy.

Foxtrots on the cover of the official naval magazine for submarines – The Periscope

CATCHING SMUGGLERS!

Post-independent India concentrated on working towards attaining self-reliance and self-sufficiency rather than depending on others, since it had all the ingredients and resources for this purpose. During the colonial era, the colonial masters took all the raw goods away, and some finished products arrived back. India, thus, had no manufacturing plants of any worth when she gained Independence. The road to progress was steady but slow. While building up a nation from scratch, and towards this end encouraging people to buy Indian goods, there were strict import restrictions in place. 'Phoren' items therefore became a very elusive attraction that many in the country coveted. Consequently, smuggling of foreign goods into the country became an attractive proposition for those looking to make quick, easy, money. Along sea routes, small innocent dhows brought in attractive smuggled items from the Persian Gulf, while passenger liners between Singapore and Madras clandestinely smuggled in goods from the orient. The air and land routes were equally busy! At that time, the country did not have a Coast Guard Force, and it was left to the Customs Department to look for, and seize, contraband goods. Whenever things got too difficult for them to handle, they would ask the Indian Navy to assist them. Such a request was placed in the early nineteen seventies, and the Navy instructed all their ships on the west coast to seize these dhows smuggling contraband goods and bring them to harbor, to hand them over to the Customs Department. Vanshali was operating off the West Coast of India, from Bombay, at that time.

During peacetime, it is customary to earmark specific areas for submarine exercises and promulgate the same through 'Notices To Mariners' so that vessels on innocent passage are forewarned and encouraged to keep clear off that area. The fleet ships then come to this area to work up anti submarine warfare skills with submarines that wait for them, one in each area at a time. Every country does this, and so does the Indian Navy. On the West Coast of India, such areas were promulgated off Bombay, off Goa, and off Cochin. They were then marked as Submarine Exercise Areas on relevant Charts. The Charts were commercially available and used by mariners plying those waters.

On a bright, calm, day with fair weather and calm blue skies promising an enjoyable outing, Vanshali headed out to sea from Bombay to her Submarine Exercise Area, to carry out some independent work up. Soon Bombay Floating Light, which marked the entrance to the harbor, was out of sight, and so were the merchant ships anchored around it, waiting for permission to enter the port. Her bulbous sonar nose lazily dipped and rose gently. A few inquisitive seagulls tailed her, hoping for some pickings from possible food waste being ditched overboard.

The South West Monsoons were over. It hadn't been a fair one. A good one is interpreted as one that tops up all water reservoirs and assists the farmers to deliver a good crop. Over fifty percent of the population was engaged in farming in rural India. From importing grain to feed a population of around 225 million mouths in the early fifties, India was now feeding close to a billion and self-sufficient at that. This particular year, the rains were sufficient in some States and very scanty in others. There was enough food reserves with the Government to tide over the disappointing downpours and now the North East Monsoons were awaited with some optimism. There were still another two months to go for that.

Vanshali chugged along, her diesels settling down to a healthy purr, and the crew to the normal sea routine. It was good to get away from harbor from time to time – no domestic chores, marketing or responsibilities to handle! The families were never happy to see the men folk go to sea, but had got used to looking after themselves for long periods while the breadwinner was playing around in the ocean, on the surface, and under it.

Landward, some fishing trawlers were at work, moving about in an uncoordinated fashion that irked the mariners in navy blue uniform. Amazingly, they managed to avoid colliding with each other – even by night. Perhaps there was some method in their madness? Warships considered them a nuisance because they would arrogantly continue with their work, even if they were in the direct path of the mighty armed vessels closing them. It was left to the navy to ensure that they didn't collide with these tiny fellows. Looked at from a different perspective, to the city of Bombay these 'tiny fellows' were more important than the stately warships. Their whole fish supply came from these trawlers. India has vast reserves of marine wealth in its Exclusive Economic Zone by way of fish, prawns, lobsters, and crabs that are hardly harvested. The nation, having a continental outlook in the main rather than a maritime one, has yet to realize the potentials of the sea and the vast reserves of food it stores.

Vanshali was now passing an offshore oilrig that was a part of Bombay High. To the ignorant, Bombay High was where the undersea oil belt was, and the Oil & Natural Gas Corporation (ONGC) drilled and extracted some oil from below the seabed for the nation's use. It wasn't enough to meet the requirements and therefore oil was still being imported, with the common man facing and feeling the financial burden of import. This may be somewhat true, but the extent of effort being put in to extract offshore oil from Bombay High is to be seen to be believed. There is a virtual city out there on stilts – large stationary platforms, some even with helicopter operating decks, accommodation for personnel working in the area, and tiny offices and workshops. Work is in progress round the clock, with cracking and distillation plants next to the bore well platforms extracting and refining the crude oil before it is piped ashore. The crew onboard Vanshali have often seen this amazing 'city' through the periscope, by day and by night, when snorting past the area. Just like cars on city streets, there is an endless stream of offshore vessels plying between the platforms, and between Bombay and the platforms, carrying equipment and personnel to support round the clock operations. That is another world out there.

A few hours beyond the oil rigs lay the Submarine Exercise Area. Once there, the submarine would repeatedly go through a series of maneuvers on the surface and underwater as part of self work-up, till she got them right. Not only did they have to be right, but they also had to be executed in the shortest possible time. Only practice and more practice would help the crew to reach the required, rigorous standards of efficiency. Throughout all these maneuvers, safety of the boat and its crew had also to be ensured.

The binoculars spotted a dark speck on the western horizon. The Lookout had sighted it before the Officer of the Watch and was pleased as punch about it. Both silently compete with each other to spot objects first. Should the Officer spot first, a reprimand was sure to come the Lookout's way? Invariably, in the case of objects in the sky, the officer would be the first to spot it. That was mainly because he was the better trained for it. An object noticed in the sky meant the next step would probably be an 'Urgent Dive', and that would have to be initiated by the officer. On a query from the Radar office, a blip was showing on the screen in the same direction. The radar is normally the first to detect such objects if it was switched on. Onboard Vanshali, it was normally kept warmed up, ready to transmit at short notice. Its use was minimized to an 'on-required only' basis. The object was too far to be identified, but as Vanshali was also heading westwards, it was a matter of time before it was recognizable. The two were closing each other steadily and when the distance between the two had reduced to about 5 miles, the outline of an Arab dhow could be discerned. These were the type of craft used by smugglers. It was, rather strangely, heading straight for the submarine. When it came close enough to recognize the submarine for what it was supposed to be, the dhow panicked, turned around, and started moving away at top speed. These were, decidedly, suspicious movements. The Captain came up the hatch and on espying the dhow, decided to chase it. He also asked for the machine gun onboard to be brought up to the Bridge. A burst of shells was fired ahead of the dhow, and it came to a halt. Vanshali's Boarding Party was called up to the Fin and the stopped dhow was boarded. She was carrying contraband goods, without a doubt.

However the submarine did not know what was to be done with the dhow? A workup in the Exercise Area was what was planned, and now this! The Master of the dhow was brought onboard for questioning. They had come all the way from Dubai with the contraband goods and were supposed to transfer the goods to a fishing trawler, which is what they had mistakenly taken the submarine to be, from afar. Their rendezvous point was slap bang in the middle of the Submarine Exercise Area! The Captain decided what he would do. He called all the other five members of the dhow's crew on board the submarine and addressed them. From their Master, he had learned that only he, and none of the others, new how to navigate the dhow.

"I am taking your Master with me for the day" he said.

"You all will stay onboard your dhow and not move. You will also not try and take the dhow away from this position or you will never see your Master again. We will return just before dusk with your Master, and then we will let you know what you are to do next."

They nodded their frightened heads and went back to their dhow. Then, right before their eyes, Vanshali dived with their Master safely accommodated in the Fore Ends. The Officer of the Watch on the Periscope related later in the Ward Room that the whites of the eyes of the dhow's crewmembers were clearly visible through the periscope as the submarine dived. Pure terror was written all over their faces.

Vanshali proceeded to carry out her assigned and planned work up for the day, out of sight of the dhow. At sunset, she surfaced next to the dhow. The dhow had drifted a little away, but had not moved otherwise. The rest of the crew was taken onboard and the submarine's Boarding Party took over the dhow. The dhow headed back to harbor with the loot that was to be handed over to the Customs Authorities along with the boat. On her return to harbor after her work up, Vanshali handed over the crew of the dhow too.

The story does not end there. Apparently, the rendezvous point had not been changed despite the dhow being apprehended, and Vanshali caught four more dhows over the next three months. This was the most number of dhows any single naval ship had apprehended since the Customs Authorities had asked for assistance! It landed the submarine with extra paper work as the civil courts were also involved in dealing with the smugglers, and reports and extracts from the submarine's Log Book, etc had to be handed over. Court appearances also had to be made by the Navigating Officer a number of times. The seizure of the last but one dhow was a bit of a surprise! The Master of the first dhow was the Master of the last vessel apprehended! He now acted very friendly and slapped the backs of the Boarding Party members as if they were long lost friends. The court had granted him bail, and he had gone back to the Middle East to bring this dhow and its contraband goods. Quite obviously these trips were worth the risks they were taking. A few months on and the Custom Authorities wrote to the navy to say that they had got their act together and would apprehend smugglers by themselves. The navy's services were no longer required.

COLLISION!

Vanshali was still relatively new in the Indian naval inventory. There was much by way of sensitive information about her that the Soviets hadn't disclosed. There may have been many reasons for this. One of them could have been that the Soviets and their other allies were still operating these 'class' of submarines and they therefore did not wish to disclose certain features. The other reason could be that the Indians hadn't simply asked or paid for them. One bit of information that the Indian Navy wanted to know was how much of self-noise the submarine emitted, and the sources that needed necessary attention to reduce these noisy emissions. A 'Noise Range' was required to determine this, but the navy had not created one. It was in their future plans. As an interim measure, scientists were asked to produce a portable piece of equipment to create a 'Noise Range' of sorts wherein the submarine's self-noise levels could be measured. This, rudimentary, portable, equipment eventually got ready and Vanshali was nominated to undergo these trials.

A platform was required for lowering the portable equipment in the water. The platform had to be a quiet one, so that it did not contribute its own noise to the readings, thereby leading to wrong conclusions. Ideally, an anchored pontoon would be most suitable, but there were 'power' and other requirements to operate the portable noise ranging equipment, and the navy could not spare a pontoon equipped with all the necessary paraphernalia at that time. So, a destroyer was chosen as the platform from which the noise ranging equipment would be lowered. The destroyer would remain stopped, and the equipment would be lowered into the water from her stern. The trials required the submarine to pass at right angles to the destroyer's bows as close as possible, at various depths and in different regimes of operation during each run. 'Different regimes' meant, that on one run she would snort past the destroyer propelling with the help of her diesel engines, on another run she would go past propelling on one motor to be followed by separate runs on two motors, three motors, economical speed motor, and repeat the motor runs below Periscope Depth at various depths, so on and so forth. On each run, she would also switch 'on' and switch 'off' various bits of machinery that are suspected to be particularly noisy. Each time, as the submarine passed the sensor, her noise emissions would be measured. As accurate readings had to be taken during each leg, suitable ranging equipment had also to be available on the platform and the submarine. Sufficient depths of water for the submarine to maneuver in, was another requirement. It was going to be a long tedious day with a spillover to the following day in case all the runs had not been completed during the first session.

It was a clear day with good visibility, blue skies, and calm seas when the submarine and the ship set out from harbor into suitable waters for the Trials. The scientists with their mysterious portable listening equipment had embarked the ship, some of them going out to sea for the very first time. As both units were going out for the day and expected to return to harbor the same evening, 'Their Lordships' had decided to send the "Long TAS" Course onboard the submarine for some underwater experience. The acronym "TAS" stood for 'Torpedo and Anti-Submarine'. This Course was a Specialist Course of a year's duration for Lieutenants who would, after graduation, go on to advising their Commanding Officers to hunt and sink submarines in any future conflict. Most of them were also going out to sea in a submarine for the very first time. The experience would stand them in good stead when they are on the other side of the fence.

Vanshali still had many of the original Commissioning Crew onboard. She also had some freshly Indian-trained personnel as part of her crew. This change in crew content was an on-going process necessitated by the fact that personnel, after some experience at sea, had to go for Courses to qualify for the next higher rank, or move out to give others, waiting in line, a chance at sea. These changes, in the interest of submarine safety, were limited in numbers. If a large turn around was required, the whole crew had to go through a proper series of work up as a team before Vanshali was permitted to operate independently. The ship chosen for these trials was exactly the opposite – a WW II veteran destroyer – a survivor- that had been handed over by the Royal Navy to the newly formed, post – independent, Indian Navy. Nevertheless, the two of them looked resplendent and ship-shape, hiding their respective ages, as they reached the Exercise Area for the Trials to begin.

The Long TAS Course that embarked onboard was a curious lot. One tall and lean Sikh officer immediately settled down in the Ward Room with a pack of cards. He had three others with the same idea, and they had visions of spending most of the day playing rummy. His roaming eyes missed nothing – not even the much-coveted tin of condensed milk in the fridge during that fleeting moment when the Steward opened it to take something out. He wanted to finish the condensed milk all by himself but was told that it had been kept for making tea, and a spare one was not readily available for consumption right then. The Education Officer on the Course nosed his way around the Officers' cabins to decide which bunk to select to sleep on. He selected the Correspondence Officer's bunk in the Starboard side cabin in the Second Compartment because it looked more cushioned than the rest. Later on he would learn that the cushiony appearance was because of the ship's files all spread out evenly on the bunk, with a blanket and bed cover over them to disguise the presence of the files. The submarine did not have filing cabinets onboard as Russians did not believe in burdening their sea-going units with paper work. Then there were another lot of officers who worked their way around the Periscope in the extremely cramped surroundings of the Conning Tower to get their first view through the famed eyepiece, at the world outside. They had to queue up and wait for their turn on the Search Periscope. Only the Captain, or whoever he (rarely) nominated, could handle the Captain's periscope. Others roved around the submarine to gaze at, and make out whatever they could of, the zillions of pipes, valves, and gadgets that filled every nook and cranny of each compartment in the boat, giving a totally different appearance to that of the insides of warships.

The submarine commenced her noise-ranging runs past the ship, with the latter stopped. The submarine Captain was on the Captain's Periscope with his eye on the 'glass'. He was conning the boat and giving course, speed, and other orders. On each run, the submarine had to pass at right angles, and quite close to, the stopped ship. Periodic ranges of the ship were being taken to update the 'plot' marking continuous relative positions of both platforms.

"Turn Main Engines as required". Those who have heard this order being passed by the Bridge to the Engine Room onboard surface ships driven by steam turbines must know that these orders are periodically, but regularly, given when the ship is stopped. The Engine Room then turns the turbine blades at an extremely slow speed so that continuous flow of steam on a single or a set of blades, when the ship is stopped, does not distort the blade/s. It is done for short and interrupted spells so that the ship does not creep ahead when she is supposed to be stopped. A Master (steam) Valve is cracked open momentarily and shut almost immediately in a smart manner, letting out a burst of steam onto the turbine blades. The turbine blades would turn and a new set of blades would be subjected to the steady flow of steam, till they were also turned awhile later. Such a procedure was practiced on the Trials ship. The Master Steam valve was also known as the Maneuvering Valve.

It takes a while for a submariner, looking through the Periscope of a submarine at Periscope Depth, to identify the fore-and-aft line of the submarine. There are no reference points visible through the Periscope. The bow, stern, and casing are not visible as these are submerged; only the horizon is visible all round. He has to frequently take his eye off the Periscope and look up at the etchings on the ring around the periscope shaft gland above that shows the relative bearings, and compare with the direction his Periscope is facing, to discern whether his Periscope is truly trained fore and aft. If it is not, he must adjust it to match the fore-and aft etchings. This is particularly to be ensured after rotating the Periscope through 360 degrees for an all-round search - a continuous requirement. Such was the arrangement on this particular submarine.

Looking through a Periscope is tiresome to the eyes. The low intensity of light inside the boat seen by one eye, and the bright light through the Periscope lens by day seen by the other eye simultaneously strains the eyes. At night, it is the other way around: through the Periscope one sees a dark or moonlit sea outside with one eye while the other eye is looking at instruments and gauges in the Conning Tower in red lighting. A Periscope watch keeper has to focus on all that his field of vision offers through the Periscope, as well as on dials and instruments inside the submarine. Frequently shifting his eyes to varying intensities of light reduces the efficiency of sight. His Periscope eyeing time has to be restricted. On this particular submarine, a Periscope 'trick' was restricted to 20 minutes at a time. After 20 minutes the Periscope Watch keeper in the Conning Tower, and the Trimming Officer in the Control Room below, exchanged positions.

A conventional submarine is designed to bottom. She bottoms, lifts herself, and moves on. If a ship bottoms, it is termed as 'Grounding' or 'Running Aground' – a maneuver definitely not recommended, as she is not designed to do this. If a submarine hits an object when coming up, she must instinctively go down again to get herself out of the mess, and not hang around at the depth where she got into trouble, or try to surface.

Each run of Vanshali's, in different regimes past the ship, took some time. By the eighth run, the Captain's eyes were red with fatigue. In a 'close quarter' situation the Captain must be on the Periscope. Going so close to the destroyer during each run amounted to placing the submarine in a 'close quarter' situation. Forget about 20 minutes on the Periscope – he had been there for hours! The efficiency of his eyes had come down drastically. Finally, not being able to see things properly, he sent for the second-in-command and asked him to take over the Periscope for a while. He left the scene after handing over the Periscope, to give his eyes some much needed respite.

The first run with the second-in-command on the Periscope was completed successfully. The second run commenced with the submarine in a 'Snorting Regime'. She was to pass the ship at right angles and less than half a cable away from her stem. The tall and lean Sikh Lieutenant from the Long TAS Course was still in the Ward Room, playing cards with the Engineer Officer and two others. The Education Officer on the course was watching on. One other Long Course officer was peering through the Search Periscope after having waited seemingly endlessly for his turn for a peep. He was a slow mover and generally ambled on terra firma in preference to moving at a military pace from place to place. Some others were in the Sound Room. The second-in-command – the Executive Officer - was peering through the Captain's Periscope. He had the 'con', meaning he was in command of the submarine. The Electrical Officer was on the

Trim.

It is difficult to say who hit whom. There was a sudden, dull, jerk and thud. Vanshali tilted to one side sharply. A sharp, unfamiliar, groaning sound followed an equally unfamiliar screeching sound of metal against metal that was heard along the entire length of the submarine. "We've run aground!" exclaimed the tall and lean Sikh officer who promptly charged to the fridge, grabbed the condensed milk tin, and proceeded to devour it in huge gulps. The Electrical Officer on the Trim – instead of taking the boat down – blew the Center Group of Ballast Tanks with 'high pressure' air, to surface the submarine. By now the Diesel engine had been stopped by the alert Watch-keeper in the Engine room instinctively, because tons of Furnace Fuel Oil had started pouring into the submarine through the Snort Mast that had ruptured the fuel tanks of the Destroyer above - a singular action that saved all onboard that day. The Engineer Officer abandoned his card game and charged into the Control Room to find the Revolution indicators of the three shafts showing all three propellers 'stopped'. He ordered the Electric Motors to 'Half Ahead'. What followed was a combination of positive buoyancy as a result of the Electrical Officer blowing tanks to bring the boat up, and speed as a result of the Engineer Officer giving 'Half Ahead' on the motors. A rasping-filing-effect, accompanied by the unending screeching sounds of tearing metal, propelled the submarine under and along the entire keel length of the destroyer, rupturing all of the latter's tanks below the water line, till they finally parted and Vanshali surfaced clear of, and behind, the ship. The submarine crew was to learn from the destroyer crew later that the old destroyer was bodily lifted a number of times out of the water. Her canvas Bridge awnings were ripped apart by the two Periscopes of the submarine that poked through them as she herself keeled over to one side. The old destroyer started shipping water and then began her battle for survival and to simply stay afloat.

Furnace Fuel Oil (FFO) (the fuel used by the destroyer to propel) poured into every compartment of the submarine through the Snort Induction Trunking that is normally used to ventilate all compartments by bringing in fresh air through the Snort mast. Furnace Fuel Oil also poured down the Periscope shaft glands as the periscopes had been damaged. There were many key actions to be executed quickly if the submarine was to come out of this catastrophic incident. These had been rehearsed in some form or the other during Damage Control Exercises both in harbor and at sea. The only difference was that while they were simulated, this was the real thing! The negative buoyancy attained due to ingress of FFO had to be neutralized. Seawater pouring into the submarine had to be stopped. The compartments and battery pits had to be sealed and made watertight. Any ingress of seawater into the battery pits would result in Chlorine gas emanating from the batteries and mixing in the air, which would be lethal to inhale. Everyone was busy doing what he was trained to do – except for the 'visitors' onboard. The Education Officer from the Long TAS Course jumped onto the Correspondence Officer's bunk and covering himself with the blanket, prepared to meet his Creator. The Chief Steward, inexplicably, proceeded to force everyone in the Compartment to drink water endlessly while he also drank jarfuls of it. One of the off-duty Watch-keeping officers grabbed his camera and headed towards the Control Room to see what he could get on film for posterity. He bumped into 'Black Sambo' – the TAS Officer who had been on the Periscope and who was now thoroughly drenched with FFO from head to toe. He forgot all about ambling and made it from the Conning Tower into the Second (Battery) Compartment in two giant leaps – a feat unequalled in the annals of Foxtrot Class submarines of the Indian navy ever thereafter. About eight tons of Furnace Fuel Oil from the destroyer's fuel tanks spread along the length of the submarine through the ventilation shafts, the Snort Induction Trunking, and Periscope glands.

A deathly silence pervaded throughout the submarine after it broke clear of the destroyer. Someone had even stopped the motors. Fortunately, the submarine had come to rest with only a slight list to starboard and with a 'forward bubble' (bow tilting upwards, clear of water, and the stern awash). An attempt was made to use the Main Broadcast and order personnel in each compartment to inspect their respective areas thoroughly, and report the extent of damage. This failed, as the Main Broadcast wouldn't work. Orders were then passed on the emergency telephones that existed to meet just such an eventuality. In the Second and Fourth Compartments, battery watch keepers were ordered to unseal the Battery Pits and inspect them for leaks or flooding. The reports that came in from each of the seven compartments were not too bad. The silence was suddenly broken with the sound of five loud explosions from outside the hull – a standard signal (with grenades) from the destroyer to the submarine to state that the latter was free to surface! Quite an unnecessary signal, as Vanshali was already on the surface and visible to all in the vicinity.

Soon 'Their Lordships' ashore came to know that a collision had taken place at sea from the SOS sent by the destroyer. A helicopter, with the senior-most submariner of the navy embarked, flew out to examine the scene. He could not establish communications with the submarine, but flew overhead and returned to inform the authorities that Vanshali would return to harbor under her own steam, but the destroyer would have to be towed back without any further delay as she was fighting to stay afloat.

Onboard Vanshali no one had any idea of the extent of damage outside the pressure hull. All the hatches leading out were shut and nothing could be seen through the periscopes. No communications could be established with anyone outside to even get an idea. The communication mast had apparently gone. It was up just before the collision. The Captain decided to conserve his precious High Pressure reserve of Air and not use it to blow the stern Ballast Tanks, to get the stern up. He decided to start the Diesel engines and use the exhaust gases of the engines, instead. The exhaust gases of the diesels could be forced into the ballast tanks in lieu of High Pressure air, to force the water out and surface the submarine. Fortunately, such a provision existed onboard. However, to start the diesels, air would be required and for this the Air Induction system would have to be opened up to get that fresh air. But it was contaminated with FFO! So it was decided that the air for the diesels would be drawn through the Upper Lid in the Conning Tower and sucked into the Engine Room through the Conning Tower, Control Room, and the Fourth Compartment by keeping the hatches between the Control Room, Fourth Compartment, and the Engine Room open.

Despite all efforts, the Upper Lid would not open – not even an inch. It was then decided that an attempt would be made for the air to be drawn through the Torpedo Loading Hatch located in the Fore-Ends, since the bows were above the waterline. That too would not open. If something did not open soon, the crew would have to be brought out after cutting the Hull and writing off the submarine! The alternative was to abandon the submarine by letting the crew swim out of the torpedo tubes. This thought, however, did not occur to anyone. An attempt was made to force open the Torpedo Loading Hatch with the help of adjustable shoring jacks, used for Damage Control. The Sonar Officer took charge of this operation. After many attempts, the hatch opened about two inches, and a rush of fresh air whistled in – a welcome, sweet contrast to the foul FFO-filled air the crew had been breathing since the collision. The Sonar Officer peeped through this gap and saw a horrifying mass of mangled steel that was once the streamlined Forward Casing and the Fin of the submarine. He also saw a round, silvery object lying on the mangled casing that was unrecognizable and reflecting sunlight. For a long while he could not speak and report what he was seeing, as the immensity of the damage hit him. He finally reported what he was seeing, on the emergency telephone.

The Diesels were prepared and started with the propeller shafts disconnected. The diesel exhaust was then blown into the Ballast Tanks. The Trim was regained, the stern rose, and the Aft Casing broke surface and was soon clear of the water. The Diesels were then stopped. Now came the moment of truth. With bated breaths the Aft Escape hatch was checked for the presence of water in the well. It was empty! The hatch could be opened, and personnel could come out of the submarine to inspect the extent of damage.

The Captain went up first with the Engineer Officer and the Second-in-

Command. After evaluating the extent of damage inside and outside the submarine, it was decided that they would return to harbor on their own, without being towed. About two miles away they could see the destroyer drifting with a dangerously heavy list to one side. They were in no position to help her. Anyway, preparations were made for the trip back to harbor, which was not too far away.

The Captain gingerly climbed his way up through mangled steel to the highest point above the Conning Tower and perched himself there. There was one man positioned just abaft the Conning Tower, on the Aft Casing, to relay his orders. Another man was positioned just above the Aft Escape Hatch, to catch the relayed orders of the Captain and pass them down the hatch. Down the hatch and directly under it, was yet another man positioned in the Aft Ends to receive the orders from top and pass them on to the Control Room through the internal communications telephone. The Sonar Officer and the Forward Casing Party made their way to the mangled Forward Casing, maneuvering through jagged pieces of steel, in preparation for passing the ropes to the jetty to secure the boat alongside on getting back. Which ropes? They were all jammed under squashed metal and couldn't be pulled out.

Captain: "Port Fifteen!"
Man just aft of the Fin: "Port Fifteen!"
Man above the Aft Escape Hatch: "Port Fifteen!"
Man in the Aft Ends on the Telephone: "Port Fifteen!"
Control Room in response, on the telephone: "Port fifteen. Fifteen of Port wheel on, Sir!"
Man in the Aft Ends, up the Hatch: " Fifteen of Port wheel on, Sir!"
Man above the Aft Escape Hatch to the man abaft the Fin: "Fifteen of Port Wheel on, Sir! "
Man abaft the Fin to the Captain perched on jagged pieces of metal: "Fifteen of Port wheel on, Sir!"

The reaction time was awfully slow, and anticipating this, the Captain had to give his next order without waiting for acknowledgement of his previous order. A lot of anticipation was required and maneuvering a submarine through restricted port waters under these conditions was something no one was ever taught. Imagine the emotional and mental tension the Captain was under! His boat was damaged, for which he would have to answer to the navy and pay in some form or the other. He was in command of a crew that was probably already looking at him in a different light. To maneuver the submarine into harbor under those conditions required a man of steel. He was just such a man.

It was sunset time when Vanshali entered harbor. Word had got around about the collision, and there were hordes of onlookers on the shoreline, staring at the damaged boat with curiosity written all over their faces.

Finally, the assigned jetty was approached: ropes were passed from the jetty to the submarine and were looped around any piece of broken steel that could hold them. It had been a difficult entry with strong tidal and riverine currents to counter. That night the Naval Base cinema hall was showing "Ice Station Zebra" – a movie about submarines. Vanshali's officers went and saw it.

The destroyer was towed into harbor and secured alongside the first jetty at the entrance of the harbor, which happened to be a commercial jetty. That night the whole naval base was active with personnel working in shifts to form a 'bucket brigade' to bail out water from the ship, while divers underwater with Cox guns were trying to patch up the holes. They continued throughout the next day and the next night ….. and the following day. At long last the flooding was arrested. Much later she was to make her way to her own homeport for major repairs. Vanshali preceded her.

The morning after the night before, the TAS Officer of the destroyer came onboard the submarine. He asked if he could take back his Sonar transducer? Which sonar transducer? The destroyer's sonar transducer was housed inside her sonar dome. The puzzle was solved when he proceeded to the mangled Forward Casing and picked up the 'round, shining and unfamiliar object' that the submarine's Sonar Officer had spotted through the Torpedo Loading Hatch when it was cracked open to blow ballast.

The usual Board of Inquiry and Courts Martial followed. Neither of them could exactly establish who hit whom. In a close quarter situation, the Captain with his swollen, red, bleary, eyes was expected to be on the Periscope. Blame was attributed to the submarine and the Captain's head rolled. He was relieved of Command. The second-in-command was exonerated. The Captain took the entire blame. Was the Periscope off-centered from the Fore-and-Aft line of the submarine during that fateful Snorting run? Had the submarine steered off course? Was it an error of judgment? Was 'Turn Main Engines as Required' the culprit? Did the destroyer creep forward unnoticeably till it was too late? Was it a combination of all these? Or was it just a strong current and drift responsible for the collision? Even after decades of the incident having taken place, there are still unanswered questions in the minds of some of those who lived through that experience.

Not so many months after the incident, both the destroyer and the submarine were repaired and returned to their respective squadrons. One bright and sunny day, the same destroyer, tied up alongside the Destroyer Wharf, was doing her Basin Trials. She was tied up Port-side-to and had her Starboard anchor out. The Maneuvering Valve was cracked open. The valve spindle burst out from its seating suddenly, causing uncontrolled steam to flow onto the turbine blades. The ship began to move forwards and strain on her ropes, which eventually parted. She took with her all the other ships that were berthed on her and rammed a tanker berthed ahead – a second disaster for the ship.

"Turn Main Engines as required?"

The old destroyer was repaired without any difficulty, as relevant drawings were available with the dockyard to copy and restore her to her original shape. Detailed drawings for Vanshali's hull were not, however, available. It was a tremendous challenge for the dockyard to get her back into shape. Without drawings, templates were made from a sister submarine that was brought and tied next to her. These were used to rebuild the outer casing. After the job was done, no one could discern that the new casing was any different to the old one. Such was the skill of the dockyard mateys and the shipwrights who worked on that submarine's hull.

A word about the submarine Captain taking the entire blame and exonerating his Second-in-Command: in an emotional moment after the incident and after entering harbor, in the Ward Room he remarked:

"Everyone looks forward to a Command at sea and doing a good job of it. I am sorry, but I just f----d mine up."

Even so, by taking the entire blame, he showed a quality that is extremely rare to find in today's world where ambition eggs one to lay the blame on others. It comes out of the traditions on which a navy is built, just like the tradition of the Captain going down with his ship when it is sinking, after trying his level best to ensure that all the men have abandoned it. This was another incident that happened on another occasion, on another ship. History is replete with accounts of such actions in the days gone by. Such actions are rare in today's world. The submarine Captain went on to do some fine work during wartime that earned him a Mahavir Chakra for exceptionable bravery, and the admiration of an entire nation.

Vanshali had gone through a very painful and trying experience. At that time, it was said that only four submarines in the world had come out 'alive' after collisions with ships while snorting. She was the fourth!

WAR PATROL !

When looked at in a lighter vein, till the acquisition of weapons of mass destruction by the two sides, wars and threatening postures between two neighboring countries of South Asia had similar patterns to the wars of yore. In the days of yore troops in armor or on horseback woke up at sunrise, had a good meal, polished their armor, swords and shields, and then engaged the enemy in battle till dusk. At sunset, the 'retreat' was sounded when both sides would withdraw, carry their wounded back, and tend to them. They would eat, medicate, and rest for the night, and repeat the process the following morning ... and the day after ... and for many days to follow - until a truce was declared, or one became the victor and the other the vanquished, or one was brought down to his knees!

Economically, the two nations had limitations and were therefore not capable of carrying on a sustained conventional war for any length of time. Both needed their crops desperately to feed their millions, and till the harvest was reaped, neither side even thought of carrying out an assault which entailed battle-tanks, tracked and conventional vehicles, and troops moving across cultivatable lands. Similarly, both sides had to stop running over these lands before the next sowing time came up, or fell due. Saber rattling and wars had therefore to take place between harvest time and sowing time, i.e. between November and February. This was euphemistically termed as 'campaign season', and threatening postures were taken up each year from November onwards, on either side of the border.

One particular year was different. The neighboring state itself was going through a very turbulent period. The oppressive actions by the Western part on their own people in the Eastern part carried on throughout the year resulting in thousands of refugees from there crossing the Indian border, seeking shelter. India fed them and gave them shelter in refugee camps close to the border, in anticipation of their going back. They didn't. In fact, the number of refugees only increased steadily. Eventually it became an economical strain for India to sustain them any longer. In the International forum, diplomacy was attempted to stop the neighbor from oppressing his eastern brethren, with little success. During the better part of that year, the Indian Armed Forces were in a semi alert stage – known in military parlance as the Precautionary Stage.

November was almost coming to an end. The 'campaign season' had arrived. Crops were harvested and fields were bare and motor-able by wheeled and tracked vehicles on either side of the borders. The situation across the eastern borders was only going from bad to worse. Refugees continued to pour daily into India in hordes and in unmanageable surges. Indian appeals in the International arena were not getting the required attention from the right quarters. The Armed Forces had been in a Precautionary Stage for an unusually long period and were feeling the strain. A military build-up was noticeable across the borders on the Western front. War was imminent.

In the Arabian Sea, an Indian submarine was patrolling in her Waiting Station - Waiting for the Precautionary Stage to transform into hostilities, and for a signal to 'go in'. She was well worked up and brand new – one of the latest in the inventory. She had been there for quite sometime and would have to return for replenishment and 'turn around' if the Precautionary Stage continued any longer. To maintain a constant presence in the Waiting Station, another submarine would have to set out and relieve her there. At that very moment, Vanshali was in harbor, preparing for this very same task. In the other part of the North Indian Ocean, in the Bay of Bengal, a lone submarine was patrolling and carrying out her assigned duties off the eastern seaboard of the Indian sub-continent.

The last week of November saw some hectic activity onboard Vanshali, in harbor. Dockyard workers worked over-time to attend to every minor defect on the boat. She had only recently come out of the terrible collision, and been repaired. That was followed by a full work up to restore confidence all round. She had gone through a rigorous fleet work up too. She now embarked her full outfit of torpedoes, embarked huge quantities of rations, and tack-welded her 'Rescue Indicator Buoys' to the deck. All submarines have Rescue Indicator Buoys that are released to float up to the surface of the sea when the submarine is in distress and cannot come up on her own. The buoy and the submarine are connected by an umbilical cord through which it is possible for a rescue vessel to communicate and feed minimal air and power supply for lighting, among other things. Tack-welding it meant that the submarine would not be in a position to release it - either in distress, or accidentally.

On the last day of November, at 1000 hrs, Vanshali set sail from her Base port, and after leaving harbor, headed in a southerly direction along the coast. The sea was calm and the sky blue – ideal for surface craft but not ideal conditions for submarines, particularly when they need to operate at shallow depths in the continental shelf. A clear blue sky spelt clear, transparent waters below, and in clear waters the dark outline of a submarine at shallow depths is easily visible to aircraft flying overhead. En route, there was a 'Shop Window' organized for the Illustrated Weekly of India for their 12th December issue. Photographers and correspondents had embarked fleet ships to take photographs and to gather material for their articles. The weather was conducive to good photography. As the submarine had sailed out well in advance of the Fleet, she had to lie in wait in a pre-assigned position for the ships to arrive. She was duly photographed on surface, at Periscope Depth, and in the act of surfacing, which was her contribution from the third dimension of the Navy to the periodical. That task over, she dived and slipped away quietly from the rest of the ships in formation, without giving even a hint of where she was bound for.

In navigation terms, no one onboard knew where they were bound for - not even the Navigating Officer! Only the Commanding Officer was aware of the boat's destination. He had his instructions in sealed envelopes locked in his safe. From time to time he would walk into the Navigator's Cabin and point out a position to the Navigating Officer on the Chart, and order him to set sail for that point. On reaching that point, he would indicate the next point to head for. And so it went on right through the patrol. This mystery was enough to sustain an air of excitement onboard, and keep the crew on their toes.

At midnight on the night of Tuesday 30 November / Wednesday 01 December, while the submarine was patrolling deep, Sound Room reported a sonar contact and Vanshali came up to Periscope Depth to have a look. It was a merchantman in Position 040° from position 'AA' at a distance of 15 nautical miles. These doubled lettered positions were marked on the Chart and used as reference positions from which ranges and bearings of contacts were calculated. It is a standard practice followed by many navies. The submarine quietly evaded the ship and continued on her course. Unknown to the crew, but known to the Captain, was that they were to get to a certain point by a certain time to meet a certain someone. Concealment, a trait that submarines possess, was to be exercised en route to the utmost.

Early morning on 2nd December, in position 'QQ', Vanshali affected rendezvous with that 'someone' - the submarine she was to relieve in her 'Waiting Station'. It was an amazing 'R / V' the likes of which the crew of Vanshali was to talk about for many years to come. Neither of the two had any accurate means of navigation which are now available onboard later-day submarines. Underwater, they navigated on 'Dead Reckoning' and nothing else. For those not familiar with this terminology, it means navigating with only speed and time being taken into consideration. Other factors like currents and drift were ignored. Quite obviously 'Dead Reckoning' had its inherent errors. But, at the appointed time and in the appointed position, the two submarines surfaced within minutes of each other, and only a mile apart! The two then maneuvered to touch each other's bows, and very generously, the returning submarine gave Vanshali all the unconsumed fruit juice, chocolates, and other attractive tinned items that were left over after so many days at sea, as they were on their way back to harbor and would replenish before sailing out again. A sheaf of hand-written manuscripts was also transferred to Vanshali - advice based on experience in the deployment area, from one Captain to another. The two then smartly dived and sped their ways – the other submarine back to her Base, and Vanshali to replace her where she had come from.

The crew settled down to a proper regimen demanded of them during a war patrol. They were to lie down in their bunks when off duty so as to minimize exertion and, consequently, consume minimum oxygen. Noise levels were to be at the lowest and extra precautions were to be taken by individuals to see that they did not drop any metallic objects like hammers, spanners, wrenches, tools, cutlery, etc on the steel deck that would make a resounding noise that could travel great distances underwater. Those on Watch were required to concentrate on doing their duty and not indulge in idle talk or distracting activities. The Chart House was strictly out of bounds for those who had no business to be there. Battery discharge rate was properly monitored and minimized to prolong the gaps between successive battery charges. Minimum consumption of electricity was resorted to. This also involved regulating the use of air-conditioning to an inescapable, minimum, as-required routine. For charging batteries later, the submarine would have to come up to Periscope Depth. In any case, charging of batteries was only going to be attempted under cover of darkness, at night. Only 'operational charges' were executed, and not the normal, prolonged, peacetime, charging procedures. 'Operational Charges' topped up batteries quickly and could be interrupted at any time to carry out an Urgent Dive, without detrimental effects on the battery cells. In the North Arabian Sea there is the presence of marine living organisms in the water that give off fluorescent light at night, when disturbed. This fluorescence marks the outline of ships in the area very distinctly, as also their wake, particularly on a pitch-dark night. It is visible from the air. It also marks the wake of a periscope moving in the water. A judicious decision had to be made as to when to charge batteries after considering factors like moonrise, moonset, periods of uninterrupted darkness available, fluorescence effects, time required to top up batteries etc, etc.

At mid-day a Sonar interception was obtained, and on classification found to be a bulk freighter. A brief maneuver up to Periscope Depth for a visual look confirmed this. The submarine carefully sidestepped and evaded the ship. Later that evening, at 1600hrs, the submarine picked up an oil tanker in Position 355° from 'BB' at a distance of 14 nautical miles, while deep. The Captain decided to work up his Attack Team and hone their skills. The Attack Team was closed up at their Stations and Vanshali carried out her deep attack maneuvers on the unsuspecting tanker without being detected. No water shots were fired. In any case, she had torpedoes in all but one tube. That lone tube was kept standby for ditching 'gash'. The submarine had a gash ejector next to the galley, but it was insufficient to meet her normal requirements. So it was decided that all waste would be disposed of through one torpedo tube. Waste food was first put into a sack that was weighed down with stones. The sack was then put into the

Torpedo Tube and fired out with a water shot. Because of the weight, the sack would sink to the bottom of the sea instead of floating up and risking a possible compromise of the submarine's position.

Again that same evening, at 2337 hrs, another tanker was detected but this time the submarine quietly evaded her. To some, the frequent number of ships encountered would appear to be abnormal, but to those used to operating in the North Arabian Sea, this would not even raise an eyebrow.

The 3rd of December proved to be an interesting day. It started early with two detections. First at 0315 hrs, and then later at 0840 hrs, Vanshali came across a freighter and an oil tanker in succession. The former was evaded but the latter was selected for another dummy attack. Once again, the Attack Team was closed up and a good, clean attack executed without firing, and without being detected. The tanker would have been a 'gonner' and sped her way down to 'Davy Jone's Locker' had it been wartime, and she, one of the enemy's merchant ships. Vanshali also tried to convert day into night and night into day on the advice of the other submarine commander in his sheaf of manuscripts which he had handed over during the R/V. This meant eating meals at night and sleeping by day. Breakfast at 2000 hrs (8PM) - Hmph ! It made sense and had its merits as conventional submarines normally stay deep by day and come shallow to charge batteries and refresh the air inboard at night. The crew also needed to be particularly alert at night, and it helped if everyone onboard was awake.

Full-fledged hostilities also broke out on 3rd December. The enemy had launched a pre-emptive air strike across the border on Indian military installations. Onboard Vanshali, this bit of news was received with some excitement and trepidation. Most of the young crew had not been to war before. A Higher Directive to all our submarines at sea followed later which said - "all suspicious merchantmen are to be positively identified as belonging to the enemy before they are attacked". Positively identified how? By closing up and reading their names and place of registration, and by comparing their silhouette with what was available in Lloyd's Register or other equivalent publications? Another signal followed a little later that stated, "All enemy Merchantmen have been disguised and are plying under neutral flags". By now, in view of the situation between the two warring countries, all merchantmen operating in the Arabian Sea, and particularly those plying between their country and the Persian Gulf with oil, had painted their national flags prominently in the mid-section of their shipside and in a prominent portion of their deck or on top of the Bridge so that they could be spotted and identified from afar by submarines, ships, and aircraft, as those who had no business in this war, and best left alone. So the only way of identifying disguised enemy merchantmen would be by going extremely close to suspicious vessels at Periscope Depth at the risk of being discovered, or by surfacing and sending a Boarding Party to physically board them and examine their papers. Submarines are not meant for such tasks during war. With the directives received in the two signals, Vanshali's and the other submarines' hands were tied in so far as attacking merchant ships was concerned! In later years, long after the conflict had ended the correctness or otherwise of issuing those two directives was long debated within the Indian Navy, and by other defense related institutions in many parts of the country, and the world.

India was at war for the third time with this country since being declared an Independent State. Vanshali started making her way north, moving out of her Waiting Station to her Patrol Area. On the 4th, Vanshali carried out a Deep Dive to her maximum operating depth to check her watertight integrity, all systems, and the soundness of the entire boat. It went off well and all systems were 'Go'. She headed for a spot in her pre-assigned Patrol Area that was known only to the Captain, but who had now divulged it to the Navigating Officer. That evening, on special requests from members of the crew, the Captain abandoned the idea of converting day into night and night into day! There were 80 of members of the crew onboard with only two 'Heads' (toilets). Strained faces and uncomfortable stomachs suggested that this was not working out, and was a bad idea. Later, much after cease fire, when the two crews were together, one of the officers from Vanshali asked the Commanding Officer of the other submarine whether he was successful in converting day into night and night into day? His reply:

"There was no problem whatsoever. My crew sleeps when I tell them to sleep, eats when I tell them to eat, and sh**s when I tell them to sh*t !".

The following morning (on the 5th), at 0440 hrs, the lights of a merchant ship were sighted through the periscope and Vanshali gave it a wide berth in pursuance of the directives she had received. She was close to the enemy coast now. Continuous transmissions were picked up at Periscope Depth by the passive SHF/DF (Direction Finder) in position 'DD', but no contacts on sonar or periscope were discerned. Nevertheless, she was forced to go deep off and on as a precautionary measure. The previous evening, the Indian Navy launched missile attacks on the enemy's main port on the west coast, and air attacks on ports on the eastern seaboard. Onboard Vanshali, the crew got the awesome news that an enemy destroyer was sunk with 222 personnel onboard, a minesweeper also sank killing 33 personnel onboard, and a frigate was hit and damaged. Off Visakhapatnam, one enemy submarine with 93 personnel onboard was sunk. This news was received in silence as the full impact of what was heard struck the crew. The Indian Navy had never sunk any ship before. Even during the liberation of Goa in 1960, the Portuguese warship - the 'Albuquerque' - had only been damaged and taken over as the crew had surrendered. Of course, more details of the attacks followed subsequently, but on the 5th of December, that was all the news that was received onboard. Submarines receive their signals at prearranged timings when they come up shallow, as radio waves do not penetrate very deep into the water. Only essential pieces of information are therefore fed to submarines by the authorities ashore so that they remain shallow for minimum, inescapable, periods to receive them.

On the 6th, Vanshali picked up transmissions on the Direction Finder in the Super High Frequency Band again, while in position "EE" but got no further with them as they got fainter and disappeared. "EE" was a classified designation given on the Chart to represent a certain Latitude and Longitude. Super High Frequencies are generally used by aircraft. Obviously, this aircraft had not detected the submarine and had move away, searching in another direction. Vanshali was safe for the moment but had to be very alert as an aircraft was in the vicinity. Later in the day she went through an exciting encounter that those onboard swear was genuine. Those ashore received this with skepticism when the incident was narrated to them after the submarine's return, much after the hostilities had ended. At a distance of 18 nautical miles, Vanshali picked up a firm sonar contact. It was classified as a platform being driven by steam turbines. All propulsion systems have their own signatures that they can be differentiated by. Steam turbines are distinctive by their characteristics. The Sonar Officer reported details to the Captain. The Captain took Vanshali up to periscope depth but he found no ship through the periscope. The periscope to horizon range was much less than 18 nautical miles. She resumed her patrol, deep, and the Captain came to the Sonar Compartment to have a look. There it was again! – The unmistakable sounds of turbines clearly audible on sonar. It was closing Vanshali. The Captain took Vanshali up to periscope depth again, for the second time, after the contact had closed to within periscope detection range. This was to identify the target in accordance with Higher Directives. Nothing was visible! The Attack Team was closed up and the attack computer switched on, as she went deep once more. Data of the 'contact' was now being fed into the Attack Computer. Two bow tubes housing anti-submarine torpedoes, and two housing anti shipping torpedoes were made ready to fire at short notice. Since the contact was not identified, and since Vanshali was in hostile territory, any firing on her part could only be reactive, and in self-defense. The 'contact' closed to as much as 2.3 nautical miles, and then her propellers suddenly stopped. This was odd. Ships do not stop suddenly in mid-ocean. A submarine holding a 'contact' would. A ship holding a submarine contact definitely would not. Vanshali also stopped her props. She had assumed Ultra Quiet State earlier. The Captain had pointed the submarine at the 'contact' so that he could fire his torpedoes at short notice if required. This was too close a range to venture up to Periscope Depth for another look. Silence! At one stage she seemed to momentarily give a kick on her props and stop. Vanshali's bow also slowly drifted away by about 30° or so, and the Captain was constrained to give a kick on the props and order full rudder to point her back at the 'contact'. Silence from both sides once again! By now the Sonar Officer and all personnel in the Sound Room were getting butterflies in their stomachs. The 'contact' was definitely another submarine. Worse! – Submarines with steam turbines meant nuclear propulsion submarines. Neither of the two platforms was moving under propulsion, and both were drifting. There was pin-drop silence in the boat. Then the 'contact' decided to go away. Her powerful props started churning water, and she could be distinctly heard revving up as she altered course, increased speed, and sped away - southwards - at an estimated speed of 23 Knots! Vanshali popped up to Periscope depth for the third time and scanned the horizon. There was nothing in sight. Turbine propulsion underwater, and at 23 knots with nothing visible on the surface of the sea! - It could have only been a nuclear submarine. Both the Captain and the Sonar Officer agreed on this.

Was it an American, British, French, or a Soviet boat? There were navies of other nations also mucking around in these waters, with their submarines in company. This was confirmed after the war when the Soviet reaction to the American aircraft carrier entering the Bay of Bengal came to light. The USS Enterprise had steamed into the Bay of Bengal and threatened to flex her muscles as a warning to the Indian government to stop the war. Apparently, at an appointed time that was intimated to the US, the Soviets had 'popped up' their submarines in the area, to disclose them to the Americans and thereby show solidarity with the Indians. There was an aside to this: when the USS Enterprise entered the Bay of Bengal, the lone Indian Foxtrot submarine operating in the Bay received a signal from the Submarine Operating Authority which read "Attack! Attack! Attack!" The submarine Captain well knew that the kind of weapons he had onboard was totally inadequate to even hurt the massive carrier or to send her back. So he broke radio silence and signaled back to his Submarine Operating Authority "Your signal ……. With what?! With what?! With what?!"

That same night, on the 6th of December, at about 2240 hrs, Vanshali came upon a merchantman that had switched off her lights and was weaving and maneuvering violently along her base course. The submarine outmaneuvered her and got into a firing position, but had to let her go, as it was dark and she couldn't be identified!

Vanshali had settled down to freely patrolling along the enemy coast. It was a large area to patrol, and enough leeway was given to go away from the coast for short spells for battery charging, and return to patrol again. What the crew didn't know at that time, but was informed later by way of an Intelligence Summary signal was that after the attack on the enemy ports and the sinking of the Destroyer and Minesweeper, the enemy warships had come out of their main port on the western seaboard, rounded the Cape near the harbor, and anchored in very shallow waters in the adjoining Bay. They even towed a floating dock out and anchored it next to them. The waters were too shallow for a submarine to venture into. They were also anchored too far away for a submarine to fire a torpedo from seaward and get them. Vanshali was now in an unenviable position few would like to be in - No merchantmen to sink, and no warships to attack. She was, however, a part of the Indian Navy's plan of exercising Sea Denial off the enemy coast. The plan was executed and achieved successfully.

On Tuesday the 7th, the Captain decided to close land, and Vanshali 'snorted' in, took photographs, hung around for a while, and 'snorted' out and away from one of their minor ports, in broad daylight. Through the periscope, the Officer of the Watch sighted a lone trawler entering the port with a long trail of seagulls in its wake, stealing whatever fish they could get. The jetty was also clearly visible through the periscope. Photographs of the jetty were taken through the periscope. This was made possible by the fact that 'Sea Denial' was total and effective.

Later that day, the submarine encountered yet another peculiar phenomenon that is written about in the 'Pilot' for that region. Underwater 'up-welling' off a portion of the enemy coast was, and is, a frequently occurring phenomenon, resulting in changing and unpredictable depths of water in the region. A very thick layer of water, with density different to that of waters around it suddenly appeared at a certain depth, making it very difficult for the submarine to penetrate and dive deeper through it. At Periscope depth, when transmissions on Super high Frequency Direction Finder (SHF/DF) indicated that an airborne platform was closing her, it was time for the submarine to go deep. This was a safety precaution taken to avoid detection and attack. Here, with the 'layer' in the way, she could not penetrate and go deep past it. Tons of water had to be taken into the Compensating Tanks to make the submarine heavier. Ultimately, with all that extra weight onboard, she pierced the layer and began to go down. Once past the layer, she began to gather momentum and go down like a stone despite all efforts to pump out that extra water taken in the Compensating Tanks earlier. Other emergency measures had to be resorted to, to get her under control and to bring her back to the ordered depth. The reverse had to be done to come shallow - past the layer - again. The crew eventually got to anticipating and handling the problem effectively as and when they passed such regions.

The night of Wednesday the 8th was a very busy one. The submarine had come up to Periscope depth to charge her batteries. There was a haze on the sea surface, and visibility was poor. At 0001 hrs, while at Periscope depth and charging batteries, the Officer of the Watch reported sighting a merchant ship through the Periscope. As it was at quite some distance and unaware of Vanshali's presence, the submarine altered Course away from her and continued with her battery charging. She picked up and lost quite a few sonar 'contacts' far away from her, as sonar conditions were not too conducive to getting good ranges that day either. Onboard, the crew picked up enemy radio programs on the Communications antenna, one of which announced that their maritime air forces were looking for an Indian submarine operating off their coast. Two days later, the same radio announced that one Indian submarine had been sunk off their coast! As Vanshali knew where the other submarines were, the crew dismissed this bit of information as a pack of lies and propaganda, probably meant for their countrymen, to raise their low morale.

On the 8th, Vanshali received a signal to intercept and sink a merchant ship by the name of AL MOHAMEDI that was expected to pass through her rather large Patrol Area. This signal was sent out much earlier and some time had lapsed before the submarine received it as she was deep for some hours that day, and received the signal only on coming up to Periscope depth much later. That same evening, at 1605 hrs and in broad daylight, she chanced upon a merchant ship. The ship was tracked, and the submarine maneuvered to get into a firing position before she closed her enough to read the name 'SS Glory' written prominently on her side and stern. The ship may have seen something to arouse her suspicion, for she suddenly increased speed and ran away. She was allowed to go. The Navigating Officer looked up all publications onboard. No ship was registered as "SS Glory". So who was she?

After the incident of "SS Glory", the submarine remained deep on the 9th and the 10th, looking for AL MOHAMADI. According to information received onboard, if she wasn't located by the 11th, she would have gone out of the submarine's area of operations. She wasn't located.

On the 11th Vanshali was back off the same minor port she had 'visited' in broad daylight. This time a positive layer threw her up to the surface!! She had to ship in one hell of a lot of water to go down again, and once past this layer had to pump out the same 'hell of a lot of water' to maintain depth. At midnight that night she picked up the sound of props on the sonar far away, and lost it as it went out of range. She remained deep on the 12th and the 13th without any excitement. Not having intercepted the merchantman – the only merchantman that she was licensed to attack – was a big disappointment. The crew was reminded of tales of 'boredom' described in submarine-related stories of the Second World War - how they sailed for days on end with nothing happening.

On the 14th Vanshali was ordered to return to her Waiting Stations. She headed southwards. On Wednesday the 15th, she surfaced for 'sights' to get an accurate reading of her position, and the crew had their first breath of fresh air in days! She entered her Waiting Stations the following day i.e. on the 16th. The enemy had surrendered to the Indian forces on the eastern seaboard that day. It was a historic surrender that would go down in the annals of military warfare. The war was over. But Vanshali had to cover her tracks and not disclose which route she took to 'go in' and which route she was taking to 'get back'. She therefore made a dived passage all the way back to Bombay, getting back only on the 21st - long after all the others had got back. The Indian Navy was relieved to see her back in one piece. During the course of the war, the enemy radio station - around the 9th or 10th - had announced that they had sunk an Indian submarine off their coast. Since Vanshali had not made a single transmission on her radio from the day she left the Indian coastline, till the day she returned, the navy was not to know of her well-being until well after the war.

The Indian Navy deployed its submarines with their hands tied behind their backs – in a manner of speaking. Why? Why were these potent weapon platforms under-utilized? In retrospect one can only surmise and conjecture that this was, perhaps, because of any or all of three factors. The first could be that the third dimension of the navy was still in its infancy, and these were new toys, and the Submarine Operating Authorities were not adept enough or confident of using them more boldly. The second reason could be that despite a very good work–up in the Soviet Union, which included tactical and weapons work–up, the crews had not succeeded in instilling confidence in their Submarine Operating Authorities about their own abilities. The third could be fear of repercussions on the diplomatic front should, perchance, a genuine neutral ship have gone down as a consequence of a torpedo hit from one of the Indian submarines on deployment. There could have been no other reasons at that stage. Of course, in later years, with familiarity in their usage and of their capabilities and limitations, these Foxtrot class submarines were exploited to their hilt, with all the complexities of submarine warfare and coordinated warfare being practiced regularly.

P.R. Franklin

BOTTOM CLEANING - IN COMPANY

Tropical waters and the warm temperatures prevalent play havoc on steel platforms in the water, necessitating periodic maintenance and annual dry-docking. And so it was that Vanshali found herself entering dry-docks one day to get her bottom cleaned. It was a very large dry-dock, and she found she had two more submarines for company.

These were not Indian submarines. They were of Soviet origin but belonging to another navy. After one of the many Arab-Israeli wars, these submarines were stranded on the wrong side of the Suez Canal and could not get back to their homeport. They were sent to India for repairs and refit. The crew was a lazy and undisciplined lot who landed themselves in all sorts of embarrassing situations, much to the amusement of the Indian Navy. Most of them were big beefy characters as compared to the Indians. Only a few of them spoke some rudimentary English.

In the dry dock, because of the lack of air-conditioning and subsequent discomfort inside the submarine, their Duty Watch took to sleeping at nights on the Casing. This was a very dangerous thing to do and was taboo on Vanshali. From the Casing of the submarine to the bottom of the cemented dry dock was around eight meters. One night, a sudden commotion onboard one of these foreign submarines resulted in the sentry on Vanshali's gangway waking up the Officer of the Day sleeping inside in the Wardroom. He came up to find that three sailors from one of the two foreign submarines had fallen off the Casing and had landed on the dock floor below! He quickly mustered help and transported them to the naval hospital, not too far away. They were groaning and moaning, and looked to be in very bad shape. The matron on duty received them. A cursory look showed that none of them had any superficial wounds or were bleeding. She was quite familiar with them as they had been reporting 'sick' in large numbers ever so often on silly and insignificant matters – ostensibly to get away from work! She felt the three of them one by one for broken bones. Then she asked them in turn as to what was wrong. She got only moans and groans in response. Enough was enough she decided. She slapped the first one hard on both cheeks. He forgot anything was wrong with him and sprang to attention. The same reaction was observed from the third sailor. The second one seemed to have had some problems and he was taken to the doctor for further attention. The other two were sent back onboard! It was subsequently discovered that there was nothing seriously wrong with the second sailor either. This was not how she normally dealt with persons reporting sick. This was her method of dealing with these foreign sailors. The Indians could not get over the events as they unfolded. The next day, these three sailors were observed working onboard their submarines in a normal manner as if the incidents of the previous night had not taken place. No Indian could expect to fall off the Casing of a submarine in dry dock and not come out with broken bones or concussion. Yet these foreigners had emerged unscathed.

Vanshali and her two other companions remained in dry dock for a little over a month. During this period, the barnacles and other underwater growth were scraped off their hulls. The hulls were then scraped to remove old paint and any rust found anywhere, and new paint with additives to prevent or delay formation of underwater growth was applied. This would result in a quieter submarine capable of moving at least two knots faster on surface and underwater. All the Ballast tanks were subjected to similar treatment. The bulbous sonar domes were also cleaned out.

This one-month also gave enough time to carry out other checks and routines on systems inside the submarine's pressure hull. A Satellite Navigation System was installed. All this work was progressed with the help of the naval dockyard. The crew, by themselves, could not have carried out the quantum of work that was required to be done in the dry dock.

The Commander-in-Chief came to visit the dry dock one day, soon after the three foreign sailors had fallen off their submarine. His Staff officers, who were preceded by the Admiral Superintendent Dockyard to the docks, preceded him. These senior 'advance' parties came to update themselves on all the jobs that had been completed, what was left to be done, and whether there were any hold-ups, the solutions to which they could propound when the Commander-in-Chief arrived! A drama of 'one up-man-ship' was in the offing! The Commander-in-Chief arrived. He didn't ask anything about the refits of the submarines. He only wanted to see for himself from what height the three foreign sailors had fallen to the bottom of the dry dock. After taking in the scene, he left, leaving the 'advance' party tongue-tied!

The day for undocking finally arrived. All three boats had clean bottoms, freshly painted. The crews were closed up at Action Stations for the dock to be flooded and the submarines to float up. All the umbilical cords leading from the dock side onto the submarines were removed – power supply from ashore, High Pressure air supply pipes, drinking water pipelines to the boats, and so on. A delay was suddenly announced. Puzzling! Someone from the Dockyard finally came and gave the reason. At the last minute, someone had discovered that one of the two foreign submarines was without an anchor! They could not find it in the dry dock or in its vicinity. The decision to undock that day was cancelled. A fresh date would be promulgated!

An anchor of a ship or submarine is a prominent piece of equipment and very heavy. It cannot get lost. Yet it had! There are enough security arrangements in dockyards to ensure that material does not get taken away without anyone's knowledge. In any case, to take an anchor out of the main gate, a number of sub-organizations have to be involved. There is the casual laborer, the crane operator, the transport pool, the truck driver, the security staff at the main gate, and so on. After hunting high and low all over the dockyard, the search was finally given up. A decision was taken to buy a second-hand anchor of similar specifications from the ship breaker's yard about a hundred miles away on the outskirts of a neighboring town. Anchors being standard items and an essential requirement for all craft moving on the high seas, there would be no problem finding a substitute, or so it was assumed. Two days later, the procurement party returned with an anchor that suited the submarine. When it was being hitched on to the cable, its pattern number was recorded which was required to be entered in the logbook. To everyone's amazement they discovered that it was the very same anchor that had been declared lost! A racket of items being smuggled out and sold as scrap was subsequently unearthed, and many heads rolled. The three submarines finally undocked, and proceeded to berths where the rest of their refits would be carried out while they were afloat.

It was a tragedy of fate that overtook one of the two foreign submarines a few months later. She was sunk in the Gulf of Aqaba during a subsequent Arab-Israel war. The Israeli Consul General in Mumbai remarked to one of the Indian admirals during a formal reception one day:

"Admiral, our two countries really work together as a team". Referring to the loss of the submarine, he went on,

"You repair them. We sink them! What better teamwork can there be?"!

SUPPORT ORGANISATIONS FOR VANSHALI

It has been found that to have a minimum effective force of two conventional submarines at sea at any given time a squadron must consist of at least six submarines. While two are out at sea, two would be in harbor getting ready to relieve the two out at sea, and the remaining two would be under some form of refit or the other.

To have a required flexibility to operate conventional submarines with a higher percentage presence in an area of interest far removed from their base, a submarine tender ship on forward deployment would provide the optimum solution. It would cut down the transit time for the submarines to and from the patrol area to the replenishment base considerably by being nearer at hand. Such a ship could quickly replenish a submarine or submarines, and turn them around for redeployment without their having to come all the way back to their base port. Initially Vanshali had no such support ship available to extend her operational capability at sea. She was based in Visakhapatnam, and operating in the Bay of Bengal was no problem. The submarine base in harbor met all her requirements. However, whenever she was required to move across and operate in the Arabian Sea, the support she got from the submarine base in Visakhapatnam was too far away, and a similar facility was lacking on the West coast of India. This deficiency was often felt. There was no shore support base for submarines located on the west coast. A quick solution was to acquire a submarine depot ship like the 'PKZ' that had supported her and her crew in Riga. The PKZ would, however, not be able to move about and provide the flexibility of supporting the submarine from any other base, or even in mid-ocean. A submarine support ship or tender that can propel on its own and move about would provide all the required options for submarine support. Apart from its own crew to run the ship, the submarine tender has a submarine support staff, workshops to carry out repairs on components that require attention onboard the submarine, torpedoes for turn around, compressors for providing High Pressure air, diesel generators for charging submarine batteries, and many such requirements to turn a submarine around for re-deployment from an 'advance base' in quick time. It could move down to Cochin to support a submarine operating near the southern shipping lanes, or up north to Bombay or even further up to the Saurashtra coast to support a submarine in the north Arabian Sea. Such a submarine tender was acquired and positioned on the west coast of India, and Vanshali was able to operate off either coasts of India with the required back up support.

Eventually, shore based submarine support organizations in the major naval ports quickly mushroomed to provide assistance to Vanshali and her mates when they were visiting these harbors. They relieved the submarines of much of the mundane but necessary work onboard in harbor so that the crew of the submarines could relax a bit or concentrate on harbor training on simulators on a regular basis.

As the submarine tender arrived well before the shore based submarine support facilities were created, the former took on the latter's role for quite a while on the western seaboard of India. In a lighter vein, as she stayed put in one harbor for months, it was often stated that she could not be moved as she had run aground on the beer cans consumed onboard and tossed overboard! But move she did after the shore facilities were developed adequately, on forward deployment in support of submarines.

Operating underwater has a certain amount of risk attached to it, and every care is taken to ensure that the material state of the boat and the state of training of the crew are maintained at an all-time high. Even so, submarine operations are not without accidents or fatalities. There are fatalities in war that are inevitable when the risks taken are the highest. There are fatalities in peacetime operations too. Should a boat come to grief especially during peacetime, the availability and timely positioning of a Rescue ship could save lives of survivors trapped in the hull. Just knowing that there is a rescue system available does much to the morale of the crew and the cadre of volunteers that the submarine world consists of. For a long time, their Lordships who run the navy could not comprehend the requirement for such a ship. Submariners were trained to wear waterproof rubber suits and breathing apparatus and crawl through the 533 mm torpedo tubes onboard and swim up to the surface where any ship could pick them up. Then why waste money to acquire a specialized vessel? The fact that after an accident, some or all of the personnel onboard may not be in a fit enough state to crawl through a torpedo tube was missed. Such people would have to be lifted out of the submarine in a dry state by other means. A specialized submarine rescue vessel is capable of lowering a 'rescue bell' onto the hatch of the submarine and affects transfer of personnel in a dry state from the submarine to the bell, and from the bell to the rescue vessel after the bell is hoisted back onboard. Untimely help resulted in all personnel onboard the Kursk come to grief in the early part of this century – an incident that caught the attention of the whole world when it happened. Vanshali operated in the initial stages without a rescue back up. The navy eventually purchased a Submarine Rescue Vessel that trained and exercised with the Foxtrot class of submarines, with the hope that it would never have to be really used for what it was designed for.

There was an area off Visakhapatnam that was earmarked for submarines to practice 'bottoming'. Most conventional submarines are designed to sit on the bottom of the sea to minimize discharge of batteries, conserve power, and wait silently for an unsuspecting enemy to pounce on, provided the bottom of the sea was reasonably flat and shallower than the maximum diving depth of the submarine. It was common practice for Vanshali to bottom in that selected area as part of her work up. The Submarine Rescue Vessel would also work up with the submarine by coming to the bottoming area after the submarine had 'sat', and lower her rescue bell in the water and onto the Aft Escape Hatch of the submarine on the Aft Casing. Once mating had taken place, the water from inside the bell would be drained out and the Hatch opened. Members of the submarine crew would enter this bell in batches, shutting the Hatch on each occasion, to be lifted up to the Rescue Vessel in a dry state. This work up was necessary to instill confidence in both those being rescued and those carrying out the operation. There was always a silent prayer sent up that this should never have to be used in a real life situation.

The old adage "All work and no play make Jack a dull boy" applied equally to Vanshali's crew. In her 'home port' in Visakhapatnam, a submarine support base sprung up. It had accommodation for living, galleys for preparation of food, huge dining halls, shore offices, and playing fields aplenty for the crew to play field and team games. Games contributed immensely towards building up a spirit of camaraderie among the submariners that became the envy of the rest of the navy in due course of time.

A shore battery commissioning and maintenance complex was created next to the submarine jetties to look after unloaded batteries and commission new ones for the boats. It also facilitated charging of the batteries onboard without the submarine having to use her onboard machinery for the purpose.

One of Asia's largest naval repair yard was built in Visakhapatnam to cater to the repair and maintenance of all Soviet acquisition ships, including submarines.

Last but not least, a huge submarine training complex was created with all the facilities for providing periodic refresher courses for qualified submariners, and for training new volunteers. It was well equipped with classrooms, simulators and training aids. It also had a hundred feet tall tower filled with water and with torpedo tubes at the bottom, for submariners to practice escaping through tubes.

Thus it can be seen that to put a boat like Vanshali out to sea, a large support organization is necessary, without which top efficiency is difficult to be ensured. The Indian Navy went about setting up these facilities with alacrity.

P.R. Franklin

OFF FOR A MID-LIFE UPDATE!

A warship takes a little less than a decade to build from the time the staff requirements are drawn up, to its commissioning into a navy. It is also expected to have a life of about thirty years or so in tropical environs after commissioning. That would roughly mean that from the concept stage till she is decommissioned, a warship would have spanned about forty years. Even with the best of crystal gazing, it is extremely difficult to predict technological advances over such a long period and ensure that her equipment, especially with respect to her fighting capabilities, is 'state-of-the-art' throughout her life. About half way through her life, she would find herself outdated and outmatched by newer platforms. It is therefore prudent to ensure at the initial design stage, that there is enough scope for giving her a mid-life update so that she is able to get it and remain competitive till the end.

Vanshali was fifteen years old when she was planned to undertake a mid-life update. She had gone through two major refits in her fifth and tenth years without any major changes to her equipment apart from the installation of some minor equipment during local refits. Both were undertaken in India. For her mid-life update, it was arranged that she was to go back to the country where she was built, as she would virtually be ripped apart and many of her equipment rearranged to accommodate new equipment as part of her modernization. She had commissioned in Riga and sailed around the Cape of Good Hope, to India. She had done years of yeoman service around Indian waters. Now she would be going to Vladivostok on the Pacific coast of the Soviet Union for a mid-life update that would take her away from India for about two years.

This was not the same young Vanshali that set out from Riga on a cold blistering day a decade and a half ago. This was a submarine needing a refit, and an upgrade along with it. She had served the navy well these past few years and had worn herself down in the process. She was a tired boat, not a hundred percent fit, and ready for a re-vamp. She was fit enough to make the passage to Vladivostok by herself, with a stopover in Manila for four days, and Hong Kong for another four days, en route.

Maritime traditions are built up over an extended period of time, and the newly formed submarine cadre had begun building up its own traditions. Submarines going away for long durations from their base-port were seen off with a bit of fanfare. The naval band would play; the Commander-in-Chief would be requested to say a few words to the crew on the jetty before they embarked the submarine to cast off. A cake would be presented to the crew. All this was gone through as Vanshali cast off one warm summer day from Visakhapatnam, and headed eastwards for the Malacca Straits. She would pass the Nicobar Islands through the Ten Degree Channel between Little Andamans and Car Nicobar, before getting to the Malacca Straits. She was loaded with little- little Indian things, not available in Vladivostok, that would make life a little easier to pass there while the long refit was on, and the corridors and every inch of space was full of these items. There was no worry about weight distribution for Trim. She was not going to dive on passage.

A day and a half out at sea and the ubiquitous Royal Australian Navy's maritime reconnaissance aircraft was over Vanshali, as inquisitive as ever. They seemed to be monitoring the central and south Bay of Bengal and the shipping through the Malacca Straits carefully. Only they could explain what their interests in this region were. As a country, they seemed to be going through an identity crisis. Racially, they associated themselves with the 'white' world that was geographically far removed from them. Geographically they were closer to the ASEAN states with which they had nothing in common. It was an officer from the Singapore navy who put it in perspective. He said:

"Everything that happens in the ASEAN states affects Australia. Nothing that happens in Australia, affects the ASEAN states".

Those of the crew onboard Vanshali who were basking in the sun in the Fin, waved out to the aircraft. She circled the submarine for some time and flew away in a southeasterly direction. Perhaps they were watch guards for a 'super power'?

Piracy on the high seas was something one read about in books that covered the period of sail. After the advent of steam and ships built of steel, this was a profession that had died a natural death. All of a sudden, it had picked up once again in the Caribbean Seas, the South China Sea, and the Malacca Straits. In the latter two areas the activities were believed to have originated from Indonesia, with a Hong Kong connection. Vanshali was going to plow her way through these very seas. The chances of her getting hijacked were remote as the pirates were on the look out for attractive cargo and ships that could be reused under a different flag, or sold. A submarine just did not qualify. Even so, some care would have to be taken when traversing these waters.

On the second night, schools of flying fish kept getting drawn to the navigational lights of the submarine and by morning there were hordes of them on the For'd and Aft casings. They were picked up and fried for lunch! By day they seem to fly away from the path of the submarine and by night they behaved in just the opposite manner, drawn like moths to the only light visible on an otherwise dark night. They do not fly too high and only skim a couple of feet above the sea. Vessels with a high freeboard are not so lucky to have them landing on their decks. Low decked vessels like fishing craft and catamarans land them, - and submarines on the surface!

As Vanshali neared the Ten Degree Channel, the radar began to pick up the many islands of the Andaman and Nicobar Islands in gradually increasing density. Ships transiting through the Malacca Straits navigate through the gap between the southernmost tip of the Nicobar island group - earlier known as Pygmalion Point, and now as Indira Point - and the northernmost tip of Sumatra Island. The latitude there is around six degrees North. That area is very busy with traffic. The Ten Degree Channel is relatively quieter, and Vanshali slipped through it into the Andaman Sea and re-shaped her course to a southeasterly one, heading straight for the Malacca Straits, her ever-reliable diesels purring away with a healthy beat. A school of dolphins escorted her for an hour or two as if they knew she was going to be away for a long time. Dolphins normally come looking for food and hang around till they are sure they cannot get any, and then go away.

The Malacca Straits lay ahead. Submarines on the surface are sluggish in the water as compared to ships. Also, being lower in the water they are difficult to spot and classify by night. For these very reasons, it was decided to negotiate the worst part of the Malacca Straits – shipping density-wise – by day. While those on duty on the Bridge were seriously going about the business of safe navigation and staying clear of the big ships navigating through the Straits, there were others off duty, perched in between the many masts in the Fin, taping FM music that was being broadcast from Malaysia. All the latest in music was available for free and would be deeply appreciated in Vladivostok where only Russian songs and music could be heard. The world of music from beyond the Iron Curtain was not available for listening there. Except for Russian broadcasting frequencies, all other frequencies were jammed. There was a surfeit of music over the next few days, as first music from Malaysia, and later music from Singapore was available. Piracy of a different kind was going on in full swing onboard Vanshali!

The sea was cluttered with ships of every imaginable size and shape, carrying every possible type of cargo. Policing these waters as part of anti-piracy measures was shared between warships of Indonesia, Malaysia, and Singapore. Despite their navies being small, they managed an almost constant, round-the-clock presence in the Malacca and Singapore Straits. The Indian naval ensign being flown prominently by Vanshali drew them curiously closer. Courtesies were exchanged in the traditional naval manner by piping. There was a special man detailed off to stand by the naval ensign to dip it in response to merchantmen showing their courtesies. Merchant ships half lower their ensigns and raise them again when passing a warship and this salute is reciprocated in similar fashion by the warship. 'Our' man was going bonkers responding to so many ships in the area, and the ensign seemingly kept sliding up and down endlessly! There was great relief when all this was left behind, and Vanshali entered the South China Sea. Care was taken to steer clear of the Spratly Islands that was the bone of contention between Brunei, China, Malaysia, the Philippines, Taiwan, and Vietnam. Each staked a claim for it. The islands were situated on top of a subterranean oil belt that promised riches, if harnessed.

She was fortunate to have had fair weather till now, but what was worrisome was that Typhoon 'Esmerelda' was building up east of the Philippines. All these typhoons move in a west, northwesterly, direction and hit the eastern seaboard of Asia, to peter out after crossing the coast. Some of them peter out at sea, being weak. Ships plying the South China Sea, the Yellow Sea, and the Sea of Japan have to be wary of these typhoons and steer well clear of the storm and its 'eye'. Anyway, weather reports were frequent and fairly accurate. The forecasts gave enough time to get out of the path of these typhoons – most of the time. 'Esmerelda' needed to be watched.

The submarine was chugging along on the surface, in the middle of the East China Sea one afternoon, when the Officer of the Watch spotted a boat some distance away. It seemed to be a derelict boat with no life onboard. He duly reported it to the Captain who asked him to alter course towards it to have a look. Vanshali swung to starboard and closed the floating object. When it was a few hundred yards away, they saw what appeared to be a lifeless man lying in the boat. Was he dead? No! Wait! His hand moved! It was trailing in the water, but there was definite movement as if he was bringing it up to wave out to the submarine. It was a catamaran, a double-hulled boat of rudimentary design and finish, and he appeared to be a fisherman. Who else would venture so far away from ashore by himself? Fishermen the world over are the true mariners of the sea. They bond with the sea, are not scared of it, and yet respect it and acknowledge it as a superior creation of nature. They know when the sea is generous enough to fill their boats with fish, and when the sea is angry and best avoided. But there was no net in this boat and neither were there any fish.

The crew sprung into action. There was a medical officer onboard. He was alerted as the catamaran was approached and tied up alongside Vanshali. Some members of the Casing Party got onto the Forward Casing with ropes, a lifebuoy, and a stretcher. Two of them had to get into the water and then lift the poor sod onboard. He was just about alive and totally unable to stand or move by himself. It took awhile for the man to be strapped onto the Neil Robinson Stretcher and lowered down the vertical submarine hatch to the Control Room and on to the Wardroom in the Second Compartment, where the doctor got down to work. It was quite obvious that he was dehydrated and parched. It was difficult to tell which country he came from. The two sheets of paper he had in his pocket were soiled by seawater and illegible. No one onboard could differentiate between a Filipino, a Chinaman, and a Vietnamese. It was clear that his identity could be established only after he had regained his strength and was able to speak. Information of the man having been picked up was also signaled to various authorities, some of whom, hopefully, were expected to respond. Indian authorities were also sent a detailed account of the events as they occurred.

The doctor worked on him like a man possessed. The patient was shifted to the Port side officers' cabin and the four officers from there shifted to the Wardroom for their sleeping arrangements. By the following morning the fisherman showed signs of improvement. He was conscious and seemed to be aware that he was being looked after. He cooperated with the doctor, and wolfed the food offered to him in small quantities after the intravenous tubes had been removed. He, however, would not speak and didn't seem to understand what was spoken to him.

The Captain was now in a dilemma. Vanshali was steadily moving towards Manila. "Esmeralda' was on the Starboard bow, slowly but surely building up but likely to cross Vanshali's path behind her as per the latest forecast. What was he to do with this man? Suppose he was ordered to turn back and offload him in one of the neighboring countries just left behind? He would be late in reaching his next destination. He could get caught up with 'Esmeralda'. Or, a diversion to avoid it could also result in his reaching Manila late. There was no news from Naval Headquarters as yet. It was still too early for the bureaucracy to find a solution or for Naval Headquarters to suggest a course of action. Picking up the man and saving his life was the right thing to do. There is a bond between mariners that make them stretch out beyond geo-politics to help a fellow mariner, whichever nation – friendly or not friendly - that he belongs to. To make matters worse, a slow swell was building up that had Vanshali rolling and pitching agitatedly. She doggedly stuck to her course and speed that she was required to stay on. After what seemed like an eternity, a message came in over the wireless from Delhi to say that the rescued man was to be landed in Manila! The Indian Embassy there had already been informed. What a relief! The patient was also improving. He was now talking and smiling. It didn't matter what he was saying. Nobody understood a word.

The Philippine Archipelago consisted of some 7100 islands of which Luzon, Mindanao, and Pal wan were the largest – all familiar to those who studied the war in the Pacific during WW II. Manila Bay was on the western seaboard of Luzon. Prone to earthquakes, these islands were largely mountainous in nature with narrow, flat, coastal strips. A strong Spanish influence remained even after the country was rid of colonial rule by the end of the nineteenth century. It was more predominant than the after-effects of Japanese occupation during WW II. Over ninety percent of them were Christian Malays, with Muslim Malays forming another five percent and the Chinese forming only one percent. Fortunately for the crew of

Vanshali, practically all of them spoke English that was the official language along with Filipino. As Vanshali entered Manila Bay, the sight ahead of her was truly breathtaking with the sky and the sea grey and the low hills dotted with houses providing a green backdrop. She was escorted in by waiting small units of the Philippine Navy to her appointed berth. Typhoon 'Esmeralda' hit the southern islands and moved into the South China Sea without affecting Vanshali in her protected berth in the sheltered Bay.

The crew quickly moved into their hotel and went through the exhilarating ritual of a warm, good, clean bath! Words cannot describe that feeling after days at sea without water. Oriental cuisines were available aplenty at very affordable rates in nearby cafeterias, and the crew tucked into some exotic seafood that involved selecting the crustacean while it was still alive and waiting for it to be cooked before your eyes. Alcoholic beverages were also available in restaurants accompanied by exciting floorshows. The crew had a wonderful four days in Manila and left with positive memories of that country. The effects of American Naval presence in Subic Bay and Manila were clearly obvious by the way the Philippines navy offered facilities for 'R & R'. It was a very small navy and an aging one that depended on the US Navy for help in any which way it was required.

The transit from Manila to the next port of call was peaceful, and soon Vanshali entered the port of Hong Kong, still under British governance, but with a distinct oriental atmosphere about it. There were myriads of vessels of all shapes and sizes crisscrossing the harbor waters. The slow sampans seemed to portray an air of oriental peace while the hydrofoil craft broke the serene waters with their churning wakes as they ferried passengers across the harbor, and some of them even on to Macao.

Just before entering harbor, one of the hull valves below the waterline had begun to leak, causing flooding in the Engine Room. The flooding took on alarming proportions when all efforts to stop the leak were coming to naught. It was barely stopped by the time Vanshali tied up alongside, but there was a lot of work to be done alongside to bring the water level in the Engine Room down to normal level. The crew stayed onboard while this was being done, and left for the hotel where they were to be accommodated, only when things were under control. The Assistant Engineer Officer was left behind, in addition to the Officer of the Day, and told to come to the hotel later after ensuring that the leak had truly stopped.

Vanshali sailed out of Hong Kong on surface in broad daylight, in full sight of all those who had a good view of the harbor, and were looking out of their homes or offices across the water, her next and final port of call – Vladivostok.

A tired and weary Vanshali entered harbor after getting all the approvals at various check-points on her way into harbor that the cautious and careful Soviets had procedurally instituted as part of the Cold War precautions. The reception was no way near the farewell she had got in Riga after commissioning. Just a handful of Soviet naval personnel and one representative from the Indian Embassy in Moscow were there to greet her. She tied up on the jetty and the crew disembarked along with their luggage, leaving only the 'duty watch' onboard. Most of the crew would now be flown back to India. They would come to take her back after the refit. Only a skeleton crew, sufficient to look after her safety requirements, the technical personnel from the crew required for overseeing the refit, and the Base Support Team from the submarine base in Visakhapatnam, would remain. She was technically an Indian naval submarine, but it would be the Russians who would be refitting her, and who would have a free run onboard to do whatever was required to do as per the Contract and agreement signed between the two nations.

Apart from renewing all her worn out equipment, replacing corroded parts, and re-strengthening her pressure hull, she was to be fitted with additional 'state-of-the-art' equipment for which a certain amount of re-siting of existing equipment would have to be done.

VLADIVOSTOK

Vladivostok was the largest Soviet port on the eastern seaboard of that vast nation. In the Russian language, the name when translated into the English language read "Lord of the East". As a city it was not very large (about six hundred square kilometers with a population of around 600,000) when Vanshali entered harbor for her mid-life update. From the center of the city, if one were to draw a circle of nineteen kilometers radius, one could envelope the whole city. It is located in the southern extremity of the very hilly Muravyov – Amursky Peninsula that is about 30 kilometers long and about twelve kilometers wide. Residential houses spread along the hill slopes down to the harbor, and so there was 'an uptown' and 'a downtown' part to the city. The flat areas along the coast were peppered with prefabricated multi-storied apartments and other high-rise buildings. The main street in the center of the city was named Leninskaya Ulitsa ('Ulitsa' means 'street'). The other main roads were Lugovaya Ulitsa (connected to the city railway station), Ulitsa Minnovo Gorodok, and Sakhalinskaya Ulitsa, to name a few. Then there were areas referred to as Akeanski Prospect that had a beach and a prominent Cinema Theatre, Pervaya Reichka and Ftaraya Reichka that translated to read the 'first and second rivulets' respectively because two streams separately wended their way from these residential areas down to the sea. Privately owned vehicles were scarce, but there were buses, trams and trolleybuses that ran along the main streets. Moving about was very convenient with these frequent and affordable forms of public transport available. Vladivostok railway station was the starting point for the famed Trans-Siberian Railway that extended all the way to Moscow, and on to Leningrad. There was a funicular from the higher reaches of the city down to the harbor area - a mountain railway on which counterbalanced cars on parallel sets of rails were pulled up and lowered by cables. Ferryboats plied across the harbor to get one across from one side to another. The city had a wide variety of institutions of learning, and therefore a considerable number of students.

The harbor was huge. It was a closed port for most Soviet personnel, and totally taboo for foreigners to visit. No one who had no business there was allowed to enter the city without specific approval, as it housed the Headquarters of the mighty Soviet Pacific Fleet that challenged the American Naval might across the Pacific Ocean. It was also the base port of the Pacific fishing fleet that came into harbor for three months in the year to offload their wares. The harbor had a deep natural Bay named 'Zolotoi Rog' that translates to read 'Golden Horn'. At one end of Leninskaya Ulitsa, not far from 'Gostineetsa Primoria' (hotel) and the railway station, a very popular restaurant existed with the same name. The

Indian crew frequented it during their sojourn in this city. Vladivostok is located seventy-five miles from the Chinese border, a hundred miles from North Korea, and six thousand two hundred miles from Moscow! This proximity had its own effect. Way back in history, at various stages, the Chinese and the Koreans had inhabited it before it fell to the Russians. It was the largest port on the western side of the Sea of Japan.

The weather in this far eastern part of the Soviet Union could be kind during certain parts of the year and extremely hostile during winter months when the cold Siberian winds blew across the peninsula. In December and January, the temperatures could go down to between - 28°C and -32°C and the wind chill factor would sometimes be unbearably high. The 'Zolotoi Rog' Bay and the adjoining seas would freeze over and vehicles plied between nearby islands and the city in selected, well-marked, portions of the frozen sea that had the thickest ice! The warmest part of the year was in July/August when temperatures rose to as high as +21°C to +23°C for a while. Buildings were all centrally heated with a steam circulating system, and some of the homes were of wooden construction to give added insulation. Cold or warm, the local people moved about outdoors with the same regularity, to and fro from offices, shopping, or queuing up for 'goodies' as and when they rarely made their appearances.

The city of Vladivostok was synonymous with what the eight initial crews called their home away from home. It was here that the crews underwent around two years of classroom training, followed by sea training onboard a Soviet Foxtrot Class submarine in and around the neighboring waters. Their training institution was on Ruskii Ostrov – an island 45 minutes away from the city by boat, and 11 minutes by bus across the frozen sea during winters. While the bachelors lived on the island and made week-end forays to the city, the married officers lived in Gostineetsa Primorya and came to the island on weekdays for instructions. They first had to learn to read, write, and speak Russian language. None of the Instructors spoke the English language. In fact, no one in the city they came across spoke in the English language. To survive, one had to speak in Russian which they soon managed very well. Fluency was achieved to required levels within the first three months. In two and a half years, they became very familiar with the language, the city, and made many friends. When they departed for Riga to commission their own submarines, they left behind some very good friends with whom the system did not allow further contact in any form. The Indians had established a very good rapport with the Soviets in this city.

It was in this environment that Vanshali's skeleton crew found themselves in, as soon as they had settled down. Most of the crew flew back to India and from those who stayed back, the bachelors (officers and men) were accommodated in appropriate barracks, and the married officers in hotel 'Gostineetsa Primoria'. Everyone was given a local identity card by the Soviets that permitted him to move within a radius of nineteen kilometers from the center of town. Working hours were from 9AM to 5PM, five days a week. Weekends were free to relax. The Commanding Officer of Vanshali passed the usual order that everyone was to move about in groups, and in any case not less than in twos. A few of the Refit Team were from the initial crews that trained here, and now had the opportunity to re-establish contact with some of their old friends who were possibly still around.

The presence of the Indian submarine crew aroused more than a little curiosity. Two decades had passed since Indians were last seen in this port. Some of the 'locals' who were around then, recalled their presence and smiled at the crew members as they passed them on the streets or brushed past them in department stores. Occasionally, the odd one would stop an Indian and enquire after the well-being of one of the original Indian crews they had met while the former had trained here.

At the nineteenth kilometer from the center of town, in a northerly direction was a 'sanatorii'. It was not a sanatorium as is generally understood. This was a place for 'rest and recuperation' for crews of Soviet naval ships. The Indians were also extended the privilege of going there, and the men made it their favorite haunt. This necessitated positioning an officer there over the weekends to keep a general eye on them and to ensure they kept away from trouble.

The year and a half stint in Vladivostok passed all too soon. Vanshali's refit and mid-life update was nearing completion. It was done quickly and efficiently by knowledgeable Soviet technicians who had the experience of refitting many different submarines of many different types. This was achieved despite the very severe winter period that hampered speed of work for three months. The Soviets had hundreds of submarines in their inventory, and a huge shore support system to keep them going. Had this refit been done in India, it would have taken much, much longer. A new set of batteries, made in India, was shipped for the submarine as Indian batteries were far superior to what the Soviets had in their submarines. These were commissioned and loaded onboard Vanshali.

The rest of the officers and men required to complete the crew flew in to receive what was now a seemingly brand new, much revived, Vanshali and put her through an acceptance program that included sailing for trials in the Sea of Japan. Trials completed, she set sail for India.

Her return journey was mostly accomplished underwater with just one stopover in Bandar Lampung in the Sunda Straits separating the Indonesian Islands of Sumatra and Java, and a second stopover in Port Blair in the Andaman Islands.

P.R. Franklin

THE INSPECTION

Vanshali returned to Visakhapatnam to a very warm reception and in time to participate in the preparation for the Annual Inspection of her supporting base. Inspections are a necessary part of naval existence. They are carried out at various levels in all moving and static formations of the navy. They could be of an administrative nature or of an operational nature. The Commander-in-Chief inspects the establishments under him, the Fleet Commander inspects the ships under him, the Commanding Officers inspect the unit under them, and Department Officers inspect their respective departments, so on and so forth. Vanshali is inspected annually administratively, and operationally in harbor and out at sea once in every operational cycle. An operational cycle covers the time she is operational and spanned the time between two consecutive refits. She is also involved in the inspection of the shore establishment that supports her, since all administrative cover emerges from there and the crew lives there, when in harbor. Being an annual feature, the shore establishment is ably supported by the submarine by lending manpower that put their shoulders to the wheel to make the Inspection a success. This is a story of one of the many such Inspections that took place during Vanshali's lifetime.

Once upon a time, the Second-in-Command of the shore establishment that supported Vanshali, got promoted and appointed as its Commanding Officer. A new Second-in-Command was appointed and assumed duties. Much of the rest of the staff of officers remained the same. Right from the beginning it was quite apparent that the new Second-in-Command had an entirely different way of working to that of his predecessor —now the Commanding Officer. The former was aggressive, active, and found everywhere – often to the dismay of the staff officers who were sometimes caught with the shoe on the wrong foot. He didn't trust his left hand from his right hand and suggested that the officers also believe in this maxim. The latter, on the other hand, left matters to his subordinate officers after instructing them as to what was expected of them believing that, given the responsibility, they would carry out their duties conscientiously. The Annual Inspection of the establishment was only a couple of weeks ahead, and energies were being channeled towards preparing the place for the event, and a consequent good report. Everything had to be in order – books, buildings, furniture, moveable and immovable assets. An Annual Inspection always precedes the event with a daunting task for those to be inspected.

One morning, a few minutes after the Commanding Officer had driven to the main Administrative building, the First Lieutenant was sent for.

"Why is the brass portion of this fire extinguisher not shining?" bellowed the Commanding Officer.

"This week we are concentrating on cleaning up 'Area B', Sir." replied the rather naïve First Lieutenant.

"What the f.... is 'Area B'?" asked the now apoplectic Commanding Officer.

"Oh, Sir – the Base Commander has divided the entire establishment into four areas – A, B, C, and D. Each week, one area will be tackled so that at least once a month everything will get a thorough cleaning."

"You mean everything was not being thoroughly cleaned earlier?" thundered the Commanding Officer, apparently taking it as a personal affront.

The dumb First Lieutenant had no answer. The Commanding Officer stomped away in a huff up to his office. The fire extinguisher was polished immediately.

About the same time a week later, the First Lieutenant was called to the same place by the Commanding Officer.

"Why are these window panes looking so dirty? Don't you believe in getting them cleaned? You want me to get after you every day?"

"Sir, we are concentrating on 'Area C' this week" replied the First Lieutenant.

"What the f.... is 'Area C'?" he started, and then suddenly recalled the earlier conversation.

"Tell the Base Commander to see me" he growled as he turned away and headed for his office. Something transpired between the two of them that day. The morning 'exchanges' ceased. But it didn't end there.

The Commanding Officer takes 'Rounds' of the establishment once a week. It is a formal Inspection and a serious event. A bugler and the Master-At-Arms, who have the route taped out, lead him. An entourage consisting of Heads of Departments, the Base Commander, the First Lieutenant, the Medical Officer etc, etc, follow him. He checks the area for cleanliness, tidiness, hygiene, so on and so forth. He inspects the galley and tastes the food prepared for the next meal. He inspects the living quarters of the men. He shoots questions and one of the entourage better have the right answer, or one that will satisfy him, or else embarrassing moments follow. Only a quarter of the area was covered when the Base Commander suddenly stepped in front of the Commanding Officer and announced with a salute that the 'Rounds' had been completed! There was a horribly confused look on the senior officer's face and he couldn't find words to say anything. He walked away in silence. From then on, on matters of cleanliness, he decided to by-pass the Base Commander and deal with the First Lieutenant directly. The latter found this very distressing as he now had not one but two 'immediate superiors', often giving contradicting orders. He would now and again appeal to the Base Commander to talk to 'The Old Man' but to no avail. The Base Commander decided to avoid any confrontation and let 'The Old Man' just get used to his way of working.

The Annual Inspection was now only a few weeks away and the Commanding Officer – seeing the seemingly lack of progress made – started feeling restless. He called the Base Commander and the conversation went as follows:

"I have been walking around the establishing and it seems to me that you are w..a..y behind schedule. The sailor's lockers have not been varnished as yet,

They need to be given time to dry after that and well before the inspection ….. ".

"Tomorrow when you walk around, the lockers will all be varnished, Sir" interrupted the Base Commander. He withdrew and sent for the First Lieutenant.

"Stop all other work in the barracks and get the men to varnish all lockers by tonight" he directed.

The 'work plan' was interrupted, and the lockers varnished.

The next day, when the Captain walked around the barracks accompanied by the First Lieutenant and the Base Commander, he found the lockers had been varnished but very little progress had been made on other things. Turning around, he addressed the Base Commander:

"The walls have not been white-washed as yet. When will that be done? - and when will they dry up?"

"You wanted to see the lockers varnished, Sir. They have all been varnished." Replied the Base Commander.

"But the walls…?" asked the very disturbed Captain.

"Tomorrow afternoon, when you walk around, the walls will be all white-washed." was the reply, and orders were passed down the line to accomplish the task.

The now very anxious Captain wanted to take matters in his own hands and personally organize cleaning up the entire establishment for the Inspection. It would be a matter of disgrace in the Command if the Inspection resulted in a bad report. Everyone would hear of it and it would be difficult to live down. He sent for the First Lieutenant and asked him to report directly to him.

"Now look here .. I want the front line for the Guard of Honour on the Parade

Ground marked subtly, so that it is not VERY noticeable, and at the same time noticeable to the men forming the front line, so that all the toes of their boots are put against the line to form a straight line. Understand?"

"Aye, Aye, Sir," replied the First Lieutenant who the called the Gunnery Instructor to his room and ordered him to ensure that the front line for the guard is marked in a straight line. He then ran off to hasten up the white washing process.

The Captain walked around the establishment in the afternoon, and summoned both the Base Commander and the First Lieutenant to his office.

"Have you seen the white wash stains on the floor?" he screamed. "It will take ages to get rid of them. Didn't you notice how I insisted on newspaper sheets being spread all along the walls last year before they began the white washing? Why wasn't it done this year?"

He went on and on about many other small but significant issues, and finally, in exasperation, popped the question:

"Does the Commanding Officer of this establishment get to see the place ready for inspection BEFORE the C-in-C, or WITH the C-in-C?"

The Second-in-Command had had enough and blurted out:

"With the C-in-C!" and realizing that he needed to sort out things, went on, "Look Sir, with all due respects to you, we were working on a work plan that would have had the establishment spick and span for you to see before the Inspection Day, but you upset the whole plan by asking to see the lockers varnished one day, the walls white washed the next day .... So on and so forth. Now, please let me do my job, and I will see that everything is ready on time." With that he stomped out of the room. As the First Lieutenant got up to follow him, he was stopped

"YOU!" thundered the Captain, "Go and have a look at the Parade Ground markings and come back and see me"

The stupid sailor – whoever he was –had used a 4-inch broad brush and white paint to mark a very wriggly front line for the front row of the Guard to put the toes of their boots to! The First Lieutenant was now miserable anticipating the wrath of a very frustrated Commanding Officer descending on him. He called for the Gunnery Instructor and gave him a piece of his mind and directed that the damage to be rectified. He, then, went back to the Commanding Officer to get his share of the dose.

"I'm sorry Sir! I should have supervised it myself. Anyway, I've lined up the

Gunnery Instructor, and the damage is being rectified," blurted out the First Lieutenant.

The gleam in the Captain's eye told him that this apology had no effect. For the next fifteen minutes he got it! – All about not ever trusting what the right hand passes to the left hand, about lack of attention to minute details, why personal supervision is always required on important issues, etc, etc, etc. A thoroughly disheartened First Lieutenant walked out of the Captain's office with his shoulders drooping and his feet heavy as lead. This past month had been full of tensions and travails. The Annual Inspection was still ahead. Being told that the job was not being done properly did not help matters. Worse! Having two bosses breathing down his neck was not helping matters either.

The Base Commander had decided to wax the cemented flooring in the sailor's barracks a dark red with Cardinal Polish. However, Cardinal Polish in such large quantities was very expensive. He decided to experiment making a cheaper substitute with Red Oxide powder and paraffin wax, and in this he was successful. So, the entire flooring of the sailor's barracks, including the corridors, were properly waxed a dark red for the Inspection. Work went on at a frantic pace with no one looking at the clock, and everyone hell bent on getting the job done.

The morning of the Inspection arrived. Everyone was up at 4 AM, getting last minute things over so as to be ready for a Parade at 9AM followed by the Inspection of the Submarine Base by the Commander-in-Chief. The Base Commander and the First Lieutenant were moving about, checking things and passing orders to attend to minor details that mattered during inspections – things that made all the difference between a mediocre and a good inspection. Suddenly, out of the darkness, the Captain loomed on the Parade Ground and sent for the First lieutenant.

"Get all the lights in the barracks switched on. I want to see from here if they are all working, or whether some bulbs need replacement."

The First Lieutenant sent a sailor off to do the job, starting from the ground floor from left to right, then to the first floor from right to left, on to the second floor from left to right once again ... so on and on till the sixth floor. The First Lieutenant sidled away from the Captain and stood out of sight but watched all the lights coming on in sequence. Suddenly out of the darkness the Base Commander came up to him and asked;

"What the hell is going on? Why are all the lights being switched on?

In hushed tones the First Lieutenant whispered that the Captain had instructed that this be done.

"With full load, the Mains may blow and we haven't got the time to rectify such a defect should it occur" said the Second-in-Command and he got a sailor to promptly go and start switching off the lights!

From the Parade Ground, it was a nice sight – while the third floor lights were being put on, the ground floor lights were being put off. While the fourth floor lights were being put on, the second floor lights were being put off .... . The First Lieutenant beat a hasty retreat from the Parade Ground and made himself scarce!

The Ceremonial Parade went off flawlessly. The front line for the Guard was painted so faintly that it was not visible till someone looked for it. Everyone went to change into working dress from ceremonial dress for the 'walk around' by the Commander-in-Chief and his Staff. It was to start from the Sailor's barracks.

The Bugler sounded the 'alert' as the C-in-C's car came into the base. The Quartermasters sounded the "Still" on their Bosun's Pipes and the 'walk around' began. With his very first step on the porch, the C-in-C slipped on the waxed floor and was airborne, tilting backwards with his feet up before him. However, before he could land in what would have been a very awkward situation indeed, he was held up by his elbows by the Base Commander on one side and the First Lieutenant on the other.

Turning to the Base Commander he asked in low tones:

"You've waxed your floors?"

"Yes Sir! We submariners wear non-skid shoes, and so there is no problem" replied the Base Commander. From then on, the C-in-C and his entourage walked around, concentrating more on not slipping than looking around.

The Inspection went off well and a glowing report came by signal from the C-in-C's office. All the officers retired to the Wardroom to celebrate with a glass of beer.

"You - come here!" bellowed a visibly happy Captain, addressing the First Lieutenant who walked up to him smiling confidently, having seen the signal from the Admiral.

"Cheers! Well done!" and they clinked their tankards.

P.R. Franklin

THE STRIPE-WETTING

Having earlier trained under the Royal Ensign, much of the Royal Navy's customs and traditions were followed by the Indian Navy of the post-independence era. Some of them logically evolved over the years and with good reason too. One of them was the custom of observing 'Make and Mend' days twice a week. As a matter of fact, they were observed on Wednesdays and Saturdays. Evenly spaced across the week, Make and Mend days were when sailors mended sails and awnings in the days before the advent of steamships. Since a stitch in time saves nine, this work was undertaken with singular regularity. All other work on deck was put to a halt while mending sails was in progress. Sailors would sit on the deck in groups or singly, and tackle one big sail or awning at a time, or small pieces that needed only one or two individuals' attention. This activity also gave them some respite from the rigors of climbing masts and furling and unfurling sails, scrubbing and 'holy-stoning' decks, heaving in the anchor, and much of the chores that demanded muscle and sweat. Make and Mend days had a light routine for all onboard His Majesty's man-o-war ships.

Came steamships, and much of life onboard changed. However, Make and Mend routines continued, but in a modified form. In fact, to this day, warships spread awnings over decks, and cover guns and boats with canvas after sunset while in harbor, though the practice of mending awnings on Wednesdays and Saturdays has taken a back seat. They are now off-loaded to the Dockyard for affecting repairs. Make and Mend days were now declared as half days, and these were the days when some 'elbow bending' was exercised before proceeding for lunch – the bachelors to the Wardroom onboard, and the married officers ashore to their homes. The English follow this practice to this day even in corporate offices, though in a somewhat different, and yet very similar, fashion. They retire to a Pub and have a drink together before going home for the weekend. It is a practice that helps immensely to maintain good inter personnel relationships. Differences are talked about, and evened out. When they leave the Pub, more often than not, everyone is in a friendly disposition. Make and Mend is not practiced at sea onboard Indian warships.

Onboard warships, and only in harbor, Make and Mend days are the days when an officer 'Wets his Stripes' on being promoted. This is another old custom. The officer being promoted sees the Captain of the ship at the start of the working day, who removes his old shoulder stripes and puts on his new stripes for him – for the first time. The officer then invites his friends and colleagues to the bar on the following Make and Mend day to drink with him to celebrate the occasion. Before partaking of liquor offered by the new 'promotee', each invitee dips his finger in his glass and wets the host's stripes, wishing him many more to come. At times the officer may seek the Captain's permission and hoist a 'Gin Pennant' on the mast. This would be a signal for any and all officers who see the Pennant, to come onboard and share the 'promotee's' happiness with him! In this case, no invitations are sent out, and the crowd is not restricted in numbers. The Navy took this practice ashore too, and 'Stripe-wetting' was a common practice in the shore Wardrooms of Establishments on Make and Mend days. To go one step further, and because of the very restricted space in a submarine's Wardroom, submarine officers normally celebrated their promotions by inviting one and all to the shore Wardroom where their stripes would be 'wetted'.

Three of Vanshali's officers, all belonging to the same batch and with the same seniority, got promoted together and decided to hoist the Gin Pennant in the Wardroom ashore on a Make and Mend day. They were well known in the Navy and quite popular in Visakhapatnam. As a result, the Wardroom was jam-packed in no time, and beer flowed freely. At first the proceedings looked like any normal stripe-wetting occasion with much clinking of tankards followed by a "Cheers!" here and a "Cheers!" there. Some eats were circulated as 'munchings' that were always welcome with beer. The noise level steadily increased in direct proportion to the volume of liquid downed, as everyone tried to converse with everyone at the same time. Nobody seemed to be in any hurry to call it a day and leave. Was it because the bill was going to be shared by three officers? One of the officers broke out in song that brought a hush for a brief moment. Others who recognized the bawdy naval tune and knew the words soon joined him. Still others tried to listen carefully to catch the words so that they could join in when the chorus was sung. The atmosphere was turning a bit raucous. It looked like it was going to be a long afternoon indeed. At about three o'clock, after some three and a half hours of good drinking and noisy singing, someone stepped out to head for the toilet. He was the only officer who made it. Others tried to follow him but were soon stopped by one of Vanshali's officers who shut the door and stood against it in a menacing pose, ready to take on anyone who tried to get past him.

"No one is going to leave this room till I say so!" he yelled. He wasn't even one of the hosts.

At first, he was taken somewhat lightly as one who had had 'quite a bit' and therefore 'inspired' to say what he said. Gradually, however, those with straining bladders discovered that he meant business. He was pushing and shoving people away from the door when they approached him. He was physically very strong. No amount of logic, sweet-talk, or reasoning was acceptable to him, however senior the man attempting it was.

"I am bursting and need to go urgently" said a senior Commodore to this young Lieutenant.

"Then go to one of the bay windows and do it through there, Sir!" was his reply. The Wardroom was on the first floor of the building, and no one could go out through the window to get to the toilets.

It dawned on one and all that there was no going through the one and only door to the toilet to ease themselves unless they overpowered the man and carried him away. This, in their 'spirited' condition, they were not quite willing to do. Three windows were opened and three desperate fellows unzipped and eased themselves, concentrating on the job in hand rather than on the splendid view of the Naval Harbor and the ships tied up on the finger jetties before them! This was a signal for more to follow. Their bursting bladders eased, they got down to more back-slapping, drinking and spinning yarns.

The party ended at five o'clock. People weaved their way through the only door, out to the lobby, and then clutching the banister gingerly made their way down to the ground floor, and out of the building. As a general statement, it would not be wrong to say that those who came in cars walked home, those who came in motorcycles left them and drove the cars of the others home, and those who had come walking took the motorcycles home for the owners. No one could recollect what he had come in, and where it was parked. One of the 'promotees' drove an officer's car home for him but did not quite make it – he banged into the Main Gate of the Married Officer's Colony while aiming to go through it carefully. Another officer, who owned a Triumph motorcycle that he had brought back from the UK after his training there, and who nursed it like a baby, decided he would drive it home. He was told he won't make it, and as a compromise agreed to take a pillion rider. The two of them went for a toss en route. Quite a few officers decided they could not go home in this state and face the wrath of their better halves. They went into the bachelors' rooms and sprawled out on their beds – some of them with their caps and shoes on!

That was a 'Stripe Wetting' party that was not forgotten by those who attended it – ever! It was also the talk of the navy in Visakhapatnam for many years to come. It was not repeated or matched ever again, though many stripe-wetting parties followed.

THE PIGGERY

During one of the weekly staff meetings in the submarine support base, how to restrict wastage of cooked food came up for discussions. Food was being cooked as per scale and the strength of personnel expected to eat. Yet, there was considerable wastage after each meal. While there would be no noise if food was in excess and got wasted, all hell would break loose if food ran short! A suggestion came up in a lighter vein that a piggery be started so that wastage was properly consumed and decent pork made available for takers to enjoy.

Military rations did not include either beef or pork, so as to preserve the sensitivities of those whose religious beliefs did not permit them to partake of either one or the other. Those who wanted beef or pork resorted to buying them from the local markets. The pork in the local market was of dubious quality and therefore to be shunned. If the submarine base had its own piggery, the pigs could be fed the substantially large quantities of waste food from the galleys (kitchens) that were now being thrown away. The sty had to be located in a discreet place, far away from areas frequented by human population moving around the base. Such an area was located and the task of going about starting a piggery began. Not far from Visakhapatnam is the town of Gannavaram where the State Government had a pig farm run scientifically and hygienically. They sold imported thoroughbreds like the 'Yorkshire' and 'Landrace'. A visit to that farm was necessary. Volunteers to look after the pigs would be required. They would have to be trained. These were all activities far removed from the business of running submarines, but would keep some of those from rustic backgrounds, who formed a part of the spare crew ashore, very busy indeed.

Contrary to common belief, pigs are not filthy animals. They wallow in mud only to provide a covering to prevent parasites from clinging on to them. They dig ditches in the ground that eventually get filled with water to form a slush in which they wallow to keep parasites away. They do not dig with their trotters, but with their snouts. Keep parasites away from them and they are quite content to keep their skins clean. They have a pack instinct, with each pack having its own distinct smell. A 'new' pig introduced into the pack invariably receives an aggressive, and sometimes fatal, welcome because of its 'new' smell. Pigs are also disciplined animals. When a litter is born, each one grabs one teat and sticks to that teat alone. The first piglet gets the nearest teat and the last the furthermost! Of course, the last to emerge has the toughest time and chances are that the furthermost teat has the least milk, and so that reduces the odds for survival. Introducing a new litter into the pack is also met with danger since a new 'smell' is invading the pack. Those who had the fortune to look after them learned all this eventually.

Volunteers were readily available, and off they were sent to Gannavaram to learn how to run a pig sty and rear pigs in a healthy environment. They learnt that kerosene oil rubbed on snouts temporarily makes them lose their smell and this was one way of introducing new pigs or piglets into a pack. By the time the effect wore off, they would all have the same smell, and each would be acceptable to the other! This trick was to be used to change piglets to different teats during feeding time so as to ensure a higher survivability rate amongst litters. They were taught how to cut off the little, soft, tusks within days of their birth, and how to inoculate them. They were given a detailed understanding of other behavioral patterns of piglets, sows, and boars. They came back with an initial number of piglets and admiration for this breed of animal. Meanwhile, a complicated pig shed was built in the designated area that comprised of a single room for the Boar, a separate room for new-born piglets, a dormitory for the sows, a common courtyard into which they could be released in turns, a good washing and drainage system, and feeding troughs. Not far away was an area marked for the pigs to wallow in mud, which was a necessary activity that their basic instincts demanded of them.

A local veterinary doctor was contacted to regularly visit the pigs and generally keep them in good health. The waste galley food was augmented with vitamins to ensure a balanced and healthy diet. Each pig was named, and differentiation markings put on them. Separate documents were maintained for each pig where its history was available in detail. The Gannavaram pig farm officials stated when they visited the submarine base pig sty, that this sty was now far superior to theirs!

The first pig to weigh in at 80 kilograms was readied for the chopping board, as that was the weight when the best meat-to-fat ratio was achieved. The pork sold out in minutes! Soon the piggery became famous amongst all the different naval establishments in Visakhapatnam and even their Lordships at the highest local level began sending for their 'cut'. The piggery now began to make huge profits that were put back into the non-public funds of the base. These funds were used entirely for the betterment of the unit and the submarines by way of augmentation of what the Service provided, with 'extras'.

The piggery became one of the Base Commander's pet projects. In fact, he insisted on being informed about every little 'happening' in the sty. Why was Sowbhagyavati (yes, they had names!) not eating properly? What was wrong with Sowarna? Why did she have fever? What was she fed over the last three days? Was that the reason for the fever? Had she been isolated? What medicines were being administered to her? Is she re-acting positively to the medicines? Which of the others are down with fever? Why did

Sowmani have a litter of less than eight? Was the Boar healthy and well when he 'did it'? .. So on and so forth! As a result, one of the officers had put a note in the Duty officer's note book that read: "If anything unusual happens in the pig sty, please inform the next of kin immediately (telephone number of the Base Commander was written next to it)".

A sow's day began with it being hustled out into the common stone tiled courtyard where it was thoroughly hosed down. The stone tiled dormitory was hosed down too after removing the straw. Both these areas had proper drainage. Then the feeding troughs were filled and while she was busy with the activity of eating, she was carefully inspected for sores, parasites, or any form of illness. (A listless sow was isolated and referred to the local vet, and suitable entries were made in her documents. Of course, the next of kin was informed!). If she was healthy, she was left in the courtyard to mix with the others and catch a bit of the sun during the forenoon while fresh straw for the day was put in the dormitory. Just when signs of drowsiness appear she and her companions are let into the dormitory to have their afternoon siesta. Early in the evening she and her companions are pulled out again for the evening feed after which all of them are taken to the mud patch to wallow. An evening hosing down follows and they are put into the dormitory for the night. Heck! These were no ordinary pigs! These were living a life of luxury and had no reasons to complain.

Getting the boar to follow the same routine was next to impossible. He did not like to be ordered around and would express his disapproval with hostility. A safe distance had to be kept from him. He grew to enormous proportions and hardly moved about. The water hose was the only thing that would get him to move, apart from his unstinted dedication to his task of keeping at least one sow pregnant all the time. He did not run to the feeding trough for his food when it was filled as he had his own separate feeding area. He ambled across and ate only what he liked and only when he felt like. But what he ate, he ate in huge quantities. The quantities were ensured. After all, he was the one responsible for filling the non- public funds coffers!

Within months of its inauguration, the piggery had its first problem! All the trotters of the pigs were going soft and bleeding. Specialists from Gannavaram arrived along with the vet. A close inspection and lengthy discussions followed. It was concluded that the tiled floors were being kept too wet, and the trotters damp for most of the time. The flooring was sloped towards a drain to reduce the 'wet time', and they were left to forage in mud for longer hours. The trotters healed and hardened once again.

The piggery was a great success, and ran for many years to come. The naval population in Visakhapatnam got spoilt eating high quality pork. It was, however, never cooked in any of the officers' or sailors' galleys. Married personnel took pork and cooked it at home. A bachelor had to visit a married colleague to taste it. The 'executioner' soon got to know which senior officer favored which portion of the pig, and the quantities that were likely to be purchased by them! Even so, there was enough pork of good quality available to all takers.

The team that looked after the piggery had a changing population, but the standards never dropped. Many of these men, after leaving the navy, went back to their villages and ran their own piggeries, and very successfully, at that.

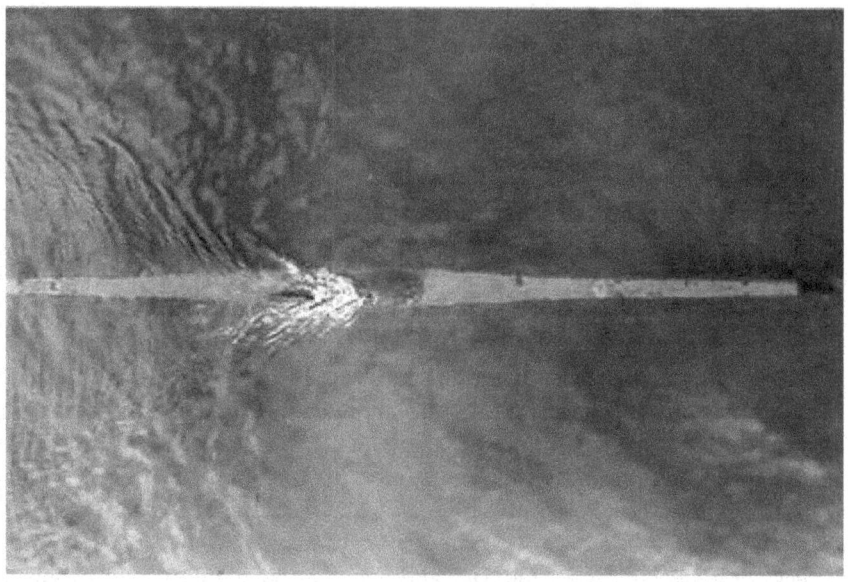

Fluorescence effect of water (Read page 136)

THE ROGUE TORPEDO

Vanshali was equipped with a fine set of torpedoes that could hit both ships and submarines. She carried more than enough of them during hostilities for prolonged operations at sea without the need to return for reloads. During peacetime, however, she carried a minimum outfit. Often, she would carry 'practice' torpedoes and go out to sea for the crew to practice attack skills. These were torpedoes that would surface after carrying out a full run without exploding, to be recovered for re-use later. They had inbuilt recorders to record data during each run that could be retrieved to carry out accurate analyses for improved performance in later firings. A target ship and a recovery ship would accompany Vanshali during such sorties.

Torpedoes are intricate by themselves in that they have their own guidance and propulsion systems, their own detection systems, their own tracking systems, and their own counter-measures and explosive systems. With zillions of parts that comprise a torpedo, in the event that any one of them misbehaves, there is no saying what the torpedo will do. They are, very carefully prepared, transported from their workshops, and loaded onboard the submarine. Even onboard the submarine, they are handled very carefully. This is a story of one of them that did not behave properly after firing.

The weather was ideal for torpedo firing – blue skies, a flat calm sea, and good visibility. Visibility even through the Periscope was going to be fine. However, there was no target ship along with Vanshali this time. There was a recovery ship to recover the torpedo after it surfaced, and there was a target submarine! – her sister submarine. This time she was going to fire a torpedo against an underwater moving target, with both dived. Then the other submarine would fire her torpedo on Vanshali. Both the torpedoes would be recovered and the team would return to harbor.

During such structured exercises, the target submarine would be permitted to move as she wished, but in a confined 'box'. The recovery ship would be kept well out of range of both submarines, but in the vicinity of where the torpedoes are expected to surface. The attacking submarine would be expected to start her run from some miles away, move through the designated 'box', detect, and attack the target submarine. Some other peacetime safety restrictions were also woven into the exercise to prevent catastrophes.

On arrival at the designated area, all units took up their respective positions, and the two submarines dived well out of sight of each other. During this first run, Vanshali was the 'attacking' submarine. The Torpedo Officer and his crew carefully loaded the practice torpedo into Torpedo Tube No 3 and carried out final checks to ensure that all was well. The

Engineer Officer in the Control Room carried out final adjustments to ensure that the submarine was trimmed properly. The Sonar Officer had all his detection systems 'on', with the best men on the job. It was important that the target submarine be detected as early as possible, at the farthest range possible, so that the Captain had enough time to carry out a good attack. It was equally important to approach the target as silently as possible so that the latter is not able to detect Vanshali and take evasive action. This was a cat and mouse game – and a very interesting one at that.

"Assume Ultra Quiet State! Assume Ultra Quiet State" announced the Second-in-Command over the Main Broadcast system. Everyone ran to their respective Action Posts and remained there, moving about minimally, and on tip-toes. The Control Room ordered the Main Motors to stop propelling, and switched on the Economic Speed Motor, which was a very silent motor that was difficult to detect by another platform. During Ultra Quiet State, the submarine is at its quietest. This is necessary to prevent its own self noise interfering and reducing the efficiency of its own sonars, and to make it more difficult for the opponent to detect her at extended ranges.

"Attack Team Close Up! Attack Team Close Up" announced the Second –in-Command over the Broadcast, his voice barely a whisper. The Fire Control System and its computer were switched 'on'.

A flurry of activities was in progress in the Fore-ends – the Torpedo Room – at the same time. Silently, they were going about the task of getting the Torpedo and its Tube Systems ready, which involved flooding the Torpedo Tube with sea water, equalizing the water pressure inside the Tube with the sea water pressure outside, then opening the Bow Cap of the Torpedo Tube, ensuring the umbilical cords from the fire Control System to the Torpedo through the Torpedo Tube were properly engaged and functioning, so on and so forth.

Now the long wait began as Vanshali inched her way towards her intended target with her ears (sonars) listening very carefully for the faint beat of the target submarine's propellers. Contrary to common belief, the sea is a very noisy environment with myriads of living organisms contributing their mite in no small measure, each at its own frequency. Through this noisy spectrum the Sonar Operators had to recognize the target submarine's own individual noise, and that too at the maximum range possible. Similar actions were sure to go on onboard the target submarine in an effort to remain as silent as possible and evade an attack. Once she detected Vanshali, she would take all possible measures to deny the latter a proper firing solution to fire her torpedo. This practice torpedo was a 'homing' torpedo, which meant it could be fired in the general direction of the target. It would then attempt to acquire the target through its inbuilt sonar and then shape course to attack the other submarine. One of the peacetime safety restrictions made was for the target submarine and the torpedo to be vertically separated by some tens of meters. The torpedo would not actually hit the target but pass under it or over it, and surface at the end of its endurance for the recovery ship to spot it and affect recovery.

"Sound Room to Control Room: A very faint object on the waterfall display: Unable to classify: Keeping watch and sweeping the ahead sector".

The Sonar Chief was an experienced hand and very shrewd. He had a good ear, but he sometimes let his imagination get the better of him. After getting the general direction of this source of noise, the Captain decided to point the submarine towards the source and close it slowly. It soon turned out to be the Torpedo Recovery ship, and therefore had to be disregarded. The 'target' submarine Captain was also a shrewd person and not one to be caught so easily. The range between the two was closing, which meant that there would be less time to carry out a deliberate attack. Sensing this, Vanshali's Captain informed the Attack Team that he was not going to carry out a 'Deliberate Attack' which took time and was more accurate, but would execute an 'Urgent Attack' with the detection of the 'target' submarine. The procedure was different, and as the nomenclature suggested, much quicker. In this case, the torpedo would have to corner the target and go for it. He also took Vanshali deeper – very close to the bottom of the sea - so as to make it more difficult for the 'target' submarine to detect Vanshali.

"Bingo!" Target... bearing Green 05 degrees. Range ….. yards" exulted the now very excited Sonar Chief. The distance was within the Torpedo's range.

"Fire Tube 3!" ordered the Captain. Fore Ends reported the torpedo leaving the Tube and a slight shudder was felt in all the submarine's compartments as it happened. With the release of the weapon, the Captain altered the submarine's course away from its present Course. He also started bringing her up. All recorders would have recorded the time of detection, the time of firing, and other such details. They would be compared with the timings and details from the target submarine during debrief and analyses that would follow in harbor.

The silence and low hum of machinery noise was disturbed by a distinct "Thunk!" sound that everyone in the Control Room heard. It did not sound again. However, it was not part of 'the usual' sounds and noises heard onboard.

"What was that?" asked the Captain, looking at no one in particular.

There was no answer and the incident was shrugged off. Vanshali crossed the 'box', informed the target submarine on her underwater sonar telephone that the attack was over, and the two submarines surfaced a few moments thereafter and closed each other.

"We did not hear the Torpedo" bellowed the Captain of the target submarine on the megaphone.

"We know it left our Torpedo Tube and headed in your direction" replied the Captain of Vanshali. On the horizon, the recovery vessel was weaving about, looking for the torpedo. All three started searching for it but it could not be found. This was not a happy situation. The loss of a Torpedo meant the loss of a tidy sum of money to the navy. A Board of Inquiry would follow which was also not a pleasant experience for all going through it. Despite a thorough search, it was not found. All three units went back to their initial positions for the roles to be reversed, and for the other submarine to carry out an attack. The attack was carried out, the torpedo recovered, and all three returned to harbor.

Vanshali's Torpedo Officer had his mother living with him at home, his father having passed away a few years earlier. On reaching home, he addressed his mother:

"Ma! How much money do you have in the bank?"

His mother asked him what the matter was.

He replied, "I fired a torpedo and it got lost at sea. I have to pay for it"

"How much?" enquired the mother, and was aghast when he told her the amount with a straight face. That kind of money was simply not there. What is going to happen to her son now, she wondered? A few hours later, she went to call on a relation of hers who was the State Finance Minister, to seek advice on how to get the money and give it to her son to pay the navy back for the lost torpedo. On her return, she found a few of her son's course mates in the house.

"See what my son has done!" she rued. "Now what is going to happen to us? Where am I going to get this money from?"

As she narrated it to the son's course mates, they burst out into laughter and went and hugged her.

"Aunty - Don't worry. No one has been asked to pay for a lost torpedo yet. Your son is only worrying you." As the son was persuaded to come out with the truth, her expression was a mixture of relief, anger and disbelief!

In harbor, after the submarines had tied up on the jetty, someone drew the attention of others to a patch of green paint and a dent on Vanshali's black painted Fin. Where had it come from? Then it all fell into place. The torpedo was painted green. If it hit the submarine, a loud "Thunk" would be heard inside. The detailed analysis concluded that the torpedo left the Torpedo Tube, switched on her 'homing head', and began her search for the target submarine. When Vanshali altered course after firing the torpedo, she left a wake of bubbles behind her to which the torpedo locked on. She then circled and came back and hit Vanshali on her Fin. The impact must have been enough for her to get damaged and sink. It never reached the target submarine.

Drills for such exercises were modified after this incident to ensure that a repeat occurrence did not happen. It never did.

OPERATIONAL MISSIONS

Operational missions are what every submarine crew looks forward to. They are different from training sorties, but regularly carried out during peacetime. This is serious business. If carried out badly, it could even lead to international incidents, diplomatic wrangles, and embarrassment to the government. Operational sorties are, however, necessary and a part of the navy's tasks. Submarines, with their ability to conceal themselves and carry out sensitive tasks, are the favored platforms to carry out such tasks. Every bit of knowledge, training, and experience comes into play during these sorties. What's more, there is ample scope for initiative and daring to be exercised. Materially, the submarine is at its best when deployed on operational sorties. These sorties are assigned to a submarine after extensive self-work up, and work up with ships and aircraft. The submarine is thus at optimum efficiency and ready to take on all eventualities that comes its way.

Preparations for an operational sortie are also carefully executed. The required fuel is embarked. The batteries are fully charged. Spares are embarked for whatever repairs can be carried out at sea so that her staying power at sea is enhanced. The boat is fully armed. Torpedoes with warheads are embarked. Vanshali carried twenty-two of them – six in the Bow Tubes, twelve on the racks in the Fore-ends that permit two reloads, and four in the Stern Torpedo Tubes in the Aft Ends that have no reloads. If it was a mining mission that she was setting out on, she would or could carry forty-four mines in lieu of the torpedoes. The mines were half the length of a torpedo. So, in lieu of every torpedo, two mines could be carried. However, as there was a need to keep some torpedoes for self-defense, a combination of mines and torpedoes would be carried.

Warships generally move about in company, communicate with each other, and keep abreast of the latest situation on almost a minute- to-minute basis, using satellites, radio channels, visual means of communications, etc, etc. They also communicate with shore authorities whenever considered necessary. Decision-making is not too difficult or challenging a task for most of them as the onus invariably falls on the senior-most officer among them to take them. In the case of submarines, being platforms using concealment and surprise to advantage, they generally communicate with no one. The Operational Orders are known only to a handful of people. Before sailing out, these orders would be received onboard in sealed envelopes that were to be opened only at specific times, in specific areas, or on special occasions. Thereafter, only information useful to help them carry out their previously assigned mission was received on wireless, for which the submarine had to come shallow. Whenever she came shallow, she risked the possibility of being detected. So she came shallow only when she was reasonably sure that it was safe to do so. In the process, some of the information transmitted to her gets overtaken by events, and sometimes get dated. The young Captain of a submarine frequently faces situations where only he must take decisions on the spot, without having any superior authority to consult. That is a privilege and challenge, that ship's Captains rarely get.

Vanshali proceeded on operational sorties in every operating cycle after a full work up and after achieving the standards laid down for independent operations. Most of the time, these sorties were independent patrols, in sensitive areas of maritime interest. Sometimes they were offensive sorties against one's own defenses to test their effectiveness and to improve them. Sometimes they were defensive sorties against 'an invading force'. To make these sorties as realistic as possible, obstacles and opposition by way of own forces acting as 'the enemy' would be presented en route and in the area of operations. Sometimes she would encounter neutral forces – the term used to refer to other navies operating in the area, or merchantmen, or even maritime patrol aircraft of other navies operating in international waters. She would have to ensure that she acted in a manner that would ensure that she carried out her assigned mission successfully without embarrassing any of the neutrals or giving them cause to accuse the Indian submarine of violating International Laws of the Seas. The 'Confidential' Submarine Charts that Vanshali used for navigation and maneuvers helped her to navigate with caution and keep on the right side of the Law.

One particular operational sortie of Vanshali's is worthy of recall. It was in the month of November. The boat was well worked up and ready for such tasks. Her 'war outfit' of weapons was embarked, her batteries charged, her fuel topped up, and her stores embarked. The night was dark as she slipped from her moorings and left harbor. She did not display even her normal navigational lights. Once she cleared harbor, she carried out a Trim dive successfully, and began to snorkel to a particular set of co-ordinates marked as her first point to pass through, by a particular time. There was a hush onboard as her task and destination were still not known. This would be known only when the Captain opens his first envelope at the designated time.

The sea was rough. She was going straight into a 'depression' that was likely to turn into a cyclone. At snorting depths the effects of rolling and pitching were less as compared to the effects on the surface. Nevertheless, it was there. If she had gone deep, the effects would have been negligible. This, she could not do because she had been directed to get to a certain point by a certain time, and that warranted a high speed of advance. She could do this dived deep by using her batteries, but they would have steadily drained in the process, warranting coming up to the surface or to Periscope depth to have them repeatedly charged. In the process, her overall speed of advance would have come down. On the other hand, she could maintain the required speed of advance at Periscope Depth using her diesels to propel, and thereby not drain her batteries. Without doubt, the latter was the better option. She surged with the swell and struggled to maintain the ordered depth. Only her wireless mast and her passive electronic signals detection masts were up, in addition to the 'Search Periscope' that was being operated by the Officer of the Watch in the Conning Tower. All three of them were raised to be barely visible above the surface of the sea. In a flat calm sea, the wakes of these three masts would be prominent and visible to the naked eye of any pilot in a reconnaissance aircraft flying over the sea on an anti-submarine mission. However, with the sea being rough, and 'white horses' aplenty, there was little risk in the wake being detected, particularly during that dark night.

Almost twelve hours passed before Vanshali got to her first point and the envelope was opened. All eyes were on the Captain as he did this in full view of those present in the Control Room. His eyebrows momentarily rose as he read the contents and returned the envelope back into his pocket. Then he called for the Navigating Officer and went with him into the Chart Room. They huddled over a Chart with a pair of 'dividers' and a ruler. Some ten minutes passed and then the Captain came back to the Control Room to respond to the enquiring eyes of the Executive Officer.

"Another long leg before the next envelope is opened", was his laconic statement as the two of them retreated to the Wardroom in the Second Compartment. How far were they going? – And what was their mission this time? While everyone was pondering over these questions that were yet to be answered, Vanshali kept snorting with her side diesels purring and her compressors replenishing the High Pressure air that had been consumed since leaving harbor. There was, however, a change of Course to get to the next point, and that was ordered. On the new Course the swell began to push Vanshali from abeam and she began to roll inconsistently but not too severely. The 'depression' was still active but had not yet turned into a cyclonic storm. The center of the depression was quite some distance away and there was no danger of Vanshali getting caught up with it. This was indeed going to be a long day albeit a quiet and uneventful one. The Courses selected were, quite obviously, going to lead her to her destination in an indirect manner and away from the shipping lanes as no ships had been encountered after leaving harbor. Sometimes it is advantageous to go along the shipping lanes and mingle with the traffic. It offers a form of concealment.

The Watches changed around every three hours: the Periscope Watches every twenty minutes. The gallant cook was gallantly churning out meals one after the other despite the effects of weather. He had to cook and control his vessels so that they did not slide off the four hot plates he used simultaneously. The weather was not so bad that food was not being fully consumed. There are two types of seasickness. There is the more commonly known one where the stomach churns and the head aches, culminating in vomiting and an urge to lie down listlessly. There is the other one where one gets voraciously hungry and is constantly on the lookout for food! Then there were those on whom all this rolling and pitching had no effect at all. Vanshali had all three types onboard.

The sun had not shown its face the whole day but it was about sunset time now and the horizon was looking murky through the periscope. The overcast sky precluded use of the periscope sextant to determine the submarine's position. This was done as a matter of practice even though the satellite navigation system had been installed onboard Vanshali. The latter could give the submarine's position with accuracy whenever required so long as she was on surface or at periscope depth.

A little into the Middle Watch, the Captain was woken up as requested, and the next envelope was opened. It directed the submarine to proceed on her next Course not at Periscope Depth but deep, maintaining a slower speed of advance. This was welcomed all round.

"Stop Snorting! Stop Snorting! Maintain Depth." was the first order. It was soon followed by;

"Dive to Safe Depth with 5° Aft Bubble." After steadying herself at Safe Depth (Safe Depth varied depending on the deployment area and nature of opposition likely to be encountered), Vanshali was ordered to go deeper and all effects of the depression above disappeared. Steady as a rock, Vanshali vended her way to her next point, the diesels now quiet and her motors silently propelling her. The crew slept peacefully for the rest of the night.

About nine o'clock the following morning, even as the day promised to be as uneventful as the preceding day, the Captain addressed the crew on the Main Broadcast.

"Do you hear there? Do you hear there? This is the Captain speaking. Most of you must be wondering where we are going and on what mission. Well, I am at liberty to disclose the details to you now. You are NOT, .. I repeat NOT, to disclose this to anyone when we return to harbor."

There was a pause, and then he continued.

"In the profession of arms that we are in, it is our business to know everything that is possible about our likely adversaries – his level of expertise, how sophisticated his equipment is, his tactics, his ability to support himself during hostilities, from where he gets his reinforcements, so on and so forth. All this forms a part of intelligence gathering, which is a never-ending process. Every little bit of information is like a piece in a jigsaw puzzle. Put them all together and a clear picture emerges. We are out this time to gather yet another piece of vital information about our likely adversary. To do this, we are going to mingle with his forces at sea for a while without our being detected. I want each one of you to remember that you are required to be extremely discreet and quiet in whatever actions you are required to do. That's all."

The Captain decided that, that was all that was required to be disclosed, and so did not go into any details. He later called the officers to the Wardroom and separately briefed them.

"Our intelligence agencies have learnt that Country X has secretly acquired a new surface-to-surface missile for its navy from its very dependable friend and ally. A demonstration of this missile's capability is being made at sea. It has been reliably learnt that the missile is going to be fired from a ship onto a target in the course of the next few days. Our task is to place ourselves in a position from where we can witness this firing, take periscope photographs, make and record electronic intercepts, and gather as much information as we can about this missile firing exercise. What I have just said need not go out of this Wardroom. It is not to be discussed in front of the men."

There was silence all round as the importance and immensity of the task was taken in by every officer. The firing may be in that country's Territorial Waters. Then what? The implications of being discovered in their Territorial Waters need not be elaborated. There will be a furore of diplomatic proportions. On the other hand, it is possible that it is conducted beyond Territorial Waters – in International Waters. If Vanshali is caught there before the firing, it will be called off. If she is caught after the firing of the missile, she would have got some data and that may lead to some aggressive behavior from the other side, apart from noises at the diplomatic level again. There was only one course of action left for Vanshali – she had to go in and mingle with their ships, gather data, and get out without getting caught!

No more envelopes had to be opened. Now, intelligence started coming in, over the air, by wireless from back home. This was expected, and Vanshali was still some distance away from being detected by the other country's naval units at sea. So, she periodically raised her radio antenna to receive vital information. One vital bit of information that came in was that their flotilla's expected departure had been postponed. Why? Had they got suspicious about a snooper in the area? Was it because of the weather? It was most likely the latter, as every effort had been made to hide Vanshali's departure and subsequent movements.

The weather had indeed eased up and the 'depression' appeared to be petering out instead of developing into a cyclone. The weather report received over the radio confirmed this. In a day or two the sea would be calm and ideal for a missile demonstration firing to be carried out. Vanshali now had two, maybe three extra days to kill.

The Captain and the Second-in-Command – the Executive Officer - got into a huddle in the Wardroom to decide on what course of action to take. It was decided that Vanshali would close the country's main harbor where their Flottila was based, remain just outside Territorial Water limits, and observe movements of vessels in and out of that harbor for a while. This, Vanshali could do as she was permitted to patrol freely without any limitations on her area of operation.

While still some distance away from the coastline, Vanshali came up at night to periscope depth, quickly charged her batteries, ran her compressors and charged High Pressure air so vital for blowing her ballast tanks to surface, as also for meeting other requirements for air inside her. Fully topped up, she went deep again and made a slow and silent approach towards the harbor where that country's Flottila was based. Her passive sonars were on full alert, and she had assumed what is termed as 'ultra quiet state'. In this condition, she is most silent and difficult to detect. Not expected to be used, but nevertheless an essential part of self-defense, a pair of torpedoes was also readied in the torpedo tubes.

The first eighteen hours passed off peacefully. A sudden 'contact' on sonar drew the attention of the Captain. It was different to the run of the mill noise produced by merchant ships. This was a vessel whose powerful engines were straining but who was making very slow headway indeed – like a tug towing something. A quick visit to periscope depth and a look through the magnified lens confirmed what was suspected. It was a tug, and she was towing a Battle Practice Target – the type that would be used as a target for missile firings! Eureka!! Vanshali had struck gold! She was followed out of harbor till she reached a point where the tug began to extend her length of tow. The tug had apparently reached her destination or thereabouts. Vanshali reversed course and headed back towards the harbor, all the while listening out on her sonar sets for the expected arrival of the Flottila. The whole night passed without any signs of them, but midway through the following morning her sonar and her wireless antenna picked up propeller noise and the familiar chatter of warships in company. The ships had emerged, and were at sea. Messages were intercepted which were being passed on frequencies normally used by aircraft. Perhaps some VIPs were coming in Helicopters to witness the firing?

The Captain, the Executive Officer and the Navigating Officer were all now huddled in the Navigator's cabin and gleaning from each other's professional knowledge on surface-to-surface missiles in general as to the likely ranges at which such missiles would be fired when giving demonstrations. Relevant books were also consulted and the performances of some of the older and dated missiles rejected. The newer generation missiles drew their attention. These were tactical missiles with very short ranges compared to strategic missiles. To fire them beyond radar horizon ranges, a platform – ideally a helicopter – would have to be positioned midway between the firing ship and the target to collate and pass on relevant target data to the firing ship, the latter being unable to gather this information by herself. Vanshali could thus expect one such helicopter to take up position between the Battle Practice Target being towed by the tug, and the nominated firing platform. When firing practice missiles during peacetime, it is the standard practice the world over to promulgate the area where such firings are to take place, and to request innocent ships on passage, deep sea trawlers, fishing vessels and the like to keep clear off that area. This particular 'demonstration firing' had not been promulgated as that country wanted to keep all details about their latest acquisition under wraps. It is more than likely, therefore, that some of their warships may be deployed between the target and firing ship, outside the line of fire, to warn other ships that may be present in the area to move away and keep clear. These 'range clearance' ships could be identified by the electronic data bank onboard Vanshali that had details of many of the electronic equipment on them and the frequencies they used.

The picture was becoming a little clearer and seemed to suggest roughly where Vanshali should position herself to get a balcony seat for the show! The frequency bands to be monitored were also clear. Vanshali would carefully and periodically raise her radio antenna to monitor all the required V/UHF frequencies. The periscope camera was also loaded with a film to take an opportune snap if it came one's way. It only remained for the sonar to hold onto the tug's noise and the noise of ships of the Flotilla so that they could complete the picture by revealing their whereabouts.

Perhaps Vanshali's 'friends' were not aware that she was around. Perhaps they did not, in their wildest imagination, think that someone else had got wind of this firing early enough to send a snooper to the area. They certainly acted as if no one else apart from themselves were around to witness the firing. Precautions were thrown to the wind and the demonstration carried out. Vanshali was a lucky submarine. She was in the right place at the right time, and managed to get a sea of data that would be examined and re-examined by experts in harbor, once she got back.

Once again, a cautious route out from the area was taken, and the submarine returned home safely, having successfully carried out yet another operational mission.

"Where did you go this time? How was it?" asked the Captain's wife when he got back. He mumbled something that was not distinguishable, and disappeared into the bathroom to have a much-needed hot bath. There would be a detailed debrief, conducted in camera, with very few present – on a need-to-know basis. The mission would not be referred to again.

INS Vela

INS Karanj with indigenous sonar sets for sea trials

A FOREIGN CRUISE

Navies the world over, are used as instruments of diplomacy during peace time by sending them to other countries on goodwill visits. This is also known as 'Showing the Flag', meaning showing one's country's flag to the country being visited, and thereby displaying a friendly disposition. Navies are also used in threatening postures by one country against another. This is not referred to as 'Showing the Flag'. It is rarely that submarines are sent on a 'showing the flag' mission, being instruments of stealthy missions and surprise assaults that they are. Some of them visit ports to break the monotony of a long journey to a far away destination and to pick up fresh victuals from friendly countries en route. Some of them are sent by a nation to broadcast its indigenous capability for design and manufacture of such platforms with the intention of either displaying the country's potential, or signaling availability of such platforms on sale. Whatever be the reason, Vanshali was picked to visit two ports in Western Australia one fine summer. She was to go alone, without any other ships in company.

There was excitement onboard and envy all round. She was to leave her base port and head for Port Blair in the Andaman Islands. A few days there and she was then to proceed to Port Hedland in northwest Australia to spend four days there. From Port Hedland she was to proceed to Freemantle, spend another four days there, and return to her base port.

In the 'check off list' for foreign cruises was the need to place orders on the Naval Chart Depot for Charts relevant to the waters being traversed and the ports being visited. The Navigating Officer duly shot off such a request. Some confusion followed as the Chart Depot said the charts had been dispatched but Vanshali had not received them. She set sail for Port Blair leaving instructions with all and sundry that the charts should be flown across to the A & N Islands by a certain date. That date was the day before she was to sail out of Port Blair for Port Hedland. The Charts did not arrive but in the merchant ship tied ahead of her was an ex-pilot of Port Hedland as her Master. He had no Charts but sketched from memory the position Vanshali must reach outside the port, for the Pilot to embark and the clearing bearings to remain safe. With only that precious scrap of paper for the final lap of the voyage, the submarine sailed out of Port Blair and dived in comfortable depths of water to make a submerged passage to the country of Oz, skillfully avoiding the myriads of vessels of all shapes and sizes emerging from, and entering, the Malacca Straits. Captain Cook had sailed to these southern islands on a voyage of discovery without any charts in the middle of the eighteenth century. He reached there safely. There was no reason why Vanshali could not do the same! She 'snorted' a good part of the way, diving only when considered necessary, to work up the crew, or to avoid shipping. At the appointed time and on the appointed date, she surfaced close to the coast and made her way to the Pilot pick-up point, as given on 'that precious scrap of paper'. The Pilot came and took her into port where the crew wined and dined the local dignitaries over the next three days.

Port Hedland was a revelation of sorts. Two streets, each about a furlong long and at right angles to each other, formed the main part of the city shopping center. That was it! The residential areas were far removed and spread out. The port handled mainly iron ore cargo and wore a dusty brown look. There was nothing there that interested Vanshali's crew - no worthy sights, and no shopping attractions: only a few bars and restaurants. As a suitable hotel to stay in was not available, the crew had to continue to live onboard. The crew was quite disappointed. However, the submarine drew the attention of the entire township, which came onboard and walked through the seven compartments in awe. A visit by an Indian naval vessel was a rare event indeed. They got intelligent answers to intelligent questions, and were more than convinced that the Indian Navy was a very formidable force.

During an official cocktail reception hosted onboard the submarine in the Aft —ends that was cleared of bunks and made spacious for the occasion, one of the invitees imbibed a good amount of Indian whisky and got very vocal and loud. He insisted that the Captain, and who ever he cared to bring along, come to his house to meet his little daughter. No amount of persuasion worked on him, and finally the Captain agreed to go along with the Indian Defense Attaché who had come from Canberra. On reaching this man's house, he led them to a photograph, and pointing to it stated

"That gentlemen, is my daughter. She lives in India, in the Indian State of Andhra Pradesh (he had difficulty in pronouncing it for more than one reason), in a small town that goes by the name of Srikakulam (he managed to pronounce that after three attempts). Her name is 'Porthali', and she is in school in class III."

The Captain looked at the framed photograph of this very Indian looking girl, and skeptically asked the gentlemen how she was her daughter?

"I pay for her upkeep and her education. I have been doing so for the past three years and will continue to support her till she gets married", he replied.

"Have you been to India or seen her?" asked the Captain.

"No! I have never been to India or seen her. Her photographs and progress in school is sent to me every year. That's all. But she is my own precious little Porthali" he cooed, lovingly looking at the frame placed in a prominent position in his house.

The Captain and his companion left his house, bidding him farewell in very respectful tones. A 'Crest' of the submarine was sent to him the following day as a souvenir.

Vanshali sailed out of Port Hedland with photocopies of Charts required for entering Fremantle, obtained after borrowing the originals for the purpose from a Chinese iron ore tanker berthed ahead. The originals were returned gratefully with a suitable gift to the Master of the vessel.

She now snorted her way on a southwesterly course through unfamiliar waters at some distance off the western seaboard of Australia, passing the Dampier Archipelago and Barrow Island at Periscope Depth to cross the Tropic of Capricorn for the third time in her life. After a very lonely and uneventful voyage bereft of any shipping on the route, Vanshali surfaced off Fremantle and entered harbor. The Photostat copies of the Charts proved to be very useful.

Fremantle was as different to Port Hedland as chalk and cheese. The crew had a good run ashore. The city of Perth was huge and provided all that the crew had hoped for by way of recreation and shopping. Some of them managed to get in a game of chasing kangaroos on horseback! The Mayor permitted them to use public transport free of cost provided they moved about in uniform, which they did. They were also accommodated in a very comfortable hotel ashore. Fremantle more than compensated for Port Hedland.

Vanshali's Captain was slated to visit the new Australian Navy's submarine base under construction in Fremantle on a Saturday. He got a call from the Commanding Officer of the base and the conversation went something like this:

"Commodore ….. here. Are you serious about visiting my base, or would you like to call it off and spend your time on more useful pursuits in Perth?"

"I would very much like to visit your up and coming submarine base, if you don't mind" replied Vanshali's Captain.

"Then would you mind too much if I am not there to receive you and be with you? It could turn out to be a nasty experience for me should you complain of my absence. I can make arrangements for you to be received by the Officer of the Day who will show you around and answer any of the questions you might have. Be a sport and say 'Yes'".

Vanshali's Captain agreed to the proposal and wondered at this man's attitude as such things are not done in the Indian navy. He was duly received by the Officer of the Day and shown around. He was also handed over a sheaf of papers and documents giving details of all construction activity that had been completed, was in progress, and slated to be undertaken in phases over the coming years. This was much more than anyone would reveal to a foreign naval officer visiting one's naval base.

"Where is Commodore ….. " asked Vanshali's Captain of the Officer of the Day on completion of the visit.

"He and his wife are on their personal yacht at sea, Sir. The Commodore spends all his weekends at sea on his yacht, and does not like to be disturbed with official matters, except in extreme emergency" he replied.

There were thousands of yachts in the many marinas in Fremantle, and the local love for the sea was quite obvious.

After a very satisfying visit to Fremantle, Vanshali set sail for home with many of those from the local Indian community on the jetty waving the submarine away. The course was set for the southern tip of Sri Lanka, passing Cocos Islands en route. The submarine snorted all the way. The selected route was a rare one as no shipping was encountered on the way. There was a long chat on the radio on VHF with a woman radio operator in Cocos Islands who did not want the conversation to end as she said she got such an opportunity only when a ship from mainland Australia visited them once in two-three months! She gave a vivid account of the islanders, their occupation, and how they spent their spare time – fishing, of course! The US Navy had an airstrip there that they used occasionally for their own nefarious activities.

The report received by the navy through diplomatic channels was that Vanshali's visit to Australia was a huge success.

VIP'S ONBOARD

A submarine always arouses curiosity in the minds of those interested in 'affaires maritime'. The very fact that it moves about underwater – unseen and unnoticed, till it decides to make its presence felt, evokes many questions and intrigues. When the Indian Navy was still in its infancy, Royal navy submarines en route to Hong Kong or Australia from the UK or on their way back, would stop over in India and exercise with the Indian Navy and give a taste of undersea warfare, at some cost to our government. This was in the late nineteen fifties and the early nineteen sixties. Visits to these submarines in harbor or at sea were not permitted, or restricted to a few very senior officers despite the fact that these were rather dated "A" Class boats that had done most of their younger years during WW II. These restrictions were taken to ridiculous proportions in the Soviet Navy where their own submariners from one class of submarines were not permitted to board other classes of submarines under any conditions. When Vanshali arrived in Visakhapatnam for the first time from the Soviet Union, the Commanding Officer refused access to the insides and placed a sentry at the gangway round the clock to enforce this restriction. Eventually, under pressure from the Headquarters, he agreed to permit only those given 'passes' by the Headquarters to board Vanshali. Passes were given to very few, and restricted to naval personnel only. By and by, these seemingly ridiculous restrictions were lifted, and more and more people were permitted to visit the boat. Some precautions were taken by way of covering the Depth Gauges (to conceal the maximum diving depth of the submarine), Revolution Counters (to conceal the maximum speed she could do), and other equipment that were likely to compromise sensitive information, before permitting people onboard. This was in harbor. Embarking and proceeding to sea onboard the submarine was taboo for non-submariners for many years. This was also relaxed in later years by making those wishing to sail on her sign an indemnity bond to absolve the submarine of any blame should a misfortune happen to the individual (it may be recalled that all who serve on submarines are volunteers from the navy. No one is forced to serve on her.).

In her early years, Vanshali had a very senior Minister of Cabinet rank from New Delhi visiting her in harbor. There was, however, a problem. This Minister was carrying on with his life with a cardiac problem, and it was feared that he might not be able to go down the vertical steel ladder, without straining himself. The navy did not want to be held responsible for any misfortune that may befall him. The vertical ladder from the Fin down to the Control Room consisted of two flights of ladders. The one leading into the Fore Ends was angled at 60 degrees (for torpedo loading) and most unsuitable. It was decided that he would be taken down the Aft Hatch which led into the Aft Ends, and which was the shortest. He had to be taken down without having to strain himself! The navy is known for its ingenuity, which now had to be exercised for this visit. The Dockyard rose to the occasion and provided the solution. They went about the business of making a cage of sorts of the right dimensions that would hold just one man, and go down the hatch with minimum fuss. Next, the submarine was moved to a special berth where only she was tied alongside. Then the most experienced crane operator with his mobile crane was positioned on the jetty to rehearse transferring an individual from the jetty into the Aft Ends of the submarine without banging the cage about. The position of the crane's tyres, the initial angle of the jib required to lift the VIP from the jetty, the angle through which the crane had to be swung to position the cage plumb over the hatch, and the final angle of the jib for lowering him down the hatch, were arrived at and marked clearly and prominently for the crane operator to see. On the appointed day, the Minister arrived, and was lowered into the submarine with a crowd on the jetty watching this very comical sight with straight faces. Vanshali had received her first VIP onboard, in harbor. The cage was stored carefully and used on one more occasion thereafter.

A few years later, the Vice Admiral charged with the task of deploying submarines at sea (Submarine Operating Authority – SOA) decided to embark Vanshali for a day at sea. This was a singular honor for the boat because on that day she would also be the Flagship for the day, authorized to fly the Admiral's personnel flag on her mast, and all other ships at sea would be 'junior' to her and have to 'pipe' the submarine first. It was a different matter that Vanshali had no mast on which she could hoist the flag! On surface, the Captain had decided that he would tie it up on the communication mast. It would be removed before diving. Traditionally, warships in close proximity of each other at sea salute each other by 'piping' (a shrill sound on the Bosun's Pipe). The junior ship pipes first and the senior ship pipes in response. The seniority of the ships is decided by the seniority of the senior most officer onboard the ships. Normally, this would be the Captain, but when an Admiral is onboard, it would be the Admiral. (Similarly, merchant ships pay courtesy to warships by always first lowering and then raising their ensign. Warships respond by performing the same action. The seniorities of the captains do not play a part in this case.). Actually, Vanshali was scheduled to go to sea for a day. The Fleet was at sea and fleet ships were carrying some VIPs onboard to show them the navy's prowess. As part of that program, a submarine was required to dive, show them the different masts she raises above periscope depth, release flairs from deep, and then surface before their eyes. That the Admiral decided to board her at the last minute gave her very little time to prepare for his visit and had everyone onboard in a dither. They need not have worried. The Admiral was a thoroughly professional man who was not impressed by 'foo-faa' and judged only professionalism. No one onboard Vanshali new this at that time. So she sailed out without white gloved stewards, a five-star menu for the VIP, and other things that go with 'foo-faa'. The Captain had a vision of dark clouds on the horizon that spelt the end of the line for him as far as his career was concerned. C'est la vie! With the Admiral embarked, Vanshali cast off and headed to sea.

"Sir, The men onboard would like you to share their meal with them. Would you consider it?" asked the Captain hopefully, with his fingers crossed.

"Of Course! Of Course!" replied the Admiral, and the Captain heaved a sigh of relief. That took care of the need for a special menu and white gloves. When sharing food with the men, these were not required. The cook was preparing a special 'biriyani' (an Indian rice preparation for special occasions) for the men, and the Admiral would not be too disappointed.

Vanshali soon left harbor and gathering speed, headed for her rendezvous with the fleet. There is a quiet and efficient air about a submarine crew when performing their duties that is taken for granted onboard and not given too much notice. Only bad drills and things going wrong are noticed immediately. Each individual goes about his job without fuss or supervision, and with a great sense of discipline that far surpasses the performance of crews on surface ships. The VIP onboard was quietly observing all this without comment. On reaching the point where the fleet was to meet up with the submarine, the Captain asked the Admiral's permission to dive, and then proceeded with the drills to fine-tune her trim.

"Diving Stations! Diving Stations!" went the main broadcast as everyone scurried out of their bunks and to their stations.

"Diving now! Diving now!" was heard next, and those on duty on the Bridge in the fin came down.

"Upper lid shut! Upper Lid shut!" yelled the Officer of the Watch as he descended to the Conning Tower and raised the Search Periscope to keep a watch all round.

"Admiral, Sir! Would you like to go up and watch through the Periscope now?" asked the Captain, " The Fleet should be coming up from over the horizon any time now. We are in radio contact with them" he went on. The Admiral climbed from the Control Room into the Conning Tower and the Attack Periscope was raised for him

"Flood End Groups" announced the Second-in-Command and the Panel Keeper proceeded to open the Kingstons followed by Main vents of the end group of ballast tanks. The normal hiss of air escaping from the tanks was heard and Vanshali took a trimmed down position. The motors were kicked off and the Center Group of ballast tanks flooded. Vanshali went down to her Periscope depth from where only the upper tip of her periscope cutting through the water, leaving a small wake, would be visible to anyone on the surface. She settled at that depth and the Engineer Officer made fine trim adjustments for an even trim.

"Make a signal to the Fleet Commander – I see you" said the visibly excited Admiral from the Conning Tower. The Captain was amused. Here was a pun from the Admiral – when a senior officer makes a signal to a junior officer using the words "I See You", it means the latter is to dress up in ceremonial rig and meet the senior officer for a right royal ticking off for something that had gone wrong. The signal was made and the Fleet Commander – an Admiral himself – took it in the right spirit. As the fleet steamed past, Vanshali proceeded to raise and lower all her masts and followed up with a high speed surfacing that looks very impressive from the surface. The Admiral was brought back to harbor later that day. He had his 'biriyani' with the men on the way back. He was to talk about this underwater trip out to sea for many years, and even after his retirement.

During Vanshali's commissioned service, she had many VIPs visiting her, both in harbor and at sea. The list included Heads of States, Governors, Prime Ministers, senior government officials, and senior officers from the three Services. While in the Andaman Islands, she had the local Rani Laxmi of Kamorta and Nancowry Islands (residing in Champin village) and her entourage coming onboard in grass skirts. (No one was permitted to stand under the vertical hatch ladder while they descended). Abroad, she had foreigners visiting her. Security factors were always kept in mind and taken care of. That which was required to be concealed was concealed, and the crew was well aware of what could be revealed and what should not be revealed. On one occasion, the Motor Panel operator was asked how fast the submarine could move underwater. His reply was that he really did not know. He was able to give whatever speed was ordered from the Control Room! Another was asked how deep the submarine could dive? His answer was that the depth gauge was not located in the compartment he worked in, but he reckoned they could dive deep enough to evade anything and to attack targets successfully!

RELEGATION TO SECOND LINE

With time comes age. The old must give way to the young. Vanshali. was now already thirty-three years old since her first launch, and quite dated despite her midlife update and the many refits. She had done thousands of hours underwater, covering thousands of nautical miles. Newer classes of submarines, and newer anti-submarine frigates with state of the art equipment had joined the force, and Vanshali's vintage was being exposed more and more. Navies in the region were also replacing their aging forces with newer and better platforms. Already whispers could be heard during exercise de-briefs, and in the corridors over a cup of tea during intermissions, that Vanshali and her clan had outlived their lives and should now be de-commissioned one by one. Apart from her diminishing operational usefulness, she was also costing the exchequer more and more to maintain. The humidity and salinity of the tropics are deadly contributors to corrosion, and Vanshali had only been operating in the tropics for most of her life. Battling corrosion over the years had finally taken its toll and made it unviable to keep her and her sisters going. A warship could be kept going as long as she floated and propelled. A submarine, however, had to be fit enough to dive, resist the enormous water pressure forces that bear on her when she is dived, and be able to fight with the advantage of surprise on her side. Corrosion systematically destroys this capability. The light was visible at the end of the tunnel. Vanshali must go to the scrap yard sooner or later.

It was about this time that a requirement came up that changed Vanshali's future. The Research and Development (R&D) department of the Ministry of Defence, having successfully designed and manufactured a SONAR (Sound Noising and Ranging) system for ships to detect submarines, had embarked on a program of indigenously designing and manufacturing a SONAR system for submarines. They needed a submarine on which they could install their system and try out the prototype at sea. This was not a requirement that could be met by the newer submarines. Installing such a system would mean ripping out the existing system onboard and replacing it with the new creation. The solution was to hand over Vanshali or one of her sister submarines for this purpose. It would be a requirement for a short duration of a year or two. Once the SONAR and its system were proved successful, they could be removed, and the submarine then scrapped. The question now was, which submarine was it going to be? Rumors were rife that it would be Vanshali. While their Lordships debated on the selection, Vanshali and her crew waited with bated breaths. The decision took a long while coming, and in the interim period, Vanshali was semi-retired. She spent more hours tied up to the jetty than out at sea. Also tied up next to her were four other sister submarines. One of them would get a few years' extension of life. The others would be sold as scrap!

The announcement came. Vanshali, a thirty-four year old submarine was selected to be the R&D platform for the submarine SONAR to be tested. She would now be relegated to the second line of service – no longer a front-line submarine. A sigh of relief could be heard in all the compartments. She was to serve the navy for a few years more as a commissioned but experimental platform, and retain the capability to lay defensive minefields (should the need arise), land clandestine parties, and take on secondary, but safer roles in event of war or hostilities.

Soon the R&D team of scientists arrived – they had been waiting for this for quite awhile – and preliminary discussions began. It slowly dawned on the officers of Vanshali that the R&D suite of SONARS that were going to be installed onboard Vanshali were based on a very sophisticated, ambitious, and futuristic design philosophy. If it proved, the navy would have a suite comparable to any, elsewhere in the world. Some skeptics doubted whether the end product would ever see the light of day and there were others who were confident that it would be all right. The proof of the pudding was in the eating, and this R&D team had already shown that they were capable of producing a successful model that was already fitted on some of the navy's surface ships, and performing exceedingly well too.

There was another surprise – a new Fire Control System was also being designed that would provide solutions for mine laying, torpedo firing, and tube-launched missile firings, et al. The SONAR would search, detect, classify, and designate targets to the Fire Control System that would offer options to the Captain on which targets to take on, which to evade, and in what sequence. After the Captain selects his options, it would recommend what was to be executed by the Command by way of maneuvers, speed changes, and depth variations based on factors like self-noise, the sound ray profile of the waters being operated in, details of the targets, as also feeding the weapon launchers with up to date inputs at the same time. These inputs would continue to be fed to either missile launchers or to wire-guided torpedoes even after they are released from the torpedo tubes, through their attached umbilical cord, till no longer required. The system was being designed to simultaneously track at least eight targets while carrying out attacks on any three of them in rapid sequence. The sophistication of the system lay in the speed with which it offered solutions – almost instantaneous!

To get all the required equipment installed onboard, Vanshali had to be dry-docked. The first phase would involve removing existing SONAR and Fire Control Systems and the extensive cabling and wiring that went along with them. This was to be termed the "Rip off Phase". Some holes through the Pressure hull would have to be sealed, and new holes drilled for cabling. This was not going to be a simple affair, as the sealing would have to withstand the enormous water pressure force that would be exerted when the submarine dived. Some structural changes would have to take place in the SONAR Dome by way of readjusting support frames and foundations. Some modifications to the outer casing would have to be carried out to accommodate new flank array transducers along the length of the submarine, on both sides. The Drawings were all ready, and so it wasn't going to be too difficult for the dockyard to execute what was required to be done in the "rip off phase" and the "installation phase" that would follow later.

Vanshali spent a hundred days in docks while all this was carried out. This time was also utilized to attend to all her other defects and to improve her diving capabilities to a limited depth, deep enough for the trials of the new system to be carried out. The work outside the pressure hull done, she undocked and tied up alongside while the scientists went about their job inter-phasing the different pieces of equipment and testing and tuning them inside the pressure hull. This took quite a few weeks, and finally she was ready from the scientists' point of view. Then the crew went about their work up and drills till the Squadron Commander declared the submarine fit to go to sea and dive. Further work up by herself followed, and another inspection by the Squadron Commander declared her fit for independent operations at sea. These are standard submarine procedures, and are followed in respect of all submarines after docking and refits.

She looked a little different to her sister submarines now, with new SONAR sensors fitted in novel cylindrical shaped housings on the forward and aft casings. These were so placed only for the trials. If and when introduced into the Service onboard later submarines as standard fit, they would be housed discreetly so as not to be visible to the naked eye, and not affect the streamline of the hull.

She was not included anymore in major naval exercises, for fleet work up, or for normal independent operational sorties that she used to go out on. She was now an R&D platform, and a submarine that was relegated to the second line. It was a sad state to be in, but in a better state than her sister submarines which were waiting for their turn on death row!

Over the months to follow, she sailed off Visakhapatnam many times over, for SONAR trials. In fact, for the next four years, extensive trials on the new systems were carried out. She was docked once to attend to some minor problem on one of the new sensors that was housed below the waterline, outside the pressure hull. Initial reports on the SONAR's performance were coming in. They were fantastic and difficult to believe. The performance was better than that of the latest submarines in the inventory, and showed remarkable consistency in all sea conditions.

P.R. Franklin

THE FINAL COUNTDOWN

"I am tired and weary. My frames are aching, and all my innards are feeling weaker and sluggish. I can now see a bright light at the end of the long tunnel awaiting me – the light that will bring me long and lasting rest. I am now 47 years old which is very old by warship standards. I have given my very best during these past four and a half decades. The Indian Navy has got more than it expected out of me. I am the 'alpha' of their submarine arm. While my 'omega' is in sight, their power and might in the undersea world is growing from strength to strength. In every conceivable field of undersea warfare, I have contributed towards enhancing their expertise. My crew, the support staff, and the Dockyard, all find it extremely difficult to keep me going. I cannot dive with alacrity or maneuver with agility any longer. Operationally also, I am not able to perform to standards expected of me. It is no longer cost-effective to refit and revive me. I find I need more and more time alongside in harbor and less and less time at sea. I hope my masters will give me that final respite and let me go." - Vanshali.

In mid-Jan 2010, a simple decision was taken by the Ministry of Defence – to let go of the Foxtrot/Kalvari Class of submarines. The last two of the Class, were to be decommissioned and consigned to the ship breakers' yard by the end of the year, and that would bring to end the lives of all the Foxtrot/ Kalvari Class submarines.

A Commander-in-Chief of the Navy who was at the helm of the Eastern Naval Command in the year 2001 had anticipated this. He had ideas of his own. Working behind the scenes, he conceived and executed the idea of beaching one of these eight submarines and keeping her there in perpetuity as a museum on the shores of Visakhapatnam, in memory of this Class. He had very little time to lose. With a team of trusted and dedicated scientists, Marine Engineers, Dockyard workers and others, and with the approval of the local government, he beached one submarine at right angles to the shore line in Visakhapatnam. He then got the team to haul all 2000 tons of her up to a safe distance away from the water line and turn her by ninety degrees to finally rest her, parallel to the coastline. After she had been firmly secured, he proceeded to convert her into a museum for the public, to be eventually handled and managed by the government. However, before handing her over, she had to be decommissioned!

The decommissioning ceremony was conducted with full service decorum and poignancy at the site where the submarine was beached. Both, serving, and retired officers who had served on her – including the Commanding Officer who had commissioned her, and many of the Commanding officers who followed – were invited and present. Also present were Senior Naval officers of Flag Rank of the Eastern Naval Command. The event was graced by a large number of sailors – past and present - who had served on her, as also their family members. Emotions ran high.

INS Kursura beached

With the sounding of the 'last post' by the bugler at sunset, the Paying off Pennant was lowered and a box containing the submarine's Naval ensign was handed over to the Flag Officer Commanding-in-Chief, Eastern Naval Command by the last Commanding Officer of the submarine, marking the official decommissioning of the submarine. A ceremonial guard was paraded on the occasion. All eight of these submarines got identical send-offs when their turn came to be paid off.

One lone Foxtrot Class submarine stands there on the beach in Visakhapatnam today, and thousands and thousands of visitors have gone through her to see for themselves how officers and men served onboard these denizens of the deep, in uncomfortable and inhospitable surroundings. It is visited in thousands to this day. The men, who served on them, like the rest of the Armed Forces, did so to protect our country and its people from harm. Theirs was truly a sacrifice of all the little comforts available in the service. They volunteered to undergo this tough, risky, and rigorous life. Not everyone can do it. No one is forced into submarine service. What's more, they set the standards, initiated traditions, and set up much needed infrastructure to support and operate submarines from both our coasts for operational deployment in our areas of interest. Not one of these submarines was lost at sea during war or peace.

P.R. Franklin

EPILOGUE

The last of the 'Foxtrot' Class submarines was decommissioned by the Indian Navy in December 2010, bringing to an end, a glorious chapter in the annals of the submarine arm. Those who trained for them, and brought them all the way from the Soviet Union to India, round the African continent - the pioneers - retired from naval service years earlier. Many of the boats outlived them in the navy. Almost all of what has been written in this book are near true accounts of what took place at some time or the other while the eight of them were serving the navy. They happened in one or the other of the boats, but have been made to appear as if all of them took place onboard one – Vanshali – submarine. One of the submarines, indeed, stands proud on the beach in Visakhapatnam as a museum. Without resorting to combining episodes to make it appear as if all of them took place onboard the same submarine, covering a period of over three decades in the life of any one of them would make arduous reading. Some sections like the War Patrol, for example, and some sections describing Fleet Exercises, are imaginary in nature, though not far from the truth.

Diesel submarines are making way for nuclear propelled submarines in navies that can afford them. However, in many of the smaller navies, they continue to serve with credit to their countries. Diesel submarines, therefore, still have a future for some years to come despite the existence of their nuclear powered counterparts.

At some futuristic date, with the purchase of new state-of-the-art conventional submarines, it is likely that they may take the names of these 'Foxtrot' class submarines. That is a tradition that was inherited from the Royal Navy, and continues in the Indian Navy to this day. So, Kalvari, Khanderi, Karanj, Kursura, Vela, Vagir, Vagli, and Vaghsheer, may sail again under the Indian Flag someday as different platforms. It is hoped they will.

Farewell To The Sea

Farewell, ye proud and rolling waters,
Farewell, though glittering, charging sea,
The blue expanse that knows no fetters,
The beauty full of majesty.

      I loved thy raucous voice, the mellow
      Play of thy waves, their darts and leaps,
      Thy evening calm, thy fitful sleep,
      Thy passionate and wrathful bellow!

A humble fishing boat doth glide
O'er thy waves, easily obeying
Their whim, but with the wind allied,
Great ships engulfest thou, displaying
Ungoverned rage and savage pride!

      Alexander Pushkin 1824

ABOUT THE AUTHOR

Commodore P.R. Franklin, AVSM, VSM, (Retd) did his submarine training in Vladivostok, in erstwhile USSR. He commissioned the third and the sixth of the eight 'Foxtrot' class submarines that the Indian Navy purchased, and sailed them from Riga, Latvia, to India round Africa in the late sixties/early seventies. He subsequently commanded two of them. After a few squadron appointments both afloat and ashore, he headed the submarine arm as Director Submarine Operations in Naval Headquarters. Among his other appointments in the navy, he commanded the Training Squadron training officer cadets of the Indian Navy, INS Venduruthy in Kochi, was Naval Assistant to the Chief of the Naval Staff, the Naval Advisor to the Indian High Commissioner in the United Kingdom, and the Naval Officer-in-Charge Tamil Nadu & Pondicherry.

A graduate of the Defence Services Staff College, he also served as Directing Staff in that institution. He did the higher command and staff course in the former Marshal A.A.Grechkov Academy in Leningrad (renamed now as the N.G. Kuznetsov Academy in St. Petersburg). He was awarded the Vishisht Seva Medal in 1995 and the Ati Vishisht Seva Medal in 2001 by the President of India.

After retiring from the navy after 36 years of commissioned service, he was a consultant for a brief spell to a private Indian company while it produced a Submarine Control Simulator for the Indian nuclear propelled submarine, INS Arihant. He is also the author of the book titled 'Submarine Operations'.

His e-mail address is jalvayufranklin1946@gmail.com

Cmde P.R. Franklin, AVSM, VSM, (Retd)

Get Published with Frontier India

Do you want to get your book or thesis published? You might even want to republish your book which is currently out of print.. Frontier India Technology as a publisher, distributor and retailer of books, offers a complete range of publishing, editorial, and marketing services that helps you as an author to take his or her book to the reader.

Getting your work published is a wish for many for reasons including profit earning, self-satisfaction, popularity and other good reasons. We will offer you choices based on your needs. Get in touch with us at frontierindia@gmail.com.

Our Recently Published Books include :

An Indian Air force Recollects by Wing Co P.K. Karayi (Retd.) ISBN: 978-8193005507

Warring Navies – India and Pakistan (International Edition) – by Cmde Ranjit B. Rai (Retd.). Joseph P. Chacko. ISBN: 978-8193005545

Basics of marriage Management by Walter E Vieira. ISBN: 978-8193005514

Beat That Exam Fever – Succeed in Examinations by Walter E Vieira. ISBN: 978-8193005538

Ordinary Stocks, Extra Ordinary Profits by Anand S. ISBN: 978-8193005521

Foxtrot to Arihant – The Story of Indian Navy's Submarine Arm by Joseph P. Chacko. ISBN: 978-8193005552

The Role of the President of India by Prof Balkrishna. ISBN 13: 978-81-930055-6-9

www.ingramcontent.com/pod-product-compliance
Lightning Source LLC
Chambersburg PA
CBHW072043160426
43197CB00014B/2610